AQA GCSE Design and Technology

GET BETTER RESULTS FOR AQA

food chnology

D1147235

Orders: please contact Bookpoint Ltd, 130 Milton Park, Abingdon, Oxon OX14 4SB. Telephone: +44 (0)1235 827720. Fax: +44 (0)1235 400454. Lines are open from 9.00 to 5.00, Monday to Saturday, with a 24-hour message-answering service. You can also order through our website www.hoddereducation.co.uk

If you have any comments to make about this, or any of our other titles, please send them to educationenquiries@hodder.co.uk

British Library Cataloguing in Publication Data
A catalogue record for this title is available from the British Library.

ISBN: 978 1 444 123 685

First Edition Published 2011
Impression number   10 9 8 7 6 5 4 3 2 1
Year   2016, 2015, 2014, 2013, 2012, 2011

Hachette UK's policy is to use papers that are natural, renewable and recyclable products and made from wood grown in sustainable forests. The logging and manufacturing processes are expected to conform to the environmental regulations of the country of origin.

Cover photo from © Dean Turner/iStockphoto.com

Typeset by DC Graphic Design Limited, Swanley Village, Kent

Printed in Italy for Hodder Education, an Hachette UK Company, 338 Euston Road, London NW1 3BH by LEGO

AQA GCSE Design and Technology

GET BETTER RESULTS FOR AQA

food
technology

series editor: **Bryan Williams**

Val Fehners

Meryl Simpson

Barbara Monks

Julie Booker (Advisory Editor)

DYNAMIC
LEARNING

HODDER
EDUCATION
AN HACHETTE UK COMPANY

Acknowledgements

Val Fehners would like to thank Helen Jones, Assistant Headteacher at Samuel Ward Academy, Haverhill, Suffolk; Rosalind Shirm, Victoria Sparrow and Sophie Walker for use of their controlled assessment work (pupils at Samuel Ward Academy Haverhill, Suffolk); Adrian Fehners for his support and patience; and Katherine Webb-Sear for help with photography.

Meryl Simpson would like to thank Margaret Johns and her students at Valley School, Worksop, Notts; Brian Simpson for his support and proofreading; Sophie Simpson for her cup cakes; and Rosie Oakes for her photograph.

Barbara Monks would like to thank GCSE food technology students Lesley Cummins (Queens School, Bushey) Adrienne Cleasby (Graveney School, London, SW17) and Rachel Richards (Hitchin Girls' School, Hitchin, Herts) for illustrations in Chapter 12.

The authors and publishers would like to thank the following for use of photographs in this volume:

Figure 1.15 Delia Clarke and Betty Herbert, Food Facts (Nelson Thornes, 1986) p. 26, ISBN 0333336135, reprinted with permission of the author; Figure 1.2 ©Morgan Lane Photography/iStockphoto.com; Figure 1.5 Photolibrary.com; Figure 1.6 Monkey Business – Fotolia; Figure 1.17 goodluz – Fotolia; Figure 1.18 © Crown copyright material is reproduced with the permission of the Controller of HMSO and Queen's Printer for Scotland; Stockdisc/Getty Images; Figure 1.21 Elena Schweitzer – Fotolia; Figure 1.23 www.purestockX.com; Figure 1.27 WavebreakMediaMicro – Fotolia; Figure 1.28 Yuri Arcurs – Fotolia; Figure 1.30 Elenathewise – Fotolia; Figure 1.32 © Jason Stitt – Fotolia.com; Figure 1.34 Bartlomiej Nowak – Fotolia; Figure 1.35 © Zilotis - Fotolia.com; Figure 1.36 Registered Trade Mark to Coeliac UK; Figure 1.40 © MP – Fotolia.com; Figure 1.44 © Jean François LEFEVRE – Fotolia.com; photo of cod In Table 1.8 on page 46 danimages – Fotolia; photo of mackerel in Table 1.8 on page 46 © purplevine – Fotolia.com; photo of prawns in Table 1.8 on page 46 muddy/© muddy – Fotolia.com; Figure 1.47 Oatly; Figure 1.50 © Igor Dutina – Fotolia.com; crème brulée in Table 2.2 on page 62 Elena Elisseeva; crème caramel in Table 2.2 on page 62 © William Berry – Fotolia.com; biscuits in Table 2.2 on page 62 Elenathewise – Fotolia; Figure 2.3 manipulateur – Fotolia; Figure 2.4 © Monkey Business – Fotolia.com; Figure 2.5 © Ashley Cooper/Alamy; Figure 2.8 Douglas Freer – Fotolia; burger press in Table 2.6 on page 74 © 2011 Photos.com; pasta maker in Table 2.6 on page 74 Comugnero Silvana – Fotolia; gingerbread man in Figure 2.11 Siede Preis/Photodisc/Getty Images; cheesecake in Figure 2.11 evgenyb – Fotolia; apple pie in Figure 2.11 Ingram Publishing; wedding cake in Figure 2.11 aytekinbey – Fotolia; bread in Figure 2.11 © Elena Elisseeva – Fotolia.com; iced cakes in Figure 2.11 Ruth Black – Fotolia; fish pie in Figure 2.11 © Monkey Business – Fotolia.com; Figure 2.12 OCR GCSE Design & Technology: Food Technology exam paper 2002, reprinted with permission from OCR; Figure 3.1 © mediablitzimages (uk) Limited/Alamy; Figure 4.4 © Elena Elisseeva – Fotolia.com; Figure 4.6 © Julián Rovagnati – Fotolia.com; Figure 4.8 © Lee Pettet/iStockphoto.com; Figure 4.9 Alexey Stiop – Fotolia; Figure 4.10 Rixie – Fotolia; Figure 4.11 © Igor Dutina – Fotolia.com; Figure 5.2 © Claudia Dewald/iStockphoto.com; Figure 5.12 iofoto – Fotolia; Figure 5.13 Digital Vision/Photodisc/Getty Images; Figure 5.15 Stockbyte/photolibrary.com; Figure 5.16 Abel & Cole; Figure 5.17 Soil Association; Figure 5.19 FrankU – Fotolia; Figure 5.21 Getty Images; Figure 5.22 The Fairtrade Foundation; Figure 5.23 Traidcraft/Richard Else; Figure 5.24 Assured Food Standards; Figure 6.1 mbt_studio – Fotolia; Figure 6.6 Photolibrary.com; Figure 6.7 FocalPoint – Fotolia; Figure 7.6 Monkey Business – Fotolia; Figure 8.1 Monkey Business – Fotolia; barcode in Table 8.2 © Colin Underhill/Alamy; Figure 8.2 © Crown copyright material is reproduced with the permission of the Controller of HMSO and Queen's Printer for Scotland; Figure 8.9 © David J. Green – food themes/Alamy; Figure 8.10 © Shaun-Finch/Alamy; glass jar in Table 8.5 Rafa Irusta – Fotolia; metal foil in Table 8.5 © Kelly Cline/iStockphoto.com; plastic tray in Table 8.5 SimpleVision – Fotolia; egg box in Table 8.5 Rob Bouwman/© Rob Bouwman – Fotolia.com; ovenable paperboard in Table 8.5 © Kelly Cline/iStockphoto.com; Figure 8.11 © broker – Fotolia.com; Figure 8.12 © Andrey Prokhorov/iStockphoto.com; Figure 8.13 © Olivier Blondeau/iStockphoto.com; Figure 8.14 Photolibrary.com; Figure 9.1 © JMD – Fotolia.com; Figure 9.2 Ingram Publishing; Figure 9.4 photka – Fotolia; Figure 10.1 © Irochka – Fotolia.com; Figure 10.7 © KVaSS – Fotolia.com; Figure 10.11 © Aleksandr Ugorenkov – Fotolia.com; Figure 10.15 © Agatha Brown – Fotolia.com; photo of boiling saucepan in Table 10.5 © Kelpfish – Fotolia.com; photo of barbecue in Table 10.5 Ingram Publishing; photo of stir frying in Table 10.5 © Steve Lovegrove – Fotolia.com; Figure 10.29 © Studioshots/Alamy; Figure 10.32 starush – Fotolia; microwaves in Table 10.6 Panasonic UK Ltd; Figure 11.1 Eye of Science/Science Photo Library; Figure 11.3 © Henrik Jonsson/iStockphoto.com; Figure 11.4 © Darko Radanovic/iStockphoto.com; Figure 11.5 © Stuart Pitkin/iStockphoto.com; Figure 11.6 © Chris Dascher/iStockphoto.com; Figure 11.7 © Sebastian Kaulitzki/iStockphoto.com; Figure 11.9 www.purestockX.com; Figure 11.14 robynmac – Fotolia; Figure 11.15 © Ernesto Solla Domínguez/ iStockphoto.com; Figure 11.17 Giuseppe Parisi – Fotolia; Figure 11.19 © Rob Gooch/Alamy; Figure 11.20 www.purestockX.com; Figure 11.22 © Dr. Heinz Linke/iStockphoto.com; Figure 11.24 © Peter Scholey/Alamy; Figure 11.25 starush – Fotolia; Figure 12.1 © David Freund/iStockphoto.com; Figure 12.2 © Dr. Heinz Linke/iStockphoto.com; Figure 12.3 Ingram Publishing; Figure 12.4 © Bulent Ince/istockphoto.com; Figure 12.6 © Dr. Heinz Linke/iStockphoto.com; Figure 12.8 © Dr. Heinz Linke/iStockphoto.com; Figure 13.1 FrankU – Fotolia; Figure 13.4 Sheff's Special.

All other photographs in this volume taken by the authors.

Illustrations by Art Construction.

Every effort has been made to trace and acknowledge the ownership of copyright. The publishers will be glad to make suitable arrangements for any copyright holder whom it has not been possible to contact.

Contents

chapter 1
Materials and components – understanding the nutritional properties of food

1.1 The nutritional characteristics of the main nutrients

Learning objectives

By the end of this section you should have developed a knowledge and understanding of:

- the nutritional properties of ingredients and food products, and the main nutrients:
  - proteins
  - fats
  - carbohydrates – sugars, starches and fibre
  - vitamins A, B, C and D
  - minerals – calcium and iron
- the fact that diets with deficiencies or excesses of particular nutrients may lead to health-related problems.

Introduction

Every living thing needs food – it is essential to keep us alive and in good health. We need food for:

- providing the energy we need to survive, to keep us healthy and to help fight disease
- growth and repair of body tissue
- all bodily functions, which depend on the energy and trace elements found in the food we eat
- stopping us feeling hungry
- keeping us happy, as we find eating a pleasurable and enjoyable experience.

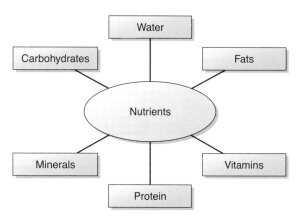

△ **Figure 1.1** Nutrients in food

Nutrients

Nutrients are substances found in foods. They are divided into two types:

- The **macronutrients**, fats, proteins and carbohydrates – these are needed by the body in relatively large quantities and form the bulk of our diet.
- The **micronutrients**, vitamins and minerals – these are found in food and are vital to health, but are required in very small quantities.

Our diet also needs to include two other important substances. These are:

- water: found in foods and drinks
- fibre: found naturally in plants foods.

1

Key terms

Nutrients – the part of a food that performs a particular function in the body

Micronutrients – vitamins and minerals that are needed in small quantities for health

Macronutrients – proteins, fats and carbohydrates providing the bulk of our diet

All foods contain a mix of nutrients. Some foods are higher in some nutrients than others. We should eat a mixture of foods every day.

△ **Figure 1.2** A variety of foods form a balanced diet

The government has produced guidelines and advice to encourage the UK population to improve their diet and lifestyle. It has set targets to reduce the number of people with diet-related medical conditions such as cancer, coronary heart disease, strokes, diabetes and **obesity**. Individuals could become healthier by increasing their intake of fruit, vegetables and fibre. Keeping physically active and maintaining a healthy body weight will also help.

Key term

Obesity – excessive fatness, measured as a ratio of weight to height

Deficiencies or excesses of any particular nutrient could result in a diet-related medical condition, so we need to eat a balance of nutrients every day.

We will look at these in greater detail later in the chapter.

Activities

Find a nutrition label from a food product and then carry out the following tasks.

1. List the nutrients in the product.

2. State which are the macronutrients and which are the micronutrients in the product.

3. State a target group for the product and give one reason for your answer.

4. Explain why it is important to have nutritional labelling on foods.

Key points

o We need a balance of nutrients in our diet every day.
o Foods contain a combination of macro- and micronutrients.

Protein

Protein is one of the macronutrients essential for growth and repair of body tissue, and is crucial to the healthy functioning of the body. Protein is made up of complex chains of molecules called amino acids. There are 20 different types of **amino acid**, each with a specific function in the body.

Key term

Amino acids – the smallest units of a protein

The functions of protein in the diet

○ Used for growth, especially in children and pregnant women.
○ Used to repair body tissue after illness, accidents and surgery; renewal of cell proteins for people of all ages.
○ Enzymes vital for metabolism are composed of proteins.
○ Hormones, which regulate some important bodily functions, are also composed of protein
○ They provide a secondary source of energy. When the body has used all the amino acids it needs for construction, the remainder are 'burnt' for energy.

The human body needs all 20 amino acids for the maintenance of health and growth. Eleven of these can be made by the body itself, but the others have to be obtained through the food we eat – these are called **essential amino acids.**

Key term

Essential amino acids – amino acids that cannot be made by the body

High biological value proteins

The foods that contain all the essential amino acids are said to have a **high biological value** (HBV). Most of these come from animal sources (meat, fish, poultry and dairy products) plus the vegetable source, soya. As the vegetarian market grows there is a large range of food products made from soya, such as soya mince, textured vegetable protein known as TVP, and tofu. Another HBV protein is Quorn®, which is the brand name for a food product made from

mycoprotein. Some sources of HBV protein foods are shown in Figure 1.3.

Key term

High biological value proteins – proteins that contain all the essential amino acids

Low biological value proteins – proteins that do not contain all the essential amino acids

Controlled assessment link

Quorn® can be used in your work; see Figure 14.13 on page 241.

Low biological value

Vegetable sources of protein include cereals, peas, beans, pulses, nuts and seeds. Because these do not contain all the essential amino acids they are said to have **low biological value** (LBV). They can easily be combined in a meal or product to provide all the essential amino acids. This is called **food combining** or complementary proteins. Some sources of LBV protein foods are shown in Figure 1.4.

Key term

Food combining – mixing different low biological value proteins to supply all the essential amino acids

Vegetarian, vegan or other limited diets rely on combining LBV proteins, for instance beans on toast, dhal and rice, hummus and pitta bread, to form proteins of higher value.

Sources of protein in the diet

Animal sources include all meats, such as poultry, offal and game, as well as fish, cheese, milk, eggs and gelatine.

Vegetable sources include soya beans and soya products, pulses, beans, cereal grains and cereal products, nuts and Quorn®.

△ **Figure 1.3** All these foods are protein sources of HBV

△ **Figure 1.4** All these foods are protein sources of LBV

Protein deficiency

Not eating enough protein can cause various problems:

○ In children, growth slows down or stops.
○ Digestive upsets are caused as enzymes are not produced.
○ The liver fails to function normally.
○ Muscles become weak, so limbs are thin and the tummy is soft and may look distended.

Exam practice questions

1. List **four** functions of protein in the diet. **[4 marks]**
2. Explain the difference between HBV and LBV proteins. **[4 marks]**
3. Explain why you would combine protein foods to complement each other. **[4 marks]**
4. Give **two** examples of complementary proteins. **[2 marks]**

Activities

1. Prepare a main course product that combines a range of LBV proteins. Use nutritional software to find out how one portion of the product meets the needs of a teenager.
2. Plan a meal that will provide 18 g of protein.

Key points

○ Protein is needed for growth and repair of body tissues.
○ Protein is made up of amino acids.
○ Good sources of high biological value proteins are meat, fish, cheese, eggs, fish and soya.
○ Good sources of low biological value protein are pulses, cereals and nuts.

Fats and oils

Lipids is a general term for both fats and oils. Oils are fats that are liquid at room temperature. Fat is one of the macronutrients essential to health. All fats and oils have similar chemical structures and functions. All are high in calories. Fat in the diet is important for health and well-being.

Key terms

Lipids – another name for fats and oils

Satiety – a feeling of fullness

The functions of fat in the diet

- Fats are used by the body for energy and also form part of the structure of cells.
- Stored under the skin, fat helps insulate the body against the cold.
- Our vital organs, such as kidneys, are protected by a layer of fat.
- Fat is a source of the fat-soluble vitamins A, D, E and K (see the section on vitamins, page 13).
- We like to eat fat because it gives foods texture and flavour.
- Fat in our diet helps to promote a feeling of **satiety** (feeling full after eating).

Sources of fat in the diet

Fats come from both plant and animal sources. Plant sources include:

- some fruits, for example, avocado pears, olives
- nuts and pulses, for example, peanuts, walnuts
- seeds, for example, sesame, sunflower and soya.

Animal sources include:

- meat and meat products, such as lard and suet
- dairy products, for example, milk, butter, cheese and cream
- fish, particularly oily fish, for example, tuna, salmon and sardines.

Visible and invisible fats

Some fats are visible, such as the fat on meat or solid fats such as butter. Other fats are invisible and form part of the food product and cannot be seen, such as in ready meals, chocolate, biscuits and burgers.

△ **Figure 1.5** Visible fats and oils

△ **Figure 1.6** Invisible fats

The chemistry of fats

Fats are large molecules made up of the elements carbon, hydrogen and oxygen. They are composed of fatty acids and glycerol. Fatty acids may be saturated or unsaturated.

Saturated fats

In saturated fats, each carbon atom in the fatty acid is combined with two hydrogen atoms. Saturated fats are solid at room temperature and are mainly found in animal foods. Too much saturated fat in the diet has been linked to high blood cholesterol, leading to an increased risk of coronary heart disease, diabetes and obesity.

Cholesterol, a type of saturated fat, has the consistency of soft wax and is produced in the liver and transported round the body in the blood. It has been found that when too much cholesterol is in the blood it is deposited on the walls of the arteries, narrowing them and making them less efficient. Narrowed arteries are one of the major causes of coronary heart disease.

△ **Figure 1.7** Sources of saturated fat in the diet

Unsaturated fats

There are two types of unsaturated fats, monounsaturated and polyunsaturated. Unsaturated fats are usually soft or liquid at room temperature and have a lower melting point.

○ **Monounsaturated fats** have one pair of carbon atoms, with only one hydrogen atom attached, so they are capable of taking one more hydrogen atom. They are soft at room temperature but will go solid when placed in the coldest part of the refrigerator. They are found in both animal and vegetable fats.

Monounsaturated fatty acids in particular are considered healthier because they can help to lower blood cholesterol, reduce the risk of diabetes and are linked with a lower rate of cancer.

△ **Figure 1.8** Sources of monounsaturated fat in the diet

○ **Polyunsaturated fats** have two or more pairs of carbon atoms, which are capable of taking up more hydrogen atoms. They are very soft or oily at room temperature. They will not go solid even in the refrigerator.

△ **Figure 1.9** Sources of polyunsaturated fat in the diet

Key terms

Monounsaturated fats – a fat molecule with one hydrogen space

Polyunsaturated fats – a fat molecule with more than one hydrogen space

Hydrogenation – the process of adding hydrogen to oils to make them into solid fats

Essential fatty acids – small unit of fat that must be supplied in the diet

Key points

- Fat is a concentrated source of energy.
- Excess fat in the diet is stored as body fat.
- We are advised to reduce our fat intake to no more than 35 per cent of our total energy intake.
- Saturated fats contribute to a high level of cholesterol in the blood.

Trans-fatty acids are man-made molecules produced when hydrogen is added to vegetable oils. This is called **hydrogenation**. This process is used to make solid fats from oil and is used in a variety of manufactured foods. Trans-fatty acids behave like saturated fats, raising your level of cholesterol. Medical research has shown that trans-fatty acids are very bad for your cardiovascular system and may increase the risk of breast cancer.

Essential fatty acids (EFAs) cannot be made by the body but are important to the healthy and efficient functioning of the body. It is important to get the right balance of EFAs in our diet. They are essential for regulating body processes, including blood clotting and control of inflammation. Two important ones are:

- *Omega 3*, found in oily fish, seeds, walnut oil, and green leafy vegetables. It helps protect the heart.
- *Omega 6*, found in vegetables, fruits, grains, chicken and seeds. It helps lower cholesterol in the blood.

Exam practice questions

1. Give **four** functions of fat in the diet. **[4 marks]**
2. Explain why high-fat food products appeal to us. **[4 marks]**
3. Explain why we should cut down on the amount of saturated fats that we eat. **[4 marks]**
4. Describe, using examples, the difference between a low-in-fat and a lower-in-fat product. **[4 marks]**

Research this on the internet.

Useful websites:
British Heart Foundation (www.bhf.org.uk)
British Nutrition Foundation (www.nutrition.org.uk)

Activities

1. Produce a poster entitled 'A guide to the fat in your diet'.
2. Visit your supermarket or a supermarket website and conduct a survey of the types of product that have a lower-fat version. Set out your findings in a chart like the one shown below.

Product name	Regular product	Lower-fat version	By how much is the fat reduced per 100 g?

3. Examine a range of butter, lard and spreads. Compare the fat content in 100 g of each.

Stretch yourself

Research the chemical structure of the different types of fats. Draw diagrams to show the molecular structure.

○ They provide dietary fibre (non-starch polysaccharide (NSP) to help digestion.
○ They sweeten and flavour foods.

They are divided into sugars and starches, also known as simple and complex carbohydrates.

Carbohydrates

Carbohydrates are important macronutrients formed from carbon, hydrogen and oxygen. They are mainly used to provide energy – during digestion they are broken down to their simplest form, glucose, which can be used for energy. There are three forms: sugar, starch and NSP (fibre).

Key term

Carbohydrate – the major source of energy in the body

The functions of carbohydrates in the diet

○ They provide the body with energy for physical activity.
○ They provide the body with energy to maintain bodily functions.

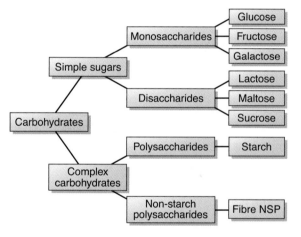

△ **Figure 1.10** Simple and complex carbohydrates

Controlled assessment link

See Figure 14.9 on page 234. This homemade gnocchi is high in carbohydrates.

Simple carbohydrates (sugars)

There are two main types of simple sugars.

Monosaccharides

Monosaccharides are also known as simple sugars. The simpler the carbohydrate, the more quickly it can be absorbed in the body and the faster energy can be provided.

- ○ *Glucose* is one of these simple sugars. Although found in some fruits and vegetables, it is often used by athletes in tablet or powder form to provide a fast energy boost.
- ○ *Fructose* is similar in structure to glucose and is found naturally in the juices of some fruits and plants, but mainly in honey. As it is the sweetest of all sugars, it is used by manufacturers to replace sucrose.
- ○ *Galactose* is formed during digestion of lactose (milk sugar).

Key terms

Monosaccharide – simple sugar

Disaccharide – two monosaccharides combined

△ **Figure 1.11** Sources of monosaccharides in the diet

Disaccharides

Disaccharides are double sugars that are made up of two monosaccharides.

- ○ *Lactose* is the disaccharide found in milk, which some people think gives milk its slightly sweet taste.
- ○ *Maltose*, another of the disaccharides, results from the fermentation of cereal grains. Sucrose is the most common disaccharide. It is known as cane sugar. It provides the body with energy but has no other benefits in the diet. It contains no other nutrients. Sucrose comes from sugar beet or sugar cane. We buy it as granulated sugar/brown sugar/syrup/treacle/castor and icing sugar.

We eat sugar in different forms:

- ○ as **intrinsic sugar**, found naturally in the cells of fruits and vegetables; it is part of the cells
- ○ as **extrinsic** sugars, which are those you can see, such as cane sugar, syrup and those added to cakes, biscuits, desserts and sweets.

Key terms

Intrinsic sugar – contained within the cell walls of plants

Extrinsic sugar – sucrose added to a product

Activity

Find four examples of foods containing intrinsic sugars and four food products containing extrinsic sugar. Display them on a poster.

The most common problems relating to sucrose are obesity and tooth decay. Tooth decay is caused when the bacteria in your mouth (plaque) feed on the sucrose to produce an acid. The acid then causes small holes in your teeth (dental caries). Intrinsic sugars are less harmful as they are less likely to lead to tooth decay and are easier for the body to absorb.

Plaque + sucrose = acid

Acid + tooth = decay

△ **Figure 1.12** Sources of disaccharides

△ **Figure 1.13** Sources of starch in the diet

Polysaccharides

Polysaccharides are complex carbohydrates formed from hundreds of glucose molecules strung together. They provide the body with energy. Modern dietary advice recommends that the dietary intake of fibre-rich complex carbohydrates be increased to provide at least 50 per cent of our daily energy needs.

Key term

Polysaccharide – complex carbohydrate, either starch or fibre

Starches

Starches are found in grain products like bread, rice, cereals and pasta, and in some fruits and vegetables. Starches take longer than sugars for the body to digest and so provide a feeling of fullness for longer, helping to avoid overeating and obesity. All starch comes from plant sources.

Functions of starch in the diet

- It is broken down slowly into simple sugars by the digestive system to provide energy.
- It adds bulk to our diet.
- It gives a feeling of fullness.
- Excess is converted to fat.

Fibre/NSP

Fibre/NSP (non-starch polysaccharide) is the non-digestible cellulose found in plant foods. It cannot be digested so it passes straight through the digestive system, absorbing moisture and providing bulk. **Dietary fibre** helps to 'push' other food through the system and helps to 'clean' the walls of the intestine of bacteria. The efficient removal of waste products from the body is vital to health.

Key terms

Non starch polysaccharide (fibre) – the part of food that is not digested by the body

Dietary fibre – material from plants, which is not digested by humans but which absorbs water and binds other residues in the intestine, thus aiding the excretion of waste material from the body

Diverticular disease – a disease caused by lack of fibre in the diet

Functions of dietary fibre

- Holds water and keeps the faeces soft and bulky.

- Helps prevent various bowel disorders, including constipation, bowel cancer, **diverticular disease**, appendicitis and haemorrhoids (piles).
- Can help people to control their body weight because high-fibre foods are filling.
- High-fibre diets are linked to lower blood cholesterol.

Too little fibre in the diet can cause constipation and, in extreme cases, diverticular disease, where the lining of the intestine becomes distorted and inflamed.

We should be eating no less than 18 g of fibre a day, although women seem to need more than men. The average person eats only about 12 g a day, which means that we should be increasing our intake by 50 per cent.

> **Controlled assessment link**
> See Figure 14.8 on page 226. One of the points in the design specification is that the product must be high in fibre.

△ **Figure 1.14** Sources of fibre in the diet

Sources of fibre in the diet

There are two types of dietary fibre, insoluble and soluble, which have different functions.

- Insoluble fibre absorbs water and increases bulk, making the faeces very soft and bulky and easy to pass through the digestive system. Insoluble fibre-rich foods are wholemeal flour, wholegrain breakfast cereals and pasta, brown rice, and some fruits and vegetables.
- Soluble fibre slows down the digestion and absorption of carbohydrates and so helps to control blood sugar levels, which helps stop us feeling hungry. Soluble fibre may also reduce blood cholesterol levels and so may reduce our risk of heart disease. Good sources of soluble fibre are oats, peas, beans, lentils, most types of fruit and vegetables. Vegetables and fruits also provide more fibre if eaten with their skins on.

(a) High-fibre diet

(b) Low-fibre diet

(c) Development of diverticula in wall of colon

Colon wall

Soft, large faeces pass easily through the intestine

Small, hard faeces do not pass easily through colon

Inner lining of colon pushes and distorts colon wall

△ **Figure 1.15** Waste passing through the digestive system

Key points

- Sugars and starches release energy into the body.
- Starches are converted to energy more slowly than sugars.
- Sugars contain no other nutrients apart from energy.
- If we eat more carbohydrates than we need for energy, the excess is stored as fat.
- Dietary fibre is a very complex structure and cannot be digested.

Vitamins

Vitamins are micronutrients because they are needed only in very small quantities. They all have chemical names, but they are usually referred to by letters.

Functions of vitamins in the diet

Vitamins are essential to the body to:

○ maintain health
○ help prevent deficiency diseases such as beri beri and rickets
○ regulate the repair of body cells
○ help combat the ageing process
○ help to process carbohydrates and release energy in the body.

There are two main groups of vitamins, fat-soluble and water-soluble. Fat-soluble vitamins A and D are found in the fat in foods. They can be stored in the liver and used by the body when needed. Water-soluble vitamins dissolve in water. They include the B group and vitamin C. They are not stored in the body, so it is important that foods containing these vitamins are eaten regularly.

Fat-soluble vitamins A and D

Fat-soluble vitamins (chemical name)	Function (its job in the body)	Good sources	Deficiency (what happens if we do not get enough)	Examples of food source
Vitamin A (retinol) (beta-carotene – an antioxidant vitamin which might protect against cancer)	Keeps eyes healthy and improves night vision Helps maintain skin	Retinol is in liver, oily fish, eggs, milk, cheese and butter Beta-carotene is in red, green and orange vegetables and fruits, especially carrots	Long-term deficiency may lead to night blindness Excess may lead to liver and bone damage	

△ **Table 1.1** Fat-soluble vitamins A and D

Cont.

Fat-soluble vitamins (chemical name)	Function (its job in the body)	Good sources	Deficiency (what happens if we do not get enough)	Examples of food source
Vitamin D (Cholecaliferal)	Works with calcium to build and maintain strong bones and teeth	Dairy products, oily fish, liver, cereals Available by exposure to sunlight	In children it can cause rickets, which is a softening of the bones. There is no Reference Nutrient Intake (RNI) for vitamin D	

△ **Table 1.1** Fat-soluble vitamins A and D

Water-soluble vitamins B and C

Vitamin B is a group of vitamins that all have similar functions. The most important B vitamins are listed in Table 1.2.

Fat-soluble vitamins (chemical name)	Function (its job in the body)	Good sources	Deficiency (what happens if we do not get enough)	Examples of food source
B1 (thiamine)	Helps the release of energy from nutrients Functioning and normal nervous system	Fortified breakfast cereals, whole grains, meat, eggs, milk, some vegetables	Slows growth and development Severe deficiency causes beriberi	
B2 (riboflavin)	Normal growth Healthy skin Release of energy	Liver, kidneys, meat, milk, eggs, green vegetables	Poor growth rate Skin and eye problems	
B3 (niacin)	Metabolism, growth and energy release Essential for healthy skin and nerves	Meat and poultry, fish, cereals, grains, dairy products, pulses	Deficiency is very rare in the UK Pellagra, rough sore skin, weakness and depression	
B9 (folate or folic acid)	Essential for the formation of red blood cells Foetal development	Liver, kidneys, wholegrain cereals, pulses, dark green vegetables	Tiredness and anaemia	

△ **Table 1.2** Water-soluble vitamins B and C

Cont.

Fat-soluble vitamins (chemical name)	Function (its job in the body)	Good sources	Deficiency (what happens if we do not get enough)	Examples of food source
Vitamin C (ascorbic acid)	Formation of connective tissue Helps wound healing and calcium absorption Blood and blood vessel formation Helps absorb iron	Citrus and soft fruits, oranges, blackcurrants, strawberries Green vegetables, cabbage, new potatoes, peppers	Spotty skin, swollen gums, loose teeth In severe cases scurvy develops	

△ **Table 1.2** Water-soluble vitamins B and C

Key points

o Vitamins are required in very small amounts.
o Vitamins promote health and help prevent disease.
o They regulate the building and repair of the body.
o They help regulate the chemical reactions which release energy in body cells.
o Fortified food products have vitamins added to improve their nutritional value.

Activities

1. Prepare a salad that would appeal to a teenager, providing as many vitamins as possible.

Make a list of the ingredients and state which vitamins are in the salad.

2. Analyse a range of orange drinks to determine the amount of vitamin C in each one. Compare the amount of vitamin C, sugar and the cost of each one.

3. List the water-soluble and the fat-soluble vitamins and their main functions.

Exam practice questions

1. State **one** vitamin that is important in the diet of the following people:

   o pregnant women
   o babies and toddlers. **[2 marks]**

2. Give **two** ways that a parent could make sure their child gets enough vitamin C. **[2 marks]**

3. Explain, using examples, why vitamins are important in the diet. **[6 marks]**

Stretch yourself

Carry out research about vitamin supplements. Would you recommend to someone that they should take them?

Minerals

Our bodies require mineral elements for a variety of functions. They are micronutrients required in very small quantities. We are going to look at two important **minerals**: **calcium** and **iron**. Sodium phosphorus and fluoride, called trace elements, are also important, and there are many more.

> ## Key terms
>
> **Minerals** – substances used by the body to control processes; they form an essential part of body fluids
>
> **Calcium** – a mineral element that is essential for strong bones and teeth
>
> **Iron** – a mineral present in the blood and stored in the liver; prolonged lack of iron leads to anaemia

Functions of vitamins in the diet

Minerals have four major functions:

- body building (bones and teeth)
- control of body processes, especially the nervous system
- they are an essential part of body fluids and cells
- they form part of enzymes and other proteins necessary for the release of energy.

Calcium and iron are the most important minerals needed by the body.

Calcium
Functions of calcium

- Calcium helps form teeth and bones and gives them strength. (An adult body contains more than 1 kg of calcium!)
- It is also needed for blood clotting after injury or surgery.
- It helps the muscles and nerves work properly.
- It is needed for normal growth in children.

People need differing amounts of calcium each day, depending on their age and gender. Pregnant women and those who are breastfeeding need an increased amount. Young children need a diet high in calcium because their bones are growing rapidly, but by about the age of 18 years bones stop growing. We reach peak bone mass at about 30 years of age, when our bones are fully calcified.

Calcium deficiency

Our body will take calcium from our bones and unless it is replaced it will cause osteoporosis. Osteoporosis is a condition of weakening and thinning of the bones, most common in the elderly, especially women.

- Blood will not clot properly after injury.
- Muscles will not work properly.
- Children's growth will be slowed, as bones will not develop normally.

Vitamin D and phosphorus work together with calcium to help maintain strong bones and teeth.

Iron
Functions of iron

We need iron as it forms haemoglobin, which gives blood its red colour and carries oxygen round the body to the cells.

Iron deficiency

Anaemia, caused by a lack of iron in the diet, is one of the most common nutritional problems worldwide. Women and children are the most at risk. Symptoms are tiredness and lack of energy.

Our bodies can store iron in the liver. The best sources of iron are liver and kidney, red meat, oily fish and leafy green vegetables. In the UK, breakfast cereals and bread are fortified with iron. Iron obtained from red meat, known as haem iron, is more easily absorbed than that from vegetables. Vegetarians need to ensure that they get an adequate supply of iron from bread, pulses and vegetables. Iron absorption is reduced by the presence of tannins found in tea and coffee, and phytates found in unrefined cereals such as bran. Iron absorption is increased by eating non-haem, iron-rich foods with foods and drinks containing vitamin C.

Mineral/ element	Function in the body	Good sources	Deficiency	Examples of food source
Iron	Production of haemoglobin in red blood cells to carry oxygen in the blood	Red meat, kidneys, liver, eggs, bread, green vegetables	Anaemia	
Calcium	Combines with phosphorus to harden bones and teeth Blood clotting Nerve and muscle function Heart regulation	Dairy products, fortified white bread, oily fish, green vegetables, nuts/ seeds, citrus fruits	Stunted growth Can cause rickets	
Phosphorus	Combines with calcium to harden bones and teeth Muscle function	Dairy products, nuts, meat, fish and foods rich in calcium	People are rarely deficient in this mineral, but deficiency causes tiredness and depression	
Sodium	Maintains water balance in the body Nerve transmission	Cheese, bacon, smoked meats, fish, processed foods, table salt	Deficiency is highly unlikely	
Fluoride	Strengthens teeth against decay	Fish, tea, drinking water, toothpaste	Tooth decay	

△ **Table 1.3** The functions and sources of minerals in the diet

Activity

Design and make a product that meets the specification in Figure 1.16 (see page 17).

Draw your design on plain paper and annotate. Explain in detail how your design meets the requirements of the specification. It is important that you label and colour your design.

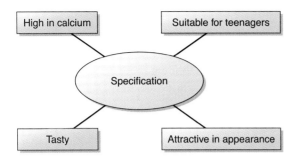

△ **Figure 1.16** Specification for a food product

 Stretch yourself

Work out the calcium content of the product you have designed in the activity on page 17:

1. for the whole product

2. for a portion size.

Exam practice questions

1. State **four** functions of calcium in the diet. **[4 marks]**

2. Explain why the requirements for calcium change with age. **[4 marks]**

3. Suggest a range of meals, suitable for a toddler, which include calcium. **[6 marks]**

4. List **four** functions of iron in the diet. **[4 marks]**

5. Give advice to a teenage girl who is a vegetarian on how to get sufficient iron in her diet. **[6 marks]**

Water

Nearly 65 per cent of the human body is made up of water. We need a lot of water every day. If someone becomes very short of water they can die in hours because the blood gets thicker and difficult to pump, so the heart stops because of overstrain. Lack of water to drink is therefore more harmful than shortage of food.

The body can protect itself to some extent against shortage of water by reducing its water output. It cannot stop losses due to breathing and sweating, but it can limit the production of urine. The medical condition known as **dehydration** occurs when more water is being lost from the body than is being replaced by drinking.

 Key term

Dehydration – a medical condition resulting from insufficient water in the diet

Functions of water in the body

○ Water helps regulate the body's temperature. Sweat evaporates and cools us. Without this cooling system we would become ill from heatstroke.

○ Water helps the kidneys flush out harmful excess or foreign substances from our blood. The kidneys filter waste products and eliminate them from the body as urine.

○ Water transports nutrients, oxygen and carbon dioxide round the body.

○ Water is needed by nearly all body processes, for example, digestion.

If we eat a lot of watery food we can drink less. Many foods are very watery, especially fruits and vegetables. On average 1 to 2.5 litres of water pass out of the body each day as urine. Some water is also removed with faeces. At least 1 litre of water is lost from the body each day as breath and sweat.

In the UK the tap water is germ-free. The water in some districts contains valuable fluoride, either naturally occurring or added.

△ **Figure 1.17** We need to replace the water lost during physical activity

1.2 Current nutritional/healthy eating guidelines

Introduction

A healthy, **balanced diet** is one that provides the correct combination of food and nutrients for optimum growth and health. To achieve a balanced diet it is important to eat a mixture of foods, as foods rich in one nutrient 'balance' the lack of that nutrient in other foods.

Carbohydrates in the form of starchy foods, such as rice, pasta, cereals and potatoes, should form the basis of our diet. These are called **staple foods**. We should also eat at least five portions of fruit and vegetables each day.

Key terms

Balanced diet – a diet that provides adequate amounts of nutrients and energy

Staple food – a food that forms the basis of a traditional diet, e.g. wheat, barley, rye, maize or rice

Eatwell Plate – a healthy eating model, to encourage people to eat the correct proportions of food to achieve a balanced diet.

The eatwell plate

The eatwell plate is a pictorial food guide showing the proportion and types of foods that are needed to make up a healthy, balanced diet. The plate has been produced by the Food Standards Agency as a guide to help people to understand and enjoy healthy eating.

The eatwell plate is based on the government's Eight Guidelines for a Healthy Diet, which are:

1. Base your meals on starchy foods.

2. Eat lots of fruit and vegetables.

3. Eat more fish, including a portion of oily fish each week.

4. Cut down on saturated fat and sugar.

5. Try to eat less salt – no more than 6 g a day for adults.

6. Get active and try to maintain a healthy weight.

7. Drink plenty of water.

8. Don't skip breakfast.

The eatwell plate is based on the five food groups and supports previous advice to reduce fat, salt, sugar and alcohol and to increase fibre.

It encourages you to choose different foods from the first four groups every day, to help ensure you obtain the wide range of nutrients your body needs to remain healthy and to function properly.

Controlled assessment link

Figure 14.1 on page 224 shows a design brief which takes the eatwell plate into consideration.

△ **Figure 1.18** The eatwell plate (Source: Food Standards Agency)

Bread, rice, potatoes, pasta and other starchy foods

Foods from this group should make up 33 per cent of the food that we eat and should be included at every meal. This is the bulk of your diet.

Fruit and vegetables

Eating at least five portions of fruit and vegetables every day is recommended for health. Fruits and vegetables do not have to be fresh or raw – they all count except for potatoes. Canned, dried, frozen, juices, soups and stews are all good and count towards your '5 a day'. You can count dried fruit, pulses and juice only once each, but you can have as many canned, fresh or frozen as you like.

Milk and dairy foods

These foods should be eaten in moderate amounts every day. Try to eat two to three servings. A serving is a 200 ml glass of milk, 150 g of yoghurt or 30 g of cheese (the size of a small matchbox!). Always choose lower-fat versions whenever you can.

Meat, fish, eggs, beans and other non-dairy sources of protein

Choose lower-fat meat products, leaner cuts of meat, and trim off any visible fat and skin. Use cooking methods that do not use any fat, and drain away fat. Grill, poach, steam, bake or microwave. It is recommended that we eat fish at least twice a week and that one of these is oily fish, such as mackerel.

Foods and drinks high in fat and/or sugar

These foods should be eaten in small amounts. Choose lower-fat or lower-sugar alternatives wherever possible. Use spreads and oils sparingly and opt for vegetable fats and oils. Try to limit your consumption of sugary foods, and drink in between meals. Try not to add any fat to foods when cooking.

Choosing a variety of foods from within each group will add to the range of nutrients you consume. Foods in the fifth group – foods and drinks high in fat and/or sugar – are not essential to a healthy diet. The eatwell plate applies to most people, including vegetarians, people of all ethnic origins and people who are a healthy weight for their height, as well as those who are overweight.

△ **Figure 1.19** Fruits and vegetables can be eaten in a variety of ways

Key points

o No more than 35 per cent of our food energy should come from fat.
o No more than 11 per cent of food energy should come from saturates.
o Carbohydrates should supply 50 per cent of our food energy.
o No more than 11 per cent of food energy should come from sugars.

5 a day

To encourage us to eat more fruit and vegetables, the UK government introduced the '5 a day' campaign. This is to ensure that you get a variety of vitamins, minerals, trace elements and fibre in your diet. This will include antioxidants and plant chemicals needed for good health. Fresh, frozen, canned and dried fruits and vegetables are all excellent sources. The Food Standards Agency has produced guidelines to help you achieve your 5 a day.

△ **Figure 1.20** 150ml of orange juice is one portion

Dietary guidelines

The eatwell plate is all about balance. There are no good or bad foods and all foods can be included in a healthy diet as long as the overall balance of foods is right. All foods supply energy and nutrients – it is achieving the correct intake of those nutrients that is important for health.

ONE portion = 80g = any of these
1 apple, banana, pear, orange or other similar sized fruit
2 plums or similar sized fruit
½ a grapefruit or avocado
1 slice of large fruit, such as melon or pineapple
3 heaped tablespoons of vegetables (raw, cooled, frozen or canned)
3 heaped tablespoons of beans and pulses (however much you eat, beans and pulses count as a maximum of one portion a day)
3 heaped tablespoons of fruit salad (fresh or canned in fruit juice) or stewed fruit
1 heaped tablespoon of dried fruit (such as raisins and apricots)
1 handful of grapes, cherries or berries
A desert bowl of salad
A glass (150 ml) of fruit juice (however much you drink, fruit juice counts as a maximum of one portion a day)

△ **Table 1.4** Guidelines on one portion of your '5 a day' (Source: Food Standards Agency)

△ **Figure 1.21** A range of healthy foods as part of a balanced diet

How do we know the amount of food that we should be eating?

COMA

The Committee on Medical Aspects of Food and Nutrition Policy (COMA) is a government committee within the Department of Health. It has put together lists of the quantities of different nutrients and energy from food needed by various groups of people. This list gives **dietary reference values (DRVs)**. This is a series of estimates of the amount of energy and nutrients needed by different groups of people in the UK population.

Dietary reference values

Included in this are:

○ **RNI** (reference nutrient intake), which shows estimated quantities needed for 97 per cent of the population. This will be far too much for a lot of people.

- **EAR** (estimated average requirements), which gives an average estimate of amounts. Some people will need more and some people will need less.
- **LRNI** (lower reference nutrient intake) is the amount of a nutrient that is enough for only a small number of people who have low needs.

Key terms

Dietary reference values (DRVs) – estimates of the amounts of nutrients needed for good health

Estimated average requirement (EARs) – the average amount of a nutrient needed

Reference nutrient intake (RNI) – the amount of a nutrient that is enough for most people in a group

When you use a nutritional software program it will usually give you the results of how your product compares with the EAR, which is the amount of nutrients needed by the average person. You must remember, though, that you will eat only one portion of your product, not the whole dish!

Activities

1. Research current dietary guidelines using the internet. Useful sites are:

   www.food.gov.uk
   www.nutrition.org.uk

2. Produce a fact sheet giving advice on a balanced diet to friends who do not study food technology.

The relationship between food intake and physical activity

This is known as **energy balance**. Energy is measured in kilo**calories** (**kcal**) or kilo**joules** (**kJ**). Carbohydrates, fats and protein from all the food and drinks we consume are broken down in the digestive system and contribute to the total daily amount of our energy:

- 1 g of fat supplies 9 kcal
- 1 g of carbohydrate supplies 3.7 kcal
- 1 g of protein supplies 4 kcal
- 1 g of alcohol supplies 7 kcal.

Key terms

Energy balance – the relationship between energy input and energy used by the body

Calorie – a unit of energy that is used to give the energy yield of foods and the energy expenditure by the body

Joule – a unit of energy used to show the energy content of foods

kcal and **kJ** – measurements of energy in foods

The amount of energy we need varies with age, gender and the amount of activity we carry out. Of the energy we consume, 70 per cent is used for all bodily functions (breathing, warmth, nerves, brain cells, digestion). This is called our basal metabolic rate (BMR). The rest of our energy is used for all other activities.

If you eat and drink foods higher in energy than your body needs, the energy is stored as fat and you gain weight. If you use more energy than the calories consumed, you will lose weight.

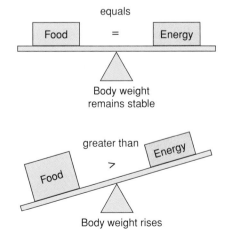

△ **Figure 1.22** It is all a matter of balance

	Males		Females	
	kJ/day	kcal/day	kJ/day	kcal/day
0–3 months	2,280	545	2,160	515
4–6 months	2,890	690	2,690	645
7–9 months	3,440	825	3,200	765
10–12 months	3,850	920	3,610	865
1–3 years	5,150	1,230	4,860	1,165
4–6 years	7,160	1,715	6,460	1,545
7–10 years	8,240	1,970	7,280	1,740
11–14 years	9,270	2,220	7,720	1,845
15–18 years	11,100	2,755	8,830	2,110
19–50 years	10,600	2,550	8,100	1,940
51–59 years	10,600	2,550	8,000	1,900
60–64 years	9,930	2,380	7,990	1,900
65–74 years	9,710	2,330	7,960	1,900
75+ years	8,770	2,100	7,610	1,810
Pregnancy	.....	.....	+0.800	+200

An additional amount is also needed by lactating mothers
Requirements given in kilojoules (kJ) and kilocalories (kcal)

△ **Table 1.5** Estimated average requirements for energy

Remember:
- If food consumed equals the energy used, your weight stays the same.
- If food consumed is greater than energy used, weight increases.
- If food consumed is less than energy used, there is weight loss.
- These are given as estimated average requirements (EAR).

Key points
- Requirements for nutrients differ for different groups.
- We need to maintain a balance of energy input and energy output.
- If too much food is consumed it is stored as fat, resulting in weight gain.

Controlled assessment link

In your controlled assessment work, you will analyse the nutritional content of existing products. See, for example, Figure 14.3 on page 227.

Exam practice questions

1. State what is meant by 'energy balance'.

   [2 marks]

2. Give **five** factors that affect how much energy someone needs. **[5 marks]**

3. Describe the effect on a person's health of being obese. **[4 marks]**

Activities

1. Use nutrition software to analyse the amount of energy that you should be consuming. Input everything that you consume in one day. Remember to include all of your drinks and snacks. Analyse your results and make a list of the ways that you could improve your diet.

2. Research how much energy you use doing each of the following activities for an hour:
   o playing squash
   o walking slowly
   o sitting at your computer
   o dancing.

1.3 Applying nutritional advice

Learning objectives

By the end of this section you should have developed a knowledge and understanding of:

o how to apply nutritional advice when analysing food products

Introduction

The eatwell plate can be applied to all main course dishes, such as lasagne, casseroles and pasta products. You will have to think carefully how to adapt desserts, snacks, cakes, biscuits and pastry products.

Remember that you are aiming to:

o lower the fat
o lower the sugar
o lower the salt
o increase the fibre.

When you develop or modify the products, you must also consider who the product is designed for, as you will need to meet their identified needs. This could mean changing the flavour, colour, texture, cost, shape or appearance, or how it is assembled or cooked. You may also need to improve the **nutritional content** or adapt it to meet cultural or dietary needs.

Key term

Nutritional content – the type and quantity of nutrition the product supplies

Analysing a product

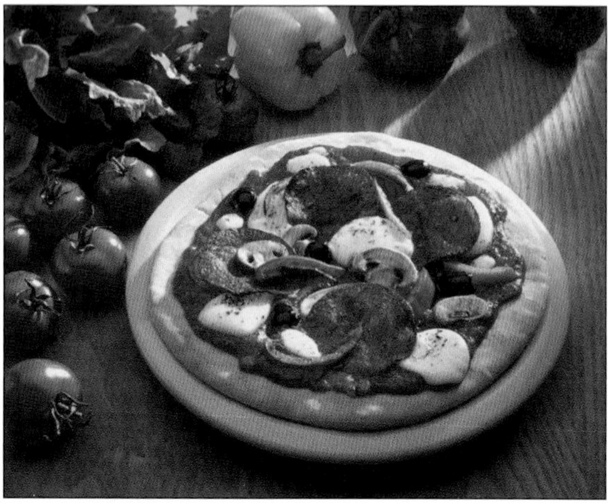

△ **Figure 1.23** Pizza – a good, balanced product

A good example of a balanced product is a pizza, which contains ingredients from the four main food groups:

- a thick dough base from the bread, rice, potatoes, pasta and other starchy food group
- tomato purée and plenty of other vegetables, such as mushrooms and peppers, from the fruit and vegetable group
- a moderate amount of cheese, or even fat-reduced cheese, from the milk and dairy group
- a moderate amount of ham or tuna from the meat, fish, eggs, beans group and other non-dairy sources of protein.

Ways to modify recipes

You can **modify** recipes to meet healthy eating guidelines by adapting or changing the ingredients or by changing the method of cooking.

> **Key term**
>
> **Modify** – change an ingredient to improve or develop a recipe

> **Activities**
>
> Design and make a pizza which follows the advice of the eatwell plate.
>
> Try using a blank eatwell plate as shown in Figure 1.24, when you are designing/adapting recipes.

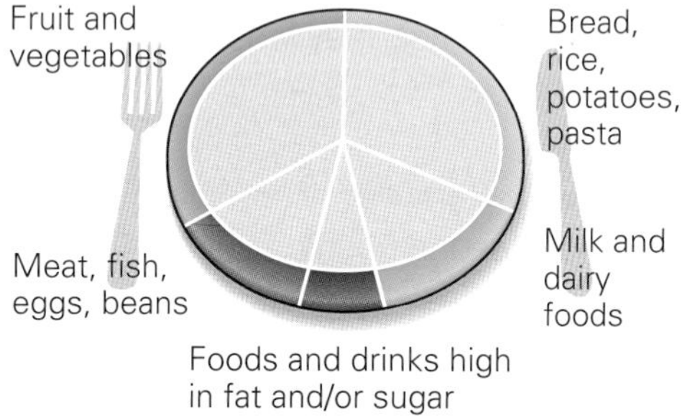

△ **Figure** 1.24 A blank eatwell plate

Bread, rice, potatoes, pasta and other starchy foods

- Use different types of flour to increase variety, for example, in bread products, such as wholemeal and granary.
- Use more pasta in relation to meat/fish sauce in pasta products.
- Use more potato in relation to meat in cottage or shepherd's pie.
- Use naan bread and plenty of rice with curries.

Fruit and vegetables

- Incorporate extra vegetables into casseroles, soups and meat sauces.
- Add salads (with low-fat dressings) and vegetables to main meals.
- Add fresh or dried fruit to puddings, cakes and biscuits.
- Use fresh and dried fruit to sweeten products instead of using sucrose.

△ **Figure 1.25** Add more vegetables to casseroles and stews

Meat, fish, eggs, beans and other non-dairy sources of protein

- Add pulses in meat dishes to increase the fibre content, reduce the overall fat content and add extra protein, for example, red kidney beans in a chilli.
- Use lean meat and remove visible fat or skin where necessary, for example, remove skin from chicken.
- Use alternatives to meat such as mycoprotein (Quorn®), tofu or textured vegetable protein to increase variety. Use eggs, nuts, pulses and seeds more frequently.
- Include fish, both oily and white varieties, in products.

Milk and dairy foods

- Switch to semi-skimmed or skimmed milk and use lower-fat dairy products.
- Use fromage frais, quark or plain yogurt in place of cream in some dishes (you may need to test this out first as the recipe may not always work).
- Use a smaller amount of a strong-tasting cheese, such as mature Cheddar or Parmesan, in cooking, instead of more of a milder cheese.

- Use reduced-fat cheese wherever possible.
- Grate cheese for use in a wide range of products, so less is used. Mix grated cheese with breadcrumbs for a lower-fat crunchy topping.

> **Controlled assessment link**
> As part of your development work, you will need to modify your recipes. See, for example Figure 14.9 on page 234, which suggests that the home-made gnocchi could be developed by adding more vegetables to make it healthier; or Figure 14.13 on page 241, where Quorn® is used as an alternative to beef and turkey mince.

Foods and drinks high in fat and/or sugar

If you make products that fit into this category, think carefully about how you can improve them. You could:

- reduce the quantity of sugar in the recipe
- replace sugar with dried or fresh fruit
- use unsaturated oils and fats instead of butter (this won't reduce the fat content but will help lower cholesterol)
- use fewer high-fat/sugar ingredients, for example, use more fruit and less topping for a crumble, use a lattice top on a pie, or change a pie into a flan
- replace cream with yoghurt
- choose lower-fat versions of ingredients.

Ways to improve the method of cooking

- Some traditional methods of cooking use a lot of additional fat, so try to avoid roasting and deep- or shallow-fat frying and choose lower-fat methods.
- Grill or oven-bake foods instead of frying, which will remove some of the fat from the foods.
- Steam fish instead of frying it.

27

- Poach, bake or boil so that no fat is added.
- Dry-fry meat in a non-stick pan to remove the fat.
- Use fats and oils sparingly. Try to spray oil, as this just puts a thin film on the pan.
- Ensure that the temperature is correct when frying so that foods absorb less fat.

△ **Figure 1.26** Change your method of cooking – try steaming

There are many ways to modify products and recipes. You will discover many more as you try different ideas.

Activity

Use basic spaghetti bolognese ingredients, but modify them to produce an innovative, healthier pasta product that will appeal to young children.

Exam practice questions

1. State **one** other method of cooking for each of the following foods that would lower the fat content:
   - fried bacon
   - fried sausages
   - fried egg
   - fried chicken
   - roast potatoes.   **[5 marks]**

2. Describe ways in which this spaghetti bolognese recipe could be adapted to meet the requirements of the eatwell plate. Consider the method of making as well as the ingredients.   **[6 marks]**

   Spaghetti bolognese
   220 g minced beef
   50 g bacon
   1 tablespoon oil
   1 chopped onion
   1 small tin tomatoes
   1 tablespoon tomato puree
   Salt and pepper to taste
   200 g spaghetti
   50 g grated parmesan cheese

3. Give **two** reasons why we should cut down on the amount of salt in our diet. **[2 marks]**

4. Suggest **two** different flavourings that could be added to a savoury product instead of salt.   **[2 marks]**

5. List **six** ways of reducing fat in a recipe of your choice.   **[6 marks]**

Key points

- Keep the balance of starchy foods and fruit and vegetables high in comparison to proteins, dairy foods, fat and sugar.
- Adapt recipes by replacing or reducing high fat, sugar and salt ingredients.

1.4 **Nutritional and dietary needs of different target groups**

Learning objectives

By the end of this section you should have developed a knowledge and understanding of the nutritional and dietary needs of different target groups, as follows:

o people of different ages and at different stages of life
o vegetarians
o those on calorie-controlled diets
o those with coronary heart disease
o pregnant women
o those with diabetes
o those with nut allergies
o those with coeliac disease
o those who are lactose-intolerant.

Introduction

Most people make a choice of food at least two or three times a day. The availability of a wide range of foods makes it easier to choose foods that are nutritionally good for us, but we are all influenced by a variety of other factors and we all have differing nutritional needs. A range of different factors affect our choice of food.

People of different ages and at different stages of life

During the different stages of life, people require different foods and quantities of nutrients to keep healthy. From a manufacturer's point of view this offers the opportunity to target groups with products designed for their particular needs.

Knowledge link
See the 'Nutrients' section at the beginning of this chapter, page 1.

Babies

Babies are totally reliant on their parents to provide food. A baby needs essential nutrients for growth and development, energy-dense,

filling food that is easy to swallow. It must be hygienic and safe. Babies initially drink only milk, but as they grow they require more energy, so they are weaned on to solid food.

Parents will want the food to be nutritious, appetising, easy to prepare, without additives, low in sugar, hygienic, safe and sold at a reasonable price.

△ **Figure 1.27** At six months babies are weaned on to solid food.

Toddlers

Toddlers are growing fast, so they require a lot of energy from their food. They need a balanced diet but a high proportion of complex carbohydrates to provide this energy. The food must be easy to hold, available in suitably sized portions, with interesting shapes, colours, textures and flavours.

School-aged children

School-aged children are still reliant on their parents, but they are influenced by the media and their peer group. They need products that meet current dietary guidelines on healthy eating and that also provide filling food, particularly for packed lunches.

Adolescents

Adolescents are becoming aware of environmental, moral, economic and health issues. They become more aware of peer group pressure and body image. Body growth is rapid, so they still require a lot of energy from their food, particularly boys during their growth spurts. Girls have a greater need for the mineral iron to replace that lost during menstruation.

Puberty is also the time when bones stop growing, and without sufficient calcium and phosphorus in the diet at this crucial time there will be a weakening of the bones, leading to rickets and osteoporosis in later life.

Food must be affordable, fashionable, quick and easy to prepare, and suited to a busy and energetic lifestyle.

Adults

Adults' needs vary the most, depending on their lifestyle and occupation. Many adults face the problem of consuming too much energy from food, leading to weight gain. They often look to buy products to help with weight loss. Some want foods that are lower in fat, salt or sugar and are eager to follow current healthy eating guidelines. They may also want luxury products as meals become more of a social occasion.

Single people

Single people will want products sold in small packs, ready or partly made products that are easy to store.

Senior citizens

Senior citizens are growing in number, and many live on a limited income. They still require a balanced diet supplying a good range of nutrients, but they often suffer from loss of appetite. They need appetising products in smaller quantities. They want easy-to-prepare, nutritional meals with easy-to-open packaging.

△ **Figure 1.28** Senior citizens enjoy cooking a meal together

Exam practice questions

List **four** specification points for a new product to meet the needs of each of the following target groups:

○ A teenage student before a game of football. **[4 marks]**
○ An office worker's packed lunch. **[4 marks]**
○ A single senior citizen's main meal. **[4 marks]**
○ Party food for a toddler. **[4 marks]**

Give reasons for each of the specification points. **[4 × 4 marks]**

Activities

1. Produce *two* design ideas that meet the specification points for one of the new products you have listed in the Exam practice questions. Develop *one* idea and, in your practical lesson, prepare one of the design ideas. Evaluate the product against the specification points.

2. Design some promotional material to give a new mum some ideas for weaning foods for a 9-month-old baby.

3. What advice would you give to a catering company that wants to start a meals service for elderly, housebound people?

Stretch yourself

1. Explain why it is important for teenagers to eat a healthy, balanced diet.

2. Explain why breakfast is an important meal for everyone.

Vegetarians

There are three main reasons why a person might become a vegetarian: for moral reasons, because of their religious beliefs or for medical reasons.

There are two main types of vegetarian:

- lacto-ovo vegetarians
- vegans.

Lacto-ovo vegetarians

Lacto-ovo vegetarians will not eat meat, meat products, fish, poultry, lard, suet, fish oils or gelatine because they involve killing an animal. They will, however, eat food products from animals, such as eggs, milk, cheese, butter, cream and yoghurt. One problem for this type of vegetarian is that cheese is made using rennin, an enzyme from a calf's stomach, but vegetarian cheese is made using a vegetable rennet (chymosin).

Lacto-ovo vegetarians can choose from a wide range of food products and recipes, and they have no problem at all in obtaining the essential amino acids for proteins or a wide range of vitamins and minerals. Quorn®, a commercially made mycoprotein, is an excellent meat substitute for lacto-ovo vegetarians, but vegans cannot eat it as it contains egg white. Cheese, eggs, nuts, beans, lentils, tofu and textured vegetable protein can all be used to make an exciting range of products.

△ **Figure 1.29** Look for the vegetarian logo

Vegans

Vegans are strict vegetarians who avoid eating all animal products, including meat, fish, eggs, cheese, dairy milk and cream. Vegans must ensure that they have an adequate nutritional balance in their diet. They have particular problems getting an adequate supply of:

- a range of proteins to ensure that they get all the essential amino acids
- vitamins A and D, which are plentiful in animal fats
- mineral elements calcium, phosphorus and iron, found in dairy products and meat
- vitamin B12, as there is no B12 in cereals or vegetables.

There are many types of nuts, pulses and cereals for vegans to use, particularly products made from soya, which is high in biological value. They need to make sure that they use herbs, spices and a variety of vegetables to avoid their diet being monotonous. A further problem is that vegan diets are sometimes very bulky and excessive amounts of fibre can cause digestive upsets. A vegan diet can include bean and vegetable stews, salads with nuts, nut roasts, pasta and rice dishes, and soya milk instead of cow's milk. Remember, though, that they cannot eat mycoprotein (Quorn®), as it contains egg white!

△ **Figure 1.30** The combination of pulses, nuts and cereals in this chickpea salad will give a vegan the essential amino acids

Exam practice questions

1. List **six** reasons why a person may become a vegetarian.

   [6 marks]

2. Explain the differences between a lacto-ovo vegetarian and a vegan. **[6 marks]**

3. Describe how the nutritional needs of a vegan can be met. **[6 marks]**

Activity

Modify a main course meat recipe to meet the needs of a vegan. Explain the reasons for your adaptation. Cook the product and evaluate it against the needs of a vegan.

Stretch yourself

Suggest two nutrients that a vegan may have missing from their diet and explain foods that they could eat to supply these nutrients.

Those on calorie-controlled diets

The number of people who are overweight or obese in the UK is increasing. People are now taking less exercise than they used to, but are still eating the same amount of food. This means that their weight gradually increases and the ratio of their weight in relation to their height is high. Figure 1.31 shows the chart that medical professionals use to check our weight.

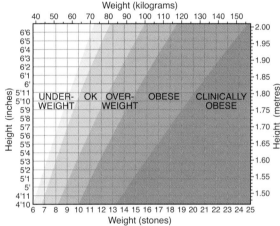

△ **Figure 1.31** Weight against height chart

Body mass index (BMI) is calculated from the relationship between your weight and height.

This is general advice for adults only – it does not apply to children. If you know your height and weight, you can work out which weight range you are in using the simple steps outlined below.

To find out your BMI

○ Take your weight in kilograms (kg) and divide it by your height in metres (m).

○ Then divide the result by your height in metres (m) again.

For example, if you weigh 70 kg and you are 1.75 m tall, your BMI would be 22.9 (70/1.75 = 40 and 40/1.75 = 22.9).

The BMI weight ranges, as set out by the World Health Organization (WHO), are outlined below.

- If your BMI is less than **18.4**, you are underweight for your height.
- If your BMI is between **18.5 and 24.9**, you are an ideal weight for your height.
- If your BMI is between **25 and 29.9**, you are over the ideal weight for your height.
- If your BMI is between **30 and 39.9**, you are obese.
- If your BMI is over **40**, you are clinically obese.

Why should we not be overweight?

Being overweight is unhealthy because it puts a strain on the organs of the body. It can cause heart disease, high blood pressure, diabetes, osteoarthritis, varicose veins, breathlessness and chest infections. It also causes unhappiness and low self-esteem and may lead to depression.

The main cause of being overweight is eating more food than the body requires so that excess energy is stored as fat. (See the section earlier in the chapter on energy balance, page 23.)

Losing weight

The only way to lose weight is to reduce the number of calories consumed and combine this with increased physical exercise. Many people try to lose weight and the 'slimming industry' is a big part of the food market. There are clubs to help and support people by group therapy, slimming magazines and crash diets in the media, but they all rely on people controlling their intake of calories.

Meals for people who are trying to lose weight should include a variety of foods and follow the eatwell plate, reducing their intake of fat and sugar. We can buy low-fat cheese, margarine-type spreads, salad dressings, low-sugar drinks,

desserts, biscuits and yoghurts. A calorie-controlled diet should consist of foods naturally low in fat, such as fruit and vegetables, white fish, poultry, skimmed milk and cheese, cereal, nuts and pulses.

People trying to lose weight should use low-fat methods of cooking, such as grilling, steaming, boiling and stir-frying.

Most foods have the amount of energy per 100 g on their nutritional label, so you can count the calories.

△ **Figure 1.32** Losing weight can be very hard work

Exam practice questions

1. List the reasons for the increase in the number of overweight primary school children in the UK.
   [6 marks]

2. Explain the ways that primary school children are being encouraged to lead healthier lifestyles. **[6 marks]**

3. Describe what the term 'obesity' means.
   [3 marks]

Activities

1. Visit the supermarket and investigate products aimed at adults on slimming diets. Using the information from the labels, compare the calories and nutritional values with similar 'non-diet' products. Collate the information in a chart.

2. Adapt a cake recipe to reduce the sugar and include more fruit and vegetables.

Healthy blood vessel   Unhealthy – blocked with cholesterol

 Figure 1.33 Plaque build-up in arteries

Those with coronary heart disease

In the UK, coronary heart disease (CHD) is a major health problem – one of the main causes of death. The risk of heart disease is increased by:

○ smoking
○ high blood pressure
○ raised levels of cholesterol
○ obesity
○ family history of heart disease
○ low levels of exercise.

Causes of CHD

CHD is related to the amount of fat in the diet. A diet high in saturated fats is also likely to be high in cholesterol. Cholesterol is a substance made in the liver and carried in the bloodstream. The cholesterol can build up and be deposited with other material as 'plaque' on the walls of the arteries, causing them to narrow. If the arteries then become blocked by a blood clot or more plaque, the person has a heart attack which, if severe, can cause death.

Animal fat → Blood cholesterol → Heart disease

The level of cholesterol in the blood depends on the amount of fatty acids in the diet. Replace saturated fatty acids with polyunsaturated fats as alternatives to animal fat-based products. Some low-fat spreads contain animal fat. Soluble fibre is thought to remove cholesterol from arteries.

To reduce your risk of heart disease, the general advice is to:

○ eat more fruits and vegetables
○ take regular physical exercise
○ do not smoke
○ eat a varied diet
○ cut back on the fat in your diet and cooking
○ eat more starchy carbohydrate
○ use monounsaturated fats (olive oil)
○ have fish instead of meat.

Does this sound familiar? It is the eatwell plate again!

Exam practice questions

1. State **two** changes that a person with heart disease should make to their diet.   **[2 marks]**

2. Explain why it is better to eat unsaturated fats than saturated fats.   **[4 marks]**

3. List **four** risk factors that cause people to have CHD.   **[4 marks]**

Stretch yourself

Discuss why coronary heart disease is a major cause of death in the Western world.

Activities

1. Your local health centre has asked for contributions to a display on 'How to reduce your risk of heart disease'. Produce a leaflet or poster about **one** of the following:

   o changes to your diet
   o recipe book ideas
   o foods to avoid
   o changes to your lifestyle.

2. Design and make a lower-fat luxury dessert suitable for someone who has CHD.

△ **Figure 1.34** Those with diabetes must control their intake of sugar

Those with diabetes

Diabetes is a medical condition where the glucose in the bloodstream is not balanced correctly. Glucose is carried in the blood to all body cells to supply them with energy. Insulin, a hormone produced by the pancreas, controls the amount of glucose in the bloodstream and stops it getting too high. Meals for those with diabetes should include high-fibre, starchy carbohydrate foods such as potatoes, rice and pasta, but should be low in sugar and sweet foods. Sorbitol (artificial sweetener) can be used instead of sucrose and glucose.

Key term

Diabetes – a metabolic disorder caused by the poor absorption of glucose. This can be due to the failure to produce insulin (in type 1 insulin-dependent diabetes) or the poor response of tissues to insulin (in type 2 non-insulin-dependent diabetes). Type 1 diabetes mellitus develops in childhood. The onset of type 2 is usually in middle age.

Pregnant women

Pregnant and breastfeeding mothers must adapt their diet to provide adequate nutrients for themselves and their baby. A new mother does not need special food products, but must ensure that she has a varied, balanced diet. She must pay particular attention to ensuring that she has the following:

o an adequate supply of protein for the growth of the baby

o calcium and vitamin D for both her and the baby's bone and tooth development – if the mother does not have sufficient calcium in her diet for the baby's needs, it will be taken from the mother's bones and teeth

o folic acid supplements before and during the early stages of pregnancy to reduce the risk of spina bifida in the baby

o iron, as the developing baby needs it for its blood supply; it also needs a store of iron in the liver as there is no iron in milk – if the mother does not get sufficient iron she will become anaemic

o a good supply of fruit and vegetables to provide vitamin C and fibre – pregnant women are prone to getting constipation

o a diet that does not include too many fats and sugary foods as it is essential that she does not put on more than 10–12 kg in weight.

Recent research has shown that mothers who follow a poor diet or who undereat both before and during pregnancy may give birth to low-birthweight babies.

Exam practice questions

1. List **four** nutrients that are particularly important during pregnancy. **[4 marks]**
2. Give **one** reason why each of the nutrients you have listed is important. **[4 marks]**
3. List **four** foods that should be avoided during pregnancy. **[4marks]**

△ **Figure 1.35** A pregnant woman

 Activities

1. Produce a leaflet for pregnant mothers – 'A guide to healthy eating in pregnancy'.
2. Design and make a main course dish that is high in iron and suitable for a pregnant mother.

 Stretch yourself

Explain why pregnant women need a good source of fibre in their diet. State four ways of incorporating more fibre.

Key points

o Pregnant women need to take care with what they eat.
o They should ensure that they have good sources of energy and nutrients.
o They should maintain levels of calcium and iron.
o Going on a slimming diet during pregnancy is not advisable.

Those with special dietary requirements

Some people cannot eat certain types of food without becoming ill. This may be because of a medical condition or a reaction to food. This is known as food intolerance or allergy.

Our bodies have an immune system to protect us from harmful things, but sometimes a person's body reacts too strongly to a particular substance. This is what happens when a person becomes allergic to a substance. Allergies to eggs, soya and certain artificial food flavours, colours or preservatives can also cause reactions.

Those with a nut allergy

Some allergies are very serious, for example, the allergic reaction to nuts. Some people have an **anaphylactic reaction** to even a minute quantity of an allergen in nuts. Their whole body reacts immediately and severely – blood vessels start to leak and they have difficulty breathing. They must be treated immediately with an injection of adrenalin, otherwise they could die. In some cases even touching or breathing in particles of the allergen can cause a reaction. Consequently, even the smallest amount of nuts or nut contact must be included on food labelling.

Controlled assessment link

See Figure 14.7 on page 233, which shows a design specification for a product suitable for those with a nut allergy.

Key term

Anaphylactic reaction – an extreme reaction to a substance needing immediate medical treatment

Those with coeliac disease

Coeliac disease is an autoimmune disease triggered by the protein gluten which is found in the grains wheat, rye and barley. Gluten damages the lining of the intestine and prevents nutrients from being absorbed. Adults with coeliac disease often have anaemia, weight loss and/or diarrhoea. One in every hundred people have coeliac disease. The medical treatment for coeliac disease is the gluten-free diet. Gluten is commonly used in bread, pasta, biscuits, cakes and pizza. Food manufacturers may also use derivatives of these grains as thickeners. There are currently two laws that relate to labelling foods with gluten. Specialist substitute gluten-free products are available. More information can be found at www.coeliac.org.uk.

Key term

Coeliac disease – a medical condition caused by an allergy to the protein gluten present in the cereals wheat, barley and rye

◁ **Figure 1.36** Look for the gluten-free logo

Those who are intolerant to certain foods

Some people develop sensitivity to certain foods, which gives them symptoms such as diarrhoea, nausea, tiredness, weakness or stomach pains. It is not an allergy, and it is often difficult to find out what foods they are sensitive to. An example of this is lactose intolerance, where a person cannot digest the milk sugar lactose. They become bloated, have abdominal pain and diarrhoea, so they have to avoid milk and milk products. Some people are intolerant to wheat, even though they do not have full coeliac disease. The list of food intolerances is getting longer and products have to list their ingredients on their packaging by law.

Key points

o People with allergies or food intolerances must read ingredients lists carefully.
o There is a wide range of products available for people with special dietary needs.

Exam practice questions

1. Describe why it is necessary for people with special dietary needs to read food labels. Give examples, using food labels. **[6 marks]**

2. Write a specification for a main course product for someone with coeliac disease. **[4 marks]**

3. Name **four** foods that are known to cause food intolerance in some people, apart from lactose. **[4 marks]**

4. State **four** foods that you could include in a packed lunch for someone with coeliac disease. **[4 marks]**

Activities

1. Make a cake product suitable for someone with coeliac disease.

2. Research a range of special dietary needs and produce a fact sheet for a supermarket to hand out.

Stretch yourself

1. Explain the function of insulin in the control of glucose levels in the blood. **[4 marks]**

2. Suggest ways that someone with a lactose intolerance could ensure that they have sufficient calcium in their diet.
[6 marks]

1.5 Nutrients found in and structure of a common range of foods

Learning objectives

By the end of this section you should have developed a knowledge and understanding of the nutrients found in and the structure of the following foods:

- cereals
- fruit
- vegetables
- meat
- fish

- milk
- cheese
- eggs
- fats and oils
- alternative protein foods.

Cereals

Cereals are an important food around the world. They are often the staple food within a country because they are cheap to produce in comparison to protein foods. The main types of cereal foods are:

- wheat
- rice
- maize
- oats
- barley
- rye.

Structure and nutritional content of cereals

Wheat

All cereal products are similar in structure. Wheat is one of the main cereals throughout the world.

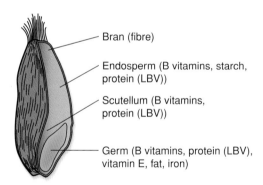

Bran (fibre)

Endosperm (B vitamins, starch, protein (LBV))

Scutellum (B vitamins, protein (LBV))

Germ (B vitamins, protein (LBV), vitamin E, fat, iron)

△ **Figure 1.37** Structure of and nutrients found in wheat

Wheat is made into flour. There is a large variety of flours available and they are used for making many different products. Flours can be described by their **extraction rate**, that is how much of the whole grain is used:

- Wholemeal flour – extraction rate of 100 per cent means that nothing has been removed from it. It is light brown in colour.

- Brown flour – extraction rate of 85–90 per cent (10–15 per cent of the grain is removed as bran). It is also light brown in colour.
- White flour – extraction rate of 70–75 per cent (the bran, germ, fat and some of the minerals have been removed). In the UK white flour has to be fortified by law with iron, calcium, thiamine and niacin. This is replacing the iron and B vitamins that have been lost in processing. It is white in appearance.

Key terms

Extraction rate – how much of the whole grain is used

Fortified – when a nutrient is added to a product to improve its nutritional value

All flours are **fortified** with calcium.

There is a large range of different flours that can be bought in supermarkets, including the following:

- Strong flour – this has a higher **gluten** content, which is needed in bread making and in flaky and choux pastry. The gluten is able to stretch after it is mixed with water and developed, for example, by kneading or rolling and folding, and helps to produce an elastic mixture.
- Soft flour – this is used for cake and pastry making and has a lower gluten content.
- Self-raising flour – this has a chemical raising agent added to it.
- Gluten-free flour – this has had the protein removed from it. It is made for people who have coeliac disease. Products that are gluten-free have a gluten-free symbol on them.

Key term

Gluten – protein in wheat products

Key point

It is important to choose the correct flour for your recipe.

Activities

1. Investigate what other types of flour are available in shops. Produce a chart or poster to show:
   - how they can be used in food products
   - their nutritional values.
2. Flour is used to make a wide range of products. Produce a mind map to show the uses of flour in food products.
3. Many children do not like wholemeal bread. Take a traditional baked product and adapt it to:
   - use wholemeal flour
   - be attractive to children.

   Evaluate how successful your product is. Suggest ways that it could be improved further.

Exam practice questions

1. Explain what is meant by the term 'extraction rate'. **[4 marks]**
2. Explain why you are encouraged to eat more wholemeal cereals. **[4 marks]**

Stretch yourself

Make 100 g quantities of short-crust pastry using a range of different flours. Carry out sensory analysis tests on them. Present your findings as a report.

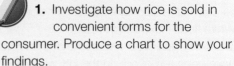
Rice

Rice is similar in structure to wheat. It is a good source of:

○ carbohydrate – starch and fibre (if brown rice)
○ B vitamins (thiamin and niacin)
○ protein (LBV).

Rice is a very versatile product and can be used as part of a main dish or in soups, starters and desserts. There is a wide variety of types of rice sold in supermarkets.

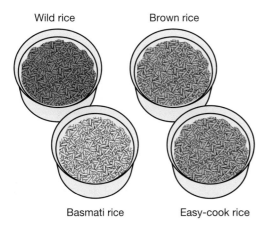

Wild rice   Brown rice

Basmati rice   Easy-cook rice

△ **Figure 1.38** Four different types of rice

There are different varieties of rice:

○ short-grain rice – used in puddings and risottos, as the grains tend to clump together when they are cooked
○ long-grain rice – the grains remain separate when they are cooked. Examples are Carolina rice and basmati.

Exam practice questions

Explain why rice is considered a healthy food to eat.

[4 marks]

Maize

The nutrient content of maize is similar to other cereals. It is also a good source of vitamin A.

Activities

1. Investigate how rice is sold in convenient forms for the consumer. Produce a chart to show your findings.
2. Rice can be used in many different types of dishes. Prepare a dish to illustrate how versatile rice is. Produce a recipe leaflet for your dish that a manufacturer could attach to the packet of rice.

Corn on the cob is a popular way to eat maize. Maize is available in a variety of forms: fresh, frozen and canned. It is also used to make breakfast cereals such as cornflakes.

In its ground form it is a white powder called cornflour, which contains starch. The other nutrients are removed during the processing of the maize. Cornflour is often used to thicken liquids and sauces.

Oats

Oats are a good source of carbohydrates (starch and fibre), B vitamins (thiamin, riboflavin and B6), calcium, iron and small amounts of folic acid.

Oats are usually rolled rather than crushed when they are processed. They are then sold by grade – coarse, medium and fine. Oats are mainly used in cereal products such as muesli, and also in baked products such as flapjacks and biscuits. Oats can be used to make a non-dairy substitute for milk.

Barley

The main nutrients found in barley are carbohydrates (fibre and starch). Today barley is mainly used in the brewing industry and for cattle food. It is used in foods as pearl barley, which can be added to stews and casseroles, or as flaked barley, which is added to breakfast cereals.

Activities

1. Other cereal products are available that can be used in food products. Investigate some of the other cereal products and produce an information leaflet about them, informing consumers about their value in the diet and how they can be used.

2. Choose one of the products from your cereals leaflet and design and make a product that shows creative use of the cereal.

3. Prepare a recipe leaflet that illustrates your dish and could be given to consumers in the supermarket.

Exam practice questions

1. List the functions of the main nutrients found in cereals.

[4 marks]

2. Explain, using examples, why cereal products are an important part of our diet.

[6 marks]

Fruit

There is a large range of fruits which come in a variety of flavours, colours, sizes and textures. They are mostly eaten raw, but on some occasions are cooked.

Structure of fruits

Fruits are made up of cells, which in turn are made up of:

o cell wall – mainly cellulose
o cytoplasm – jelly-like substance that contains the colour pigments and fat droplets
o vacuole – the largest part of the cell, which contains sugar, pigments and salts.

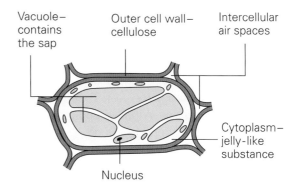

△ **Figure 1.39** Structure of fruit

Fruits can be categorised by their type. There are four main types:

o citrus – lemons, limes, oranges
o soft or berry fruits – raspberries, strawberries, blueberries, blackcurrants
o hard fruit – apples, pears
o some fruits which do not fall into any category, such as kiwi, pomegranate, melon, banana.

Nutritional content of fruit

The nutritional content of fruit varies depending on the type of fruit it is. In general, fruits are high in vitamins, carbohydrates (sucrose, fructose and fibre) and minerals. They are low in protein and fat.

Activity

We are being encouraged to eat more fruit. Prepare a dish that would be interesting and appealing to young children who claim they do not like to eat fruit.

Nutrient	Sources
Vitamin C	Rich sources – blackcurrants, rosehips Good sources – citrus fruits, strawberries, gooseberries, raspberries Remember, vitamin C is destroyed by heat
Vitamin A	Apricots
Carbohydrate	Found in the form of sucrose and fructose in ripe fruit Fibre is found in the skin and fibrous parts of the fruit

△ **Table 1.6** Nutrients found in different types of fruits

Vegetables

There is a wide variety of vegetables available for us to use all through the year. They include those which are grown in the UK and those that are imported from around the world. You are also able to buy these in a variety of forms, such as fresh, frozen and canned.

Structure of vegetables

Vegetables are similar to fruit in structure. However, they do vary depending on the type. For example, the cellulose which makes up the cell walls is thin and delicate in leaf products like spinach and lettuce, while in older vegetables it becomes thicker. The cells also contain a lot of water; if the water is lost, the leaves become limp.

Vegetables also come in a variety of colours. The colour depends on:

○ chlorophyll – provides the green colour, for example, in cabbage, sprouts, lettuce
○ carotenoids – yellow and orange, for example, in carrots
○ anthocyanins – red and blue, for example, in beetroot, red cabbage.

Nutritional value of vegetables

Vegetables are eaten mostly as part of main meals, though we are being encouraged to eat them as snacks instead of high-calorie foods.

△ **Figure 1.40** Many vegetables are brightly coloured

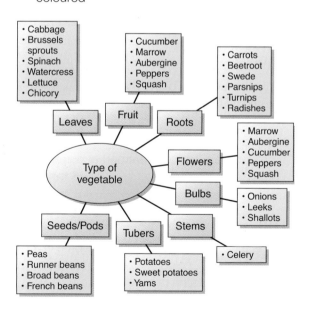

△ **Figure 1.41** We eat different parts of the vegetable plants and this is how they are classified

Protein	Only found in pulses and beans. It is of a low biological value except in soya beans, which are HBV
Carbohydrate	Root vegetables and tubers are the best sources of carbohydrate, in the form of starch Vegetables are a good source of fibre
Vitamin C	Rich sources – sprouts, cabbage, green peppers, spinach, watercress Reasonable sources – peas, beansprouts, potatoes (because we consume them in quite large quantities)
B Vitamins	Pulses provide a good source of thiamine Most vegetables contain some of the B group
Vitamin A	Carrots and dark green vegetables
Calcium and iron	Found in some vegetables such as watercress, cabbage and spinach, but it is not always available to the body

△ **Table 1.7** Nutrients found in vegetables

The nutrient content of vegetables varies depending on their type and how they are cooked. Many vitamins are water-soluble and destroyed by heat.

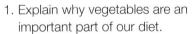

Key points

o Fruits and vegetables provide us with important vitamins, carbohydrates and fibre.
o We need to prepare and cook them carefully so that their nutrients are not lost. Remember that vitamin C dissolves in water.

Exam practice questions

1. Explain why vegetables are an important part of our diet.
   [4 marks]

2. Describe how vegetables should be prepared and cooked to preserve the vitamin content. **[6 marks]**

Activities

1. Some vegetables can be eaten raw. Design and make an interesting salad using a range of vegetables and other ingredients.

2. Calculate the cost and nutritional value of the salad using a nutrition program.

Meat

There is a large range of meat and meat products available to purchase in the shops. The quality of the product will depend on how the animal has been kept, what it was fed on, its age, and how it is processed and cooked.

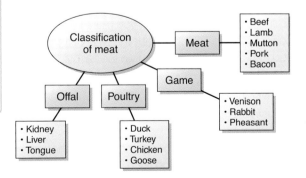

△ **Figure 1.42** Classification of meat

Structure of meat

Meat is the muscle tissue of animals. The muscles are fibres bundled together and surrounded by **connective tissue**. Connective tissue is called **collagen**.

 Key terms

Collagen – protein found in meat

Connective tissue – surrounds the muscle fibres

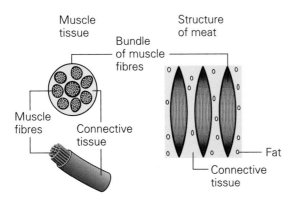

△ **Figure 1.43** Structure of meat

The parts of the animals that do the most work, that is, the neck and the shin, have large, long fibres. These tend to be tougher cuts of meat. They need long, slow methods of cooking to make them tender. Mincing breaks down the fibres and means shorter methods of cooking can be used. The meat that comes from young animals or the parts of the animal that do not do as much work, such as the breast, rump or ribs, have shorter fibres and can be cooked quickly.

To make sure meat is tender, you must choose the correct method of cooking for the type of meat. You can also help to make meat tender by:

○ reducing the length of the muscle fibres by mincing or cutting across the muscle fibres
○ using long slow methods of cooking, for example, stewing
○ marinading meat, for example, in alcohol or with vinegar or lemon juice.

Fat is found between the bundles of tissues. The fat helps to keep the meat moist when cooked and it adds flavour. Myoglobin is the colour pigment that gives red meat its red colour.

Poultry muscle fibres are similar to those of meat except that the fibres are shorter and there is very little connective tissue, which means that the meat is more tender.

Look at Figure 1.44. Can you recognise the different types of meat?

△ **Figure 1.44** Different types of meat

Exam practice questions

1. Describe how muscle fibres affect the tenderness of meat.

[6 marks]

2. Explain why tough cuts of meat are cooked by long, slow methods of cooking.

[4 marks]

Key points

1. Meat is made up of bundles of muscle fibres. Lean meat comes from young animals and the parts of the animal that do not do as much work.

2. Meat is a good source of protein in the diet and also contains other important nutrients.

Nutritional value of meat

The main nutrients found in meat are:

- protein – high biological value
- fat – the amount varies and many farmers are now producing meat that has a lot less fat than in the past
- vitamins – fat-soluble vitamins remain stable, while B vitamins may leach into the cooking liquid
- iron – red meat is a good source of iron, as is offal (liver, kidney)
- water – makes up approximately 74 per cent meat.

Poultry is similar to meat in nutritional value except that it generally contains less fat, except in goose and duck. Poultry also contains less iron than meat.

We can also eat the internal organs of animals. This is called offal and includes:

- kidneys
- liver
- heart
- tongue
- tripe.

Offal contains similar nutrients to meat but:

- it is usually lower in fat than meat
- liver is a good source of vitamins
- liver is a good source of iron.

Exam practice questions

1. List the main nutrients found in meat. **[4 marks]**
2. If you were anaemic, which types of meat would you try to include in your diet? **[4 marks]**
3. If you were trying to reduce the amount of fatty foods you consume, which types of meat would you choose? **[2 marks]**

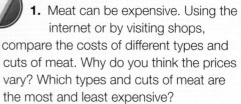

Activities

1. Meat can be expensive. Using the internet or by visiting shops, compare the costs of different types and cuts of meat. Why do you think the prices vary? Which types and cuts of meat are the most and least expensive?

2. Cheaper cuts of meat can be made into interesting, filling and nutritious dishes. Using a cheaper cut of meat, make a dish that would appeal to a family. Calculate the nutritional value and cost per portion.

Fish

There are many varieties of fish available and it can be bought in many different forms, for instance, fresh, frozen and canned.

Structure of fish

Fish is similar in structure to meat. It is made up of fibres and connective tissue. However, the fibres are much shorter and the connective tissue is much finer, which makes it quicker to cook. This means that it is a more delicate and tender food.

Nutritional value of fish

The nutritional value of fish depends on its type. Fish can be classified into three groups:

- white – for example, cod, haddock, coley, whiting, plaice
- oily – for example, sardines, tuna, mackerel, sardines, trout
- shellfish – for example, prawns, crab, lobster, shrimps, oysters.

Fish is a good source of:

- protein – fish is high in biological value protein
- fat – white and shellfish contain very little fat; oily fish are good sources of essential fatty acids that the body cannot make

Nutrient	White (cod)	Oily (mackerel)	Shell (prawns)
Energy	322.00 kJ	926.00 kJ	321.00 kJ
Energy	76.00 kcal	223.00 kcal	76.00 kcal
Protein	17.40 g	19.00 g	17.60 g
Carbohydrate	0 g	0 g	0 g
Fat of which saturates	0.70 g 0.10 g	16.30 g 3.30 g	0.60 g 0.10 g
Water	82.10 g	64.00 g	79.20 g

△ **Table 1.8** Nutrients found in raw fish per 100 g

○ minerals – calcium is a good source in fish where the bones are eaten, for example, in sprats and tinned fish when the bones are softened in processing
○ vitamins A and D – oily fish are good sources.

Controlled assessment link
Figure 14.11 on page 236 shows an example of a student's fish pie.

Key points

1. Fish can be classified by:
  ○ habitat – sea, fresh water
  ○ fat content.
2. Fish is a good source of protein and iodine.
3. The government advises that we should try to eat two portions of fish a week and one of these should be an oily fish.

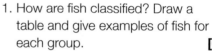

Exam practice questions

1. How are fish classified? Draw a table and give examples of fish for each group. **[6 marks]**
2. Explain why are we being encouraged to eat at least two portions of fish a week. **[4 marks]**
3. Explain why fish takes less time to cook than meat. **[2 marks]**

Activity
Many children say they do not like fish. Design a dish that would encourage children to eat fish.

Stretch yourself

Many families eat fish fingers because they think that they are good value for money.

1. Disassemble a fish finger and calculate the weight of the actual fish in it.
2. Using the current cost of fish in the supermarket, calculate whether the fish finger is good value for money.

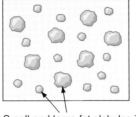

Small and large fat globules in milk which rise to the top of milk that has not been homogenised

Small fat globules evenly dispersed through the milk

△ **Figure 1.45** Comparison of milk and homogenised milk

Milk

There is a wide variety of milks available. Cow's milk is the most popular milk consumed in the UK. Other sources of milk come from goats and sheep. There are also milk-type products made from oats, rice and soya.

Structure of milk

Milk is mainly water. It is an emulsion and has tiny drops of fat suspended in it. As oil and water do not mix, the fat will rise to the top of the milk. This is seen as the cream line in the milk. Today much of the milk we buy is homogenised so that the fat is distributed evenly throughout the milk and therefore this fat line is not visible.

Homogenisation involves forcing the milk at high pressure through small holes. This breaks up the fat globules in order to spread them evenly throughout the milk.

Nutritional value of milk

Milk contains the following nutrients:

o water
o protein
o fat
o carbohydrate
o vitamins and minerals.

Milk provides you with energy.

Milk is often described as a perfect food because it is designed to feed the young of the animals it is produced from.

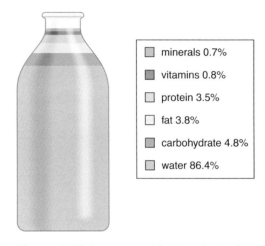

minerals 0.7%
vitamins 0.8%
protein 3.5%
fat 3.8%
carbohydrate 4.8%
water 86.4%

△ **Figure 1.46** Average nutrient content of milk

Key terms

Homogenisation – involves forcing the milk at high pressure through small holes. This breaks up the fat globules in order to spread them evenly throughout the milk and prevent separation of a cream layer

Lactose – a type of carbohydrate found in milk

Varieties of milk

There are many different types of milk available for us to buy. These vary according to how they have been produced and in their fat content.

o Whole milk has had nothing added or removed.

Nutrients	Information
Protein	○ High biological value protein
Fat	○ The amount of fat depends of the type of milk ○ By law whole milk must contain 3 per cent fat ○ Contains both saturated and unsaturated fats ○ The sales of reduced-fat milks have increased as we are encouraged to consume less fat
Carbohydrate	○ In the form of **lactose** ○ It does not taste sweet ○ Can now purchase lactose-free milk for those people who have intolerance
Vitamins	○ Vitamin A (retinol and carotene) – the amount varies – more in summer ○ Skimmed milk contains fewer vitamins as the fat is removed and vitamin A is fat-soluble ○ Vitamin D – it contains more in summer ○ Water soluble vitamins riboflavin (B2), thiamine (B1) and nicotinic acid (B3)
Minerals	○ Calcium and phosphorus ○ Approximately 43 per cent of the calcium intake of adults is provided from milk and milk products

△ **Table 1.9** Nutrients found in milk

○ Semi-skimmed milk:
  ○ is the most popular type of milk in the UK
  ○ has a fat content of 1.7 per cent.
○ Skimmed milk:
  ○ has a fat content of 0.1–0.3 per cent
  ○ contains slightly more calcium than whole milk
  ○ has lower levels of fat-soluble vitamins
  ○ is not recommended for children under the age of five.
○ Channel Island milk:
  ○ is higher in calories and fat than whole milk
  ○ has a higher content of fat-soluble vitamins
  ○ has a visible cream line and is commonly sold in supermarkets as Channel Island or Jersey milk. There are also products sold as breakfast milk – this is Channel Island

milk which has been homogenised so that the cream is evenly distributed throughout the milk. The milk has a very creamy flavour throughout.

Exam practice questions

1. Explain why milk is a valuable food in the diet. **[4 marks]**
2. Explain why the fat content of different milks varies. **[4 marks]**
3. The sales of semi-skimmed and skimmed milk have increased. Explain why this has happened. **[2 marks]**
4. Which type of milk would you recommend for children under five years of age? Give **one** reason for your answer. **[2 marks]**

Nutritional content	Channel Island	Whole, pasteurised, winter	Semi-skimmed	Skimmed
Energy	327.00 kJ	275.00 kJ	195.00 kJ	140.00 kJ
Energy	78.00 kcal	66.00 kcal	46.00 kcal	33.00 kcal
Protein	3.60 g	3.20 g	3.30 g	3.30 g
Carbohydrate of which: sugars starch	4.80 g 4.80 g 0.00 g	4.80 g 4.80 g 0.00 g	5.00 g 5.00 g 0.00 g	5.00 g 5.00 g 0.00 g
Fat of which: saturates unsaturates polyunsaturates	5.10 g 3.30 g 1.30 g 0.10 g	3.90 g 2.50 g 1.10 g 0.10 g	1.70 g 1.00 g 0.50 g trace	0.10 g 0.10 g trace trace
Sodium	54.00 mg	55.00 mg	55.00 mg	54.00 mg
Vitamin A Retinol Carotene	 46.00 µg 71.00 µg	 41.00 µg 11.00 µg	 21.00 µg 9.00 µg	 µg trace
Vitamin D	0.03 µg	0.03 µg	0.01 µg	trace
Thiamin	0.04 mg	0.04 mg	0.04 mg	0.04 mg
Riboflavin	0.19 mg	0.17 mg	0.18 mg	0.17 mg
Calcium	130.00 mg	115.00 mg	120.00 mg	120.00 mg
Phosphorus	100.00 mg	92.00 mg	95.00 mg	94.00 mg

△ **Table 1.10** Nutritional value of different types of milk (kJ = kilojoules; kcal = kilocalories; g = grams; mg = miligrams; µg = micrograms)

Stretch yourself

Explain why vitamin A (retinol and carotene) is reduced in skimmed and semi-skimmed milk.

Activities

1. Milk can also be obtained from other sources, for example, sheep, goats and soya. Using a nutrition software package, investigate the nutritional content of three different types of milk.

2. How does their nutritional content compare with the types of milk shown in Table 1.10?

3. Why do you think there is a market for different types of milk?

Milk can be processed to produce other types of milk, such as dried milk powder, condensed and evaporated milk. It can also be made into other products such as yoghurt, cream and cheese.

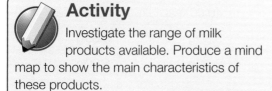

> ## Activity
>
> Investigate the range of milk products available. Produce a mind map to show the main characteristics of these products.

Alternatives to animal milk

△ **Figure 1.47** Alternatives to animal sources of milk

Some people have problems digesting cow's milk, being allergic or lactose-intolerant. This means they may want to find an alternative that will give them similar nutrition.

○ Rice milk is dairy-free, low in fat and calories, and cholesterol-free. It is a source of easily digestible carbohydrates, but it is lower than normal milk in protein and essential fatty acids.

○ Oat milk is a dairy-free alternative to milk and soya products that can be used in the same way as cow's milk. Research has shown that oats can help reduce cholesterol, are rich in folic acid and vitamin E, low in saturated fat, and, unlike other milks, oat milk is a good source of fibre.

○ Soya milk has a lower fat content than full-fat cow's milk. It is low in carbohydrate and provides a good source of HBV protein. It can be bought sweetened or unsweetened. Soya milk can be used as a straight substitute for cow's milk when cooking.

Heat treatment of milk

Most milk sold is heat-treated to kill harmful bacteria and to increase its shelf life.

> ## Key points
>
> ○ Milk is a good source of protein, calcium, vitamin B12 and riboflavin.
> ○ Vitamins A and D are found in whole milk and its products.
> ○ Milk can be processed in a variety of ways to produce other products.

> ## Activities
>
> **1.** There is a wide variety of other types of milk available to buy in shops. Investigate the range of products available and produce a chart to show information on:
>
> ○ their nutritional values
> ○ how they are packaged
> ○ their uses in food preparation
> ○ how they are processed and produced.
>
> **2.** Some children do not like to drink milk. Prepare an interesting milk-based product that uses milk as its main ingredient.

Method of heat treatment	Treatment	Effect of the treatment
Pasteurised milk	○ Heated to a temperature of at least 71.7 °C for a minimum of 15 seconds and maximum of 25 seconds ○ Milk is cooled quickly to below 6 °C	○ Kills harmful bacteria ○ Little effect on the nutritional value of the milk ○ Extends the shelf life of the milk
Sterilised milk	○ Heated to a temperature of 113–130 °C for approximately 10–30 minutes ○ Then cooled quickly	○ Destroys nearly all the bacteria in it ○ Changes the taste and colour ○ Destroys some vitamins ○ Unopened bottles or cartons can be kept for several months without being in a fridge ○ Once opened it must be treated as fresh
UHT milk (ultra heat-treated)	○ Heated to a temperature of at least 135 °C for 1 second ○ Put into sterile, sealed containers	○ Unopened packs have a long shelf life ○ Once opened it must be treated as fresh ○ Little effect on flavour or nutritional value

△ **Table 1.11** Heat treatment of milk

Cheese

There are many different varieties of cheese you can buy, some traditionally produced in the UK and others from around the world. They are made by different methods and with different types of milk, such as cow's, sheep's and goat's milk.

Structure of cheese

All cheese is made from milk. To change it from a liquid to a solid, rennin is added to the milk. In cheeses suitable for vegetarians, chymosin is added which, unlike rennin, does not come from animals. The milk then separates into curds and whey. It is the curd that is used to make the cheese. The cheese is then pressed. The harder it is pressed, the less water it contains.

Nutrients found in cheese

Cheese is made from milk solids and therefore contains similar nutrients. However, their amounts depend on the type of cheese. A hard cheese will contain more fat and protein as more of the liquid has been pressed out during the processing.

Cheese is a concentrated source of protein and also a good source of calcium, vitamin A and riboflavin. However, some types – the harder varieties and cream cheeses – have a high fat content. There are many reduced-fat varieties available today.

> Controlled assessment link
> Figure 14.11 on page 236 shows an example of a student's product that contains cheese.

Nutritional content	Cheddar (hard)	Brie (soft)	Cream cheese	Cottage cheese – reduced fat
Energy	1708.00 kJ	1323.00 kJ	1807.00 kJ	331.00 kJ
Energy	412.00 kcal	319.00 kcal	439.00 kcal	78.00 kcal
Protein	25.50 g	19.30 g	3.10 g	13.30 g
Fat of which: saturates	34.40 g 21.70 g	26.90 g 16.80 g	47.40 g 29.70 g	1.40 g 0.90 g
Water	36.00 g	48.60 g	45.50 g	80.20 g

△ **Table 1.12** Composition of cheese per 100 g

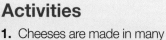

Activities

1. Cheeses are made in many different parts of the world. Plot where different types of cheese come from on a map of the world.
2. Investigate which varieties of cheese can now be purchased with reduced-fat options.

Exam practice questions

1. State **three** nutrients found in cheese. **[3 marks]**
2. Explain why cheese is an important food in our diets. **[4 marks]**

Eggs

Most of the eggs we use come from hens. However, we can also use duck, goose and quail eggs. They are a very versatile food and can be used in a wide variety of ways in food preparation.

Structure of eggs

Eggs are made up of three parts:

○ Shell – the colour of the shell does not affect the nutritional value of the egg.
○ Egg white – there are two parts to the egg white, the thick and thin.
○ Egg yolk – the colour of the yolk is related to what the hens are fed on. The yolk also contains lecithin, which is an emulsifier. This is useful when combining ingredients that would normally separate, for instance, when it is used in mayonnaise to prevent oil and water separating.

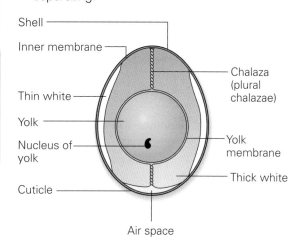

△ **Figure 1.48** Structure of an egg

The air space in the egg will get larger as the egg gets older. This is because the shell of the egg is porous. A stale egg will float in a bowl of water. The chalazae are two spiral bands in an egg that extend from the yolk to the inner membrane and help to keep the yolk in the centre of the egg. As the shell of the egg is porous, eggs should be stored away from strongly flavoured foods.

Because of their structure, eggs are a very useful food in preparing other dishes. They are particularly useful for setting, combining, aerating and thickening mixtures. (See Chapter 2, page 57, on the function of ingredients.

Nutrients found in eggs

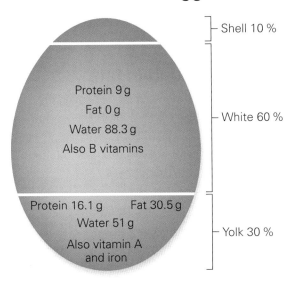

Shell 10 %

Protein 9 g
Fat 0 g
Water 88.3 g
Also B vitamins

White 60 %

Protein 16.1 g   Fat 30.5 g
Water 51 g

Also vitamin A and iron

Yolk 30 %

△ **Figure 1.49** Nutritional composition of eggs (nutrients per 100 g)

Eggs are a good source of protein and fat-soluble vitamins. They are also a high-risk food and must be stored and used correctly. They should be stored in the fridge. Eggs that are stamped with a lion mark come from hens that are salmonella-free.

Key points

o Eggs are a good source of protein, vitamin A, vitamin D, niacin and vitamin B12.
o It is possible to change the nutrient content of eggs by manipulating the feed of hens.
o Eggs have a wide variety of uses in food preparation.

Activities

Eggs have many uses in food preparation.

1. Produce a mind map to show how they can be used.
2. Prepare a range of dishes which show the different uses of eggs.

Exam practice questions

1. Explain why eggs are considered to be a valuable food in your diet.
[4 marks]
2. Explain where you would store eggs in your home. **[2 marks]**
3. How can you tell if eggs are fresh?
[2 marks]

Fats and oils

There is a great variety of fats and oils that we can purchase, and the market is continuing to expand. Fats and oils have lots of different uses in food preparation.

Structure of fats and oils

Fats and oils can come from both animal and vegetable sources. Oils are a liquid and fats are solid. Oils come from vegetables sources such as olives, corn, rape, nuts, soya, ground nuts and fish. Fats also come from animal sources.

The more saturated fatty acids a product has, the more solid the fat will be. Animal fats contain more saturated fats than vegetable and fish oils.

Fats
Animal fats

These make butter from milk, animal suet from cattle and lard from pigs. They are traditionally high in saturated fats. Today manufacturers make lighter varieties of butter by adding ingredients such as water and vegetable oil.

Low-fat spreads

There are many low-fat spreads available to buy. These contain a lower fat content than butter or margarine. The percentage of water in these products is higher. Often they cannot be used for cooking, so the labels on these products need to be read carefully.

White fats

These are made from oils and can be used to replace lard. They can be used in products such as pastry and for frying. The consistency of the products can vary. Some have air added, making them softer and easier to combine in ingredients, for instance when rubbing in pastry.

Oils

Oils contain 100 per cent fat. They mostly contain unsaturated fats from vegetable sources.

Activities

1. Use the following headings to investigate the different fats and oils that can be purchased:
   o name of fat
   o ingredients
   o uses in food preparation.
2. Record your results.

Nutrients found in fats

The main nutrient in fats is fat. However, the amount of different types of fat they contain varies.

Fats also contain fat-soluble vitamins. Vitamins A and D are added to margarine by law.

Nutrients	Olive oil	Corn oil	Butter	Low-fat spread
Energy	3378 kJ 822 kcal	3408 kJ 829 kcal	3031.00 kJ 737.00 kcal	1605.00 kJ 390.00 kcal
Protein	nil	less than 0.1 g	0.50 g	5.80 g
Carbohydrate	nil	0.0 g	trace	0.50 g
Fat of which: saturates monounsaturates polyunsaturates	91.3 g 15.2 g 60.7 g 11.4 g	92.1 g 13.3 g 27.5 g 47.3 g	81.70 g 54.00 g 19.80 g 2.60 g	40.50 g 11.20 g 17.60 g 9.90 g
Cholesterol	nil	nil	230.00 mg	6.00 mg
Water	trace	trace	15.60 g	49.90 g

△ **Table 1.13** Nutrients found in a variety of common fats and oils (per 100 g)

Key points

o Fats that are liquid at room temperature are called oils.
o Fats contain fat-soluble vitamins.
o Fats have different sensory characteristics.

Exam practice questions

1. List the main sources of fats and oils. **[2 × 4 marks]**

2. Explain why many people are choosing to use vegetable fats and oils. **[4 marks]**

3. What sort of fat would you recommend for the following people:

   o a vegan?
   o someone wanting to reduce the amount of fat they eat? **[2 marks]**

   Give reasons for your answers.

   [2 × 2 marks]

Stretch yourself

Some oils are hydrogenated. What does this mean?

Alternative protein foods

Alternative protein foods provide protein from sources other than animals. There is a variety of meat-like products available in supermarkets. They have been developed to resemble meat products.

Types of alternative protein foods

Soya beans are made into a variety of products, including milk, soy sauce and tofu.

Textured vegetable protein is made from soya beans. The soya beans are made into a flour-like substance and then mixed with water so that the starch can be removed. The mixture is then made into a variety of shapes. It can be bought as a dried or frozen product. It is very bland and

△ **Figure 1.50** Range of soya products – soya beans, chunks, milk and tofu

needs ingredients with strong flavours to be added to it to make it into an interesting product.

Tofu is made from ground soya beans. It resembles a soft cheese in texture. As it is soft it absorbs flavours.

Mycoprotein (Quorn®) is produced from micro-organisms. When it is made into a food product it has egg white added to it to bind it together. The mycoprotein is then shaped into a variety of shapes, such as mince, slices and fillets. It is also used to make ready-to-use products such as sausages.

Nutrients found in alternative protein foods

Alternative protein foods contain the following nutrients:

o protein – soya beans are a high biological value protein
o vitamins and minerals – often they have been enriched with these, for example, soya fortified with vitamin B12
o fibre, often found in soya mince and Quorn®.

They are low in fat.

Nutrients	Quorn®	Tofu	Soya mince (frozen)
Energy	433 kJ/103 kcal	438 kJ/105 kcal	727 kJ/175 kcal
Protein	14	12.1 g	18.0 g
Carbohydrate of which sugars	5.8 g 1.3 g	0.6 g 0.5 g	3.0 g 2.0 g
Fat of which saturates	2.6 g 0.6 g	6.0 g 1.0 g	10.0 g 1.0 g
Fibre	5.5 g	0.5 g	3.0 g
Sodium	0.4 g	trace	0.12 g

△ **Table 1.14** Nutrients found in a range of alternative protein foods (per 100 g)

Key points

o Soya and mycoprotein (Quorn®) foods provide protein and are low in fat.
o They are a valuable source of protein for vegetarians.
o Vegans cannot eat mycoprotein.

Activities

Many people are choosing not to eat meat.

1. Investigate the range of soya and mycoprotein foods available in supermarkets.

2. Design a dish using either a soya or mycoprotein which a supermarket could use to promote these alternative meat products. Produce a recipe leaflet that could be given out with the product.

Exam practice questions

1. Give **two** reasons why someone might eat mycoprotein instead of meat. **[2 marks]**

2. Explain why alternative protein foods are important to vegetarians. **[4 marks]**

3. Quorn® is not suitable for a vegan to eat. Give reasons for this. **[2 marks]**

Controlled assessment link

The content of this chapter will also help improve your understanding of practical work situations.

Introduction

Every ingredient used in a recipe has a specific function, for example, to thicken, aerate, coagulate, add nutritional value. You need to understand the function of ingredients in order to choose the correct ingredients when designing and making food products. It will be important that you can explain these functions when making decisions about your choice and development of products for your controlled assessment. It is the way we prepare, combine and cook ingredients that gives us the vast range of food products that we can eat.

When foods are prepared and cooked you are often able to see one or more of the following changes:

○ changes in colour – toast becoming brown
○ food increases in size – rice swells, cake mixtures rise
○ food decreases in size/shrinks – meat
○ food becomes thicker – sauces
○ food curdles – eggs
○ foods become firmer – fish.

Other ways foods change, that are not visible, are:

○ loss of nutritional value
○ food becomes tender
○ foods absorb other substances, such as water (a visible effect of this is that the structure and appearance of the food changes).

Most food products that we purchase and make contain more than one ingredient. The technical term **colloidal structure** is what is formed when at least two ingredients are mixed together. It is these structures that often give the texture to the food products.

Key terms

Colloidal structure – when two substances are mixed together

Colloids – these are formed when one substance is dispersed through another

Table 2.1 shows the function of a range of common ingredients we use when preparing food.

Ingredient	Function	Example
Flour	Forms the main structure of a product due to its gluten content	Bread – strong plain flour – high gluten content Cakes – soft plain flour – low gluten content to give a soft, tender crumb
	Bulking	Crumble – topping Pastry – casing
	Raising agent if self-raising flour is used	Cakes
	To thicken (gelatinisation)	Sauces
Fat	Adds colour and flavour if butter is used	Cakes, biscuits
	Holds air bubbles during mixing to create texture and volume	Cakes, biscuits
	Helps to extend shelf life	Pastry
	To shorten a flour mixture and make crisp or crumbly in texture	Pastry
	Shortening	Certain types of biscuits and pastry
	Frying/sautéing	Stir-fry
	To form emulsions	Salad dressing
Oils	Binds ingredients	
Egg	Adds colour and flavour	Cakes
	Holds air when whisked	Meringue, whisked sponge
	Forms an emulsion when mixed with fat	Mayonnaise
	Binds ingredients together	Beefburgers, fishcakes
	Coagulating/setting	Quiche Lorraine
	Glazing	Pastry
	Coating/enrobing	Holding dry coatings such as breadcrumbs onto a surface and forming a barrier during cooking processes, e.g. fried breaded fish
	Enriching – thickening	Sauce
	To give a smooth, glossy finish to aid piping	Choux pastry
	Adding nutritional value	Quiche

△ **Table 2.1** Functions of ingredients in mixtures

Cont.

Ingredient	Function	Example
Sugar	Sweetens	Desserts, cakes
	Develops flavour	Soft brown sugar, or treacle in gingerbread
	Increases bulk of the mixture	Cakes
	Holds air	When creamed with fat, e.g. Victoria sandwich
	To aid fermentation	Bread
	To preserve	Jam
Liquid	Acts as a raising agent when converted to steam	Cakes, batters
	Binds ingredients together	Pastry
	Glazing (milk)	Scones
	Enrich (milk)	Bread
Salt	Helps develop flavour	Pastry
	Strengthens gluten in flour and controls the action of yeast	Bread
	To preserve	Fish, meat
Baking powder	To aerate	To make cake rise
Yeast	To aerate	To make bread rise
Herbs and spices	Improve and add flavour	Curry, chilli
	To garnish	Parsley
Gelatine	Setting	Jelly, chilled desserts, e.g. cheesecakes, soufflé

△ **Table 2.1** Functions of ingredients in mixtures *continued*

2.1 **Carbohydrates**

Starch

Starch is mainly used to thicken mixtures.

Flour

There are many different types of flour available in the shops. Flour forms the main structure of many products, including cakes, bread, pastry and biscuits. The type of flour used will vary depending on the desired texture and product being made.

Wheat flour is one of the most common starchy foods used in cooking. It is often used to bulk out a recipe. The way it reacts to heat depends on the type of heat applied and the ingredients it is mixed with.

Dry heat on flour

When dry heat is applied to products such as baking bread, the crust of the product becomes brown – this is called **dextrinisation**.

Moist heat on flour

When flour is mixed with a liquid, as in a sauce, the mixture will thicken. This is known as **gelatinisation**. This occurs because:

o   the starch grains cannot dissolve in the liquid, so they form a **suspension**
o   as the liquid is heated the starch grains swell (60 °C), and as more heat is applied the starch grains break open, causing the mixture to thicken (80 °C). The mixture must be stirred as it is being heated to prevent lumps forming.

Cornflour

Cornflour is often used as an alternative to flour in sauces. It is obtained from maize kernels. It is virtually tasteless. Unlike other flours, it blends to a smooth cream with liquid; it still needs to be stirred when it is being heated so lumps do not form.

Other starch sources

Other starch foods that thicken mixtures are:

o   potatoes – potato flour is used to thicken sauces, soups and casseroles, as the starch is released from the potatoes into the cooking liquid
o   other root vegetables, for example, swedes and sweet potatoes, will thicken soups and stews; tapioca is made from the cassava plant and is used in puddings, stews and soups
o   rice – rice flour is used to thicken sauces, useful to those who are on a gluten-free or wheat-free diet; rice thickens milk puddings such as rice pudding and savoury dishes such as risotto
o   arrowroot – made from the maranta plant, used to make clear glazes which are often used on fruit tarts.

△ **Figure 2.1** Different types of thickeners

Use of modified starches

Food manufacturers use a lot of starches in products. They have been adapted (modified) to meet specific requirements. These starches are called **modified starches**.

Knowledge link
See Chapter 13 for further details on modified starches (page 219).

Activities

1. In groups, prepare a variety of dishes which show how carbohydrate foods can be used to thicken mixtures.

2. Carry out an investigation to look at the effect of different flours on bread. Prepare a variety of batches of bread using different flours.

   (a) Make sure you knead the mixtures for the same amount of time so that you carry out a fair test.

   (b) Use a digital camera to record your results. Include photographs of the texture of the bread.

   (c) Produce a sensory analysis chart to show results of your tasting of the bread.

   (d) Explain which type of flour you would use for making bread products.

Stretch yourself

1. Make a variety of different sauces using different types of starches.

   (a) Carry out a sensory analysis on the sauces.

   (b) Write a detailed evaluation explaining your results and suggesting when consumers may choose to use the different sauces.

2. Food manufacturers use many different thickeners in food products. Produce a chart to show the range of thickeners used in different food products.

Sugars

There are many different types of sugars used in food production. Sugars add flavour and bulk out ingredients.

△ **Figure 2.2** Different types of sugars (caster, demerara, granulated, soft brown, icing)

Adding flavour

Most sugars taste sweet and are added to products for this purpose. Some savoury products do contain sugar, for example, baked beans. There are sugars that do not taste sweet, such as lactose, which is the sugar found in milk.

Adding colour

Sugar helps with the browning of sweet foods.

Moist heat on sugars

When moist heat is applied to sugar, the following happens:

○ The sugar melts and becomes syrup. It is sometimes used in this syrup state, for example in fruit salads, though most people today put fruit salads into fruit juices to reduce the sugar and calorie content of the product.

○ At 154 °C the sugar starts to change colour – this process is called **caramelisation**.

| Sugar which has been browned under a hot grill to create the hard caramel on top of a crème brûlée. | Sugar which has changed to a syrup and caramelised in a crème caramel. | Maillard reaction, which occurs in biscuits when they contain carbohydrate and protein. |

△ **Table 2.2** How sugar has changed colour in three different products

○ The longer the sugar is heated, the deeper the colour of the caramel and the harder it will set when it is cooled.

Dry heat on sugars

Sugars will also caramelise when dry heat is applied to them. When sugars are mixed with other products, such as eggs and flour (which both contain protein) in baked products, browning occurs in these products. This is called a **Maillard reaction**.

Aerating

Aerating means adding air to mixtures. When sugar is beaten with a fat or with egg, air is added to the mixture. This helps to make cakes rise and gives them a light texture. Examples of this are whisked sponges, creamed or all-in-one cake mixtures.

Preserving

Sugars are also used to help preserve foods. In jams and chutneys the concentration of sugar is high and this prevents the growth of micro-organisms.

Activities

1. Produce a chart to show the different types of sugars, their description and how they are used in food preparation.
2. Make a small batch of buns using different sugars. Compare the colour, flavour and texture of the finished products.

Key terms

Dextrinisation – when dry heat is applied to flour and it browns as the starch is changed into a sugar

Gelatinisation – this is what happens to starches and water when cooked together

Suspension – a solid held in a liquid

Key terms

Caramelisation – process of changing the colour of sugar from white to brown when heated

Maillard reaction – this happens when foods containing proteins and carbohydrates are cooked by dry methods

Gells – a small amount of a solid mixed in a large amount of liquid that then sets, for example, jam

2.2 **Protein foods**

We use a wide variety of protein foods when cooking and preparing different dishes. Animal protein foods include:

- meat
- fish
- eggs
- milk
- cheese.

Vegetable protein foods include:

- soya
- tofu
- Quorn®
- nuts
- pulses.

Properties of eggs
Coagulation

When moist or dry heat is applied to protein foods they **coagulate** (set). If they are overheated they become tough and more difficult to digest. In cooking we often use eggs in mixtures to set them, for example, quiches and egg custards. We also coat products with eggs and breadcrumbs, for example, for fishcakes or Scotch eggs. When the food is heated, the egg and breadcrumbs form a protective barrier to stop any other liquid entering the food.

Key terms

Coagulate – to set; the change in structure of protein brought about by heat, mechanical action or acids

Syneresis – usually refers to eggs; if overcooked, the proteins shrink as they coagulate and separate from the watery liquid

What happens to eggs when they are heated?

The egg white begins to coagulate at 60 °C. It changes from an opaque colour to a white colour. The egg yolk begins to coagulate at 70 °C. If eggs are heated too quickly, the liquid in them separates out and the protein becomes tough. This is called **syneresis**. It is sometimes seen when cooking scrambled eggs. This has little effect on the nutritional value of eggs when they are heated.

Aeration

The process of trapping air in a mixture is called **aeration**. When egg whites are whisked, the protein in them, **albumin**, is stretched and traps the air, for example, when eggs are whisked when making meringues. If the whisked egg whites are left to stand they will eventually collapse and become a liquid again. Once they have collapsed they cannot be whisked again. If they are heated then they will set. An example of this is in meringues. Whisked egg whites can also be called a foam, as they are a mixture of gas (air) and a liquid (egg white).

Key terms

Aeration – the process of trapping air in a mixture

Albumin – protein in egg white

△ **Figure 2.3** The protein in the egg white stretches and incorporates air

Binding

Eggs are used to bind ingredients together, for example, binding rubbed-in cake mixtures and fishcakes. The egg will then set and hold the ingredients together when they are cooked

Glazing

Egg is used to glaze products such as scones and pastry. When the product is cooked, the egg adds colour to the product and produces a shiny surface.

Activity
In groups, produce a range of sweet and savoury dishes to show the functional properties of eggs.

Properties of milk

When milk is heated a skin develops on its surface. This is the protein setting. Milk is also used to:

○ bind ingredients together, for example, in scones
○ act as a raising agent when it is converted to steam, for example, in cakes and batters
○ enrich products, for example, bread mixtures.

Properties of cheese

Cheese is added to food products to add:

○ flavour, for example, in a quiche
○ colour, for example, in a sauce.

When cheese is heated, the fat in the cheese melts and the proteins coagulate. If the cheese is heated at a high temperature or for a long time the cheese will become stringy and more difficult to digest. You may be able to see the fat that has been squeezed out of the cheese. If cheese is added to a cheese sauce it should be added at the end of the sauce-making process and should be grated – this will make the melting process quicker and less heat will be required.

Gluten – the protein in flour

When making cakes, a soft flour is used which has a low **gluten** content so that the cakes have a soft crumb. When making bread, strong flour with a high gluten content is used to provide the structure. The gluten is developed in the bread dough when it is being kneaded.

Key term
Gluten – the protein in flour and so in most bread

Exam practice questions

The ingredients used in a lemon meringue pie are shown below.

Pastry	Filling	Meringue
150g plain flour 75g fat 1 egg yolk	2 lemons 2 egg yolks 50g cornflour 50g sugar 125ml water	2 egg whites 100g caster sugar

1. (a) Explain in detail the function of the egg yolk in the pastry. **[2 marks]**
   (b) Explain in detail the function of the egg yolks in the filling. **[2 marks]**
   (c) Explain what happens to the egg whites when they are whisked. **[2 marks]**
   (d) Explain what happens to the egg whites when they are cooked. **[2 marks]**
2. When the sauce was made for the filling it became lumpy. Give **two** reasons why this might have happened. **[2 marks]**

△ **Figure 2.4** Kneading bread to develop gluten

Stretch yourself

1. Investigate the different types of flour available and their gluten content.
2. Explain what effect this will have on bread products.

2.3 Functional properties of fats

There is a wide variety of different fats available for consumers to choose from. They are produced from animals, fish and vegetables. Different fats are used for their different properties in food.

Aeration

When a fat and sugar are creamed together air is trapped. When the product is heated the air will expand, causing the mixture to rise.

Shortening

When fat is used in making rubbed-in mixtures such as pastry, biscuits, scones and cakes, it coats the grains of flour. This gives it a waterproof coating and prevents the gluten in the flour from developing. This means the finished product will have a short, crumbly texture.

Emulsions

An **emulsion** is formed when oil and a liquid are mixed together, such as in salad dressings. Sometimes when oils and a liquid are mixed together they will separate when left to stand, as is seen in salad dressings.

An **emulsifying agent** is sometimes added to these ingredients to prevent them from separating. For example, egg yolk, which contains lecithin, is used in some salad dressings, mayonnaise and low-fat spreads.

△ **Figure 2.5** Low-fat spread

Flavour and moisture

There are many different types of fats and oils available. We use some of these because of the flavour they give to a product, for example, butter for a rich flavour in shortbread biscuits. Fats also add moisture to a product, which helps to extend the product's shelf life.

Cooking

Fats and oils are often used to cook foods in. Examples of this are:

○ shallow- deep- and stir-frying – this gives food a crisp texture and added flavour
○ sautéing – this helps to bring out the flavour in the food by cooking it for a longer, for example, the sweetness in onions
○ roasting – foods are baked in the fat and this helps develop the flavour. Meat, poultry and vegetables are often roasted.

We should, however, try to reduce the amount of fried foods we consume.

Activities

1. Investigate the range of fats and spreads available. Copy and complete the chart below. The first one has been done for you

Name of fat	Fat source	Can be used for
Butter	Animal – milk	Spread for bread, used in cooking and baked products

2. In groups, make small batches of shortbread biscuits using 100 g flour and a variety of different fats, for example, butter, hard margarine, low-fat spread, vegetable fat.
3. Produce a chart to show how the flavour, colour and texture of the products varied.
4. Write a conclusion explaining which type of fat produced the best biscuit. Give reasons for your conclusion.

Key terms

Shortening – when fat coats the flour grains and prevents the gluten from developing and absorbing water, resulting in a crumbly mixture

Emulsion – a mixture of two liquids

Emulsifying agent – a substance that will allow two liquids which do not mix to be held together, for example, lecithin in egg yolk

Emulsifier – a substance that stops oil and water separating

2.4 Raising agents

A raising agent is added to a cake and bread mixture to give lightness to the mixture. The lightness is based on the principle that gases expand when heated. The gases used are:

o air,
o carbon dioxide
o or water vapour.

These gases are introduced before baking or are produced by substances added to the recipe before baking.

Air

Air expands very quickly. Figure 2.6 shows the different ways that air can be added to mixtures.

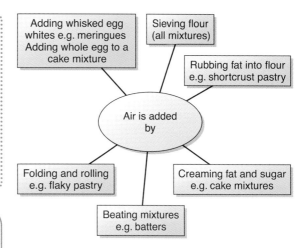

△ **Figure 2.6** Ways of adding air to mixtures

Whisked egg whites have the property of holding air, as in soufflés, meringues, and so on. Whole eggs do not hold air as easily because of the fat in the yolk.

Dishes almost entirely dependent on air as a raising agent include:

o whisked sponges
o soufflés
o meringues.

Carbon dioxide

This may be introduced by the use of:

o bicarbonate of soda (sodium bicarbonate) used alone, for example, in gingerbread – a strong flavour of washing soda is produced and a dark colour, but the flavour and colour are disguised by the use of spices, such as ginger, or treacle
o bicarbonate of soda plus acid, for example, bicarbonate of soda and cream of tartar
o baking powder – this is usually a commercial preparation of bicarbonate of soda and cream of tartar or tartaric acid, with rice flour or a similar substance added to absorb any moisture and prevent lumps. The quality of commercial baking powder is controlled by law and is of standard strength.

Self-raising flour

This is a prepared mixture of a soft flour and a raising agent. It will give good results for plain cakes or scones, but there is too much raising agent for rich cakes. *Never* use self-raising flour for bread, pastries, biscuits and batters.

Yeast

When yeast is given the right conditions – food, warmth, moisture and time – it can break down food into carbon dioxide by a process known as fermentation. Yeast is used to make bread. You can either use fresh or dried yeast.

Water vapour (steam)

This is produced during cooking from liquids in the mixture. It is used, for example, in éclairs, batters, choux pastries, flaky and puff pastry, and cakes.

Using raising agents

It is important that raising agents are used in the correct proportion so that the product is successful. Table 2.3 shows what happens if too much or too little raising agent is used.

It is also important to:

o buy a reliable brand
o store chemical raising agents in an airtight container, in a cool dry place, to prevent loss of strength and reaction
o add and distribute moisture evenly to the mixture to ensure an even reaction.

> ### Key point
> Bubbles of gas expand when heated and make food mixtures rise.

> ### Stretch yourself
> Investigate the different types of colloidal structures. Produce a chart that:
>
> o names the type of structure
> o states the two main components of the structure
> o gives at least one example of a food product.

> ### Exam practice questions
>
> 1. List the raising agents used in the following mixtures:
>   (a) Yorkshire pudding
>   (b) rough puff pastry
>   (c) Victoria sandwich cake.　**[3 marks]**
> 2. Why are strong spices used in a cake mixture that contains bicarbonate of soda?　**[2 marks]**
> 3. State the conditions yeast needs in order for it to produce carbon dioxide.　**[4 marks]**
> 4. Describe **three** ways in which air can be added to a mixture.　**[3 marks]**

Too little raising agent	Too much raising agent
Lack of volume	Over-rising, then collapsing, giving a sunken cake, or sunken fruit
Close texture	Coarse texture
Insufficient rising	Poor colour and flavour
Shrinkage	

△ **Table 2.3** Using a raising agent

2.5 The effects of acids and alkalis on food products

Acids and alkalis are found in a range of food products. When they are combined with other ingredients they will affect the flavour, texture, appearance and nutritional content of the food product.

Acids

Acids are chemicals that are found in some foods. The flavour these give foods is a sour or sharp taste. Acids also have other functions when preparing foods.

△ **Figure 2.7** A range of foods that contain acids

Acetic acid

Vinegar is a type of acetic acid. It is used to:

○ preserve foods such as pickled beetroot, cabbage, onions – the acid condition prevents micro-organisms from growing
○ tenderise meat, as the acid softens the meat tissues – this is often done to meat before it is barbecued as it will make it cook more quickly and prevent it from being tough as this is a dry method of cooking meat

○ provide a soft texture – if a small amount of vinegar is added to a meringue mixture the centre of the meringue remains soft and similar in texture to marshmallows.

Lemon juice is also an acetic acid. It is used to:

○ prevent foods going brown – foods such as apples and bananas go brown when they have been cut. This is called **enzymic browning**. If the fruit is put in a lemon juice solution the browning does not take place. This improves the appearance of the food
○ set mixtures that contain protein, for example, cheesecakes. Lemon juice is also added to some jams to help them set (form a gel).

Key term

Enzymic browning – reaction between a food product and oxygen resulting in a brown colour, for example, potatoes or apples going brown

Ascorbic acid (vitamin C)

Ascorbic acid is often added to bread mixtures when these are manufactured industrially. The ascorbic acid speeds up the fermentation process when making bread.

Other acids are used in food production; for example, in cheese making an acid is added to coagulate the milk and to make the curds that are used for the cheese.

Alkalis

The main alkali used in food production is bicarbonate of soda. This is used as a raising agent in products such as gingerbread and parkin. The bicarbonate of soda has a strong taste and is therefore only used as a raising agent in foods that have strong flavours to mask the soapy taste of the bicarbonate of soda.

△ **Figure 2.8** Gingerbread, which uses bicarbonate of soda as a raising agent

Activities

Find a recipe and make a:

o cheesecake or dessert product which illustrates the effect of acid on a protein
o cake which uses bicarbonate of soda (alkali) as a raising agent.

Stretch yourself

Acids are found naturally in some foods. Find the names of the acids found naturally in:

o apples
o grapes
o lemons
o vinegar.

2.6 Processes and techniques used in food preparation

First impressions play an important part in how successful a food product is going to be. Initially we rely on the senses of sight and smell when we judge a product, and then taste as we eat it. The aim when you produce food is to make it:

o attractive in appearance
o thoroughly/correctly cooked – to make it safe to eat
o appetising – mix of flavours.

How different products can be finished

Some products have a finish applied to them to make them more attractive. Figure 2.9 shows some different ways that foods can be finished.

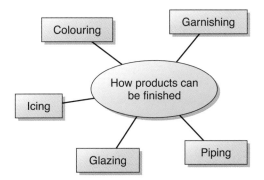

△ **Figure 2.9** How different foods can be finished

Icing

Many cakes are iced to improve their appearance. They will be iced in different ways to:

o attract the target market
o suit the type of cake mixture used.

The main types of icing used on cakes are:

o glacé
o butter
o fondant
o royal
o melted chocolate.

Glazing

The **glaze** is a finish usually applied to the food before it is cooked. It will help to improve the colourful appearance of the food, therefore making it more attractive to consumers. Glazes can be used on both sweet and savoury foods.

Garnishing

Both sweet and savoury products can be garnished. When garnishing foods you should consider the following points:

o the neatness of the product – it should improve the appearance of the product, not dominate it

o the type of **garnish** – it should improve the colour, flavour and texture of the dish.

Type of glaze	How it is used/works	Example of foods
Egg wash	Usually a mixture of egg and milk applied to the product before baking – the product will have a shiny finish	Pastry Scones
Egg white	Used on sweet pastry products with sugar sprinkled on top – this gives the product a light golden appearance and a crunchy texture.	Sweet pastry products
Milk	Helps with the browning of the product but does not give a shiny appearance	Bread Pastry Scones
Sugar and water	The sugar and water are boiled until syrup is formed; when the product is cooked the syrup is brushed over it – this gives the product a shiny and sticky glaze	Sweet bread products, e.g. Chelsea buns
Arrowroot glaze	Arrowroot is mixed with water and/or fruit juice and boiled to make a clear glaze	Fruit flans and tarts
Aspic	This is used on savoury products; it is made from gelatine and stock and sets as a clear jelly (vegetarian versions can be bought)	Used on savoury meat and fish dishes that are served cold
Jam – usually apricot or redcurrant	The jam is warmed and sieved if necessary and used to cover fruit	On French apple tart

△ **Table 2.4** How different ingredients can be used to glaze food products

Controlled assessment link
Figure 14.12 on page 237 looks at how to develop a pie using different methods of glazing.

Key term

Glaze – a finish applied to the surface of a product to improve the colour and appearance

Garnish – something added to improve the appearance of a dish, usually savoury

△ **Figure 2.10** A range of garnishes that can be used on foods

Piping

Piping can be used on both sweet and savoury products. Examples of ingredients that can be piped are:

○ whipped double cream
○ butter icing
○ royal icing
○ creamed biscuit mixtures – Viennese fingers
○ choux pastry – for making éclairs and choux
○ mashed potatoes
○ mayonnaise.

There are different types of nozzles available. The type and shape of the nozzle used will depend on:

○ the ingredient being piped
○ the purpose of the piping
○ the type of finish required.

Enrobing or coating

Some food products can be coated with other ingredients to create an attractive finish on the product or to create a layer to separate foods.

Key term

Decoration – something added to improve the appearance of a dish, usually sweet

Colouring

Sometimes colours are added to food products to improve the appearance, for instance, colours added to icing on cakes. There is a lot of debate about adding artificial colours to foods as these are linked to hyperactivity in some people, particularly young children.

Shaping

There are various tools and equipment that can help you to cut and shape foods. Table 2.6 shows a range of equipment and what it can be used for.

When using sharp equipment, take care to ensure that it is used safely.

How?	Why?	What?	Examples
Applying a coating of another food	Adds texture	Batter/sugar batter	Fritters, doughnuts
	Protects delicate food	Batter	Fish
	For **decoration** or to improve appearance	Melted chocolate	Biscuits
Applying layers of ingredients	Nutrition and texture	Egg and breadcrumbs	Scotch eggs

△ **Table 2.5** Coating food products to improve their appearance

Equipment	Name of equipment	What is can be used for
	Food processor	Slicing, grating and chopping foods
	Piping bags	For piping icings, choux pastry, potato
	Cutters	For creating shapes for biscuits and pastry

△ **Table 2.6** A range of equipment used for shaping foods   *Cont.*

Equipment	Name of equipment	What is can be used for
	Presses	For burgers
	Pasta makers	To make different-shaped pasta
	Rolling pins	To roll out mixtures such as pastry

△ **Table 2.6** A range of equipment used for shaping foods *continued*

Activities

The pictures in Figure 2.11 show a range of food products that have different finishing techniques applied to them.

△ **Figure 2.11** Different finishing techniques applied to products

1. Produce a chart to:
   - name the different finishing techniques used on each product
   - evaluate how successful they have been in improving the appearance of the product
   - suggest any further improvements.
2. Plan to prepare and make a range of dishes that will illustrate a variety of finishing techniques.
3. After you have made the dishes, evaluate how successful they are as ways of improving the appearance of food products.

Exam practice questions

1. Different finishes are often applied to food products to improve their appearance.

   Complete the chart below.

Food product	Finish used	Reason for using this finish
Apple pie		
Savoury flan		
Shepherd's pie		

2. Figure 2.12 shows a birthday cake that has been designed to appeal to children. **[3 × 3 marks]**

   (a) List **three** different finishing techniques that h

   (b) The cake was made by hand (job production). Explain **three** different ways be made by batch production.

△ **Figure 2.12** Novelty cake

Exam tips

Refer to Chapter 12 for information on batch production (page 206).

Controlled assessment link

The content of this chapter will also help improve your understanding of practical work situations.

When a question asks you to explain something, remember to make a statement, develop the point further and, if possible, give an explanation to clarify your answer.

Learning objectives

By the end of this chapter you should have developed a knowledge and understanding of:

○ the use of standard components.
○ the advantages and disadvantages of using standard components.

Introduction

The word 'components' is used to describe an individual part that makes up a product. For example, flour is a standard component of pastry, and pastry is a standard component of apple pie.

Key term

Standard components – pre-prepared ingredients that are used in the production of another product

○ spices, for example, coriander seeds
○ raising agents, for example, baking powder
○ thickeners, for example, cornflower
○ flavourings, for example, vanilla essence
○ juices, for example, lemon juice
○ ready-made pastry
○ tinned tomatoes
○ ready-to-serve custard
○ pre-washed and prepared vegetables
○ dried cheese sauce
○ crumble mix
○ frozen cream decorations
○ part-cooked base
○ ready-to-roll icing.

3.1 Types of standard

Manufacturers often find it quicker, cheaper or simpler to 'buy in' ready-prepared ingredients or parts to make their food product. These are called standard components. For example, when producing a pizza a manufacturer may buy in ready-made pizza bases, grated cheese, chopped ham and vegetables.

There is a wide range of standard components used in manufacturing food products in industry and in the home. Some of them are listed below:

○ concentrates, for example, tomato purée
○ stock, for example, cubes
○ seasonings, for example, salt
○ herbs, for example, parsley

△ **Figure 3.1** Ready-prepared vegetables are an example of a pre-manufactured component

3.2 Advantages and disadvantages of using standard components

The table below shows the advantages/benefits and disadvantages/limitations of using pre-manufactured components when preparing food products.

Key term

Consistent – the same quality each time a product is made

Advantages/Benefits	Disadvantages/Limitations
Save preparation time, therefore speed up production time	You rely on a manufacturer to supply the product, so their problems become yours
Less skilled staff need to be employed, which may save on wages	The taste and quality may not be as good as using your own ingredients
May not need to purchase expensive equipment	Other food companies may use the same components
You get the same result every time (**consistent** results), e.g. in flavour, weight, colour, texture	The components may be expensive
The quality is guaranteed	May contain certain ingredients consumers wish to avoid, e.g. artificial colourants
You are getting the components from experts who know how to make them	May contain added fat, sugar or salt
Some have a relatively long shelf life	Could have poor proportions, e.g. little meat relative to sauce
Can be used as part of more complex products	Special storage conditions may be required, e.g. freezer or chilled storage
It saves relying on several suppliers to provide the separate ingredients	
It can make food preparation safer because the high-risk processes – such as vegetable preparation that needs soil removal – are carried out in another place	
If egg products are cooked elsewhere, this removes the risk of contamination from raw egg	

△ **Table 3.1** Advantages/benefits and disadvantages/limitations of using pre-manufactured components

Exam practice questions

A savoury flan is made using the following basic ingredients:

Pastry	Filling
150 g plain flour	200 ml milk
75 g fat	2 eggs
6 tsp water	75 g grated cheddar cheese
	1 g pepper

1. (a) Identify **one** standard component that could be used in the savoury flan. **[1 mark]**
   (b) Give **two** benefits to a manufacturer of using standard components. **[2 marks]**
   (c) Give **one** limitation to a manufacturer of using standard components. **[1 mark]**
2. State **two** ways in which pre-manufactured components can maintain the consistency of a food product. **[2 marks]**
3. (a) Name **one** standard component other than grated cheese. **[1 mark]**
   (b) State **three** different food products in which it could be used. **[3 marks]**

Activities

1. A pizza is made by using the following basic ingredients:

Base	Topping
100 g strong plain flour	100 g cheddar cheese
100 g wholemeal flour	1 onion
2 tablespoons oil	8 chopped tomatoes
125 ml warm water	1 teaspoon fresh herbs

Draw an annotated sketch to show how standard components could be used when making the pizza.

2. In groups, compare the making of the following food products using standard components with making them from scratch.

   o pizza
   o fruit pie
   o decorated cake.

Produce a table to show your results. Include a sensory analysis as part of your results.

Stretch yourself

1. For activity 2 on page 79, compare the cost of producing the product using fresh ingredients with using the standard components.

2. Compare the nutritional value of the dishes you made for activity 2.

Controlled assessment link

The content of this chapter will also help improve your understanding of practical work situations.

Key points

o Standard components help to produce products of a consistent standard.
o Standard components are used by the food industry to save preparation time and costs.

chapter 4
Food skills and processes

Learning objectives

By the end of this chapter you should have developed a knowledge and understanding of:

○ baked products:
  ○ cakes and biscuits
  ○ pastry
  ○ bread
○ rubbing in, creaming, melting, whisking, all-in-one, kneading, folding, rolling, shaping, cutting
○ sauce making – roux, blended, all-in-one
○ fruit and vegetable preparation
○ preparation of meat, fish, alternative protein foods.

Introduction to baked products

There are a large number of baked products that can be successfully prepared in the home and at school. When making any baked product, such as cakes, biscuits, pastry and bread, it is important that the ingredients are added in the correct proportions and that the mixtures are handled correctly.

Knowledge link
See Chapter 2 for the function of these ingredients in cakes.

△ **Figure 4.1** Ingredients used in cake making

Key points
When producing baked products it is important that ingredients are weighed accurately so that the ingredients will work correctly together.

4.1 Cake and biscuit making

Ingredients and methods of cake making

The main ingredients used in cake making are:

○ fat
○ flour
○ sugar
○ eggs
○ raising agent.

There are four main methods of cake making. Each method produces products that have a different texture. The amount of fat in the product will determine how long the cake will stay fresh without drying out. Cakes cannot be successfully made with reduced-fat spreads, as the water content of these is too high. It is important to check on the labels of the different types of fats to see whether they are suitable for cooking. The nutritional profile of the products also varies depending on the ingredients used.

Table 4.1 shows you the main information and basic recipes for the different methods of cake making. You will need to be able to adapt these recipes to make interesting and innovative dishes and products.

Method of making	Example of product	Ratio of fat to flour	Raising agent	Basic recipe	
Creaming	Victoria sandwich, small buns	1:1	Self-raising flour – contains baking powder; air is also beaten into the mixture in the creaming process	100g self-raising flour 100g fat (margarine or butter) 100g sugar 2 eggs	
All-in-one	Victoria sandwich, small buns	1:1	Self-raising flour – contains baking powder; air is also beaten into the mixture when all the ingredients are beaten together	100g self-raising flour 100g fat (margarine or butter) 100g sugar 2 tsp baking powder 2 eggs	
Whisked sponge	Swiss roll Fruit flan Gateau Sponge cake	No added fat	Air Steam	50g flour 50g sugar 2 eggs	
Rubbed in	Scones Rock buns	1:4 in scones 1:2 in cakes	Self-raising flour – contains baking powder; some air is also introduced when the fat is rubbed into the flour	Cakes: 200g self-raising flour 100g fat (margarine or butter) 100g sugar 2 eggs 50ml milk	Scones: 200g self-raising flour 50g fat (margarine or butter) 125ml milk
Melted	Flapjack Gingerbread	Varies depending on the product being made	Bicarbonate of soda in gingerbread Flapjack does not contain a raising agent	Varies depending on the product	
Batter	Muffins		Baking powder Steam	225g plain flour 120ml vegetable oil 2 tsp baking powder ¼ tsp salt 1 egg 250ml milk	

△ **Table 4.1** Information on the methods of cake making

Fault	Cause
Cake has sunk in the middle	Too much sugar or syrup is used. This affects the gluten (protein in the flour), making it soft so it collapses.
	Too much raising agent was added to the mixture and the gluten collapses.
	The cake has not been cooked for enough time and the mixture has not set.
	The oven door was opened and closed before the cake mixture had set.
Cake has risen to a peak and cracked on top	Oven temperature was too high and the mixture had set on top before the cake had finished rising.
	Too much mixture was used for the size of the tin.
	The cake was cooked too near the top of the oven.
Has a heavy texture	The mixture was too wet.
	Not enough chemical raising agent or air was added to the mixture.
	The oven temperature was too low.
	When mixing, the mixture curdled and therefore could not hold as much air.
Has a hard sugary crust	Too much sugar was used.
	A coarse sugar, such as granulated sugar, was used and did not have enough time to dissolve.
	The mixture was not creamed enough, so the size of the sugar crystals was not sufficiently reduced.
Has an open and coarse texture	Too much chemical raising agent was used.
	Flour had not been thoroughly mixed in.
Has risen unevenly	Oven shelf is not level.
	The cake was placed too near the heat source and it therefore rose more quickly on one side.

△ **Table 4.2** Common faults in cakes

Activity

Produce mind maps or charts to show:
○ the functions of ingredients used in cake making
○ how the recipes can be adapted to make interesting and innovative food products.

Avoiding common faults

If cakes are not prepared in the correct way or ingredients not measured carefully then you will not get a successful product. Table 4.2 shows some common faults in cakes.

Biscuits

The basic ingredients in biscuits are the same as those in cakes, but the **proportions** of fat to flour differ.

○ Flour – a soft plain flour is usually used for biscuits as a strong gluten content is not required.
○ Fat – this can be butter or animal or vegetable oils. The type of fat used will depend on the method of making and the flavour required.
○ Sugar – the more sugar a biscuit contains the harder it will be. When biscuits are cooking the sugar also softens the gluten, causing the mixture to soften and spread. Some biscuits are

made with a coarse sugar, such as granulated sugar, as this gives a cracked appearance on the top, for example, in cookies and gingernut biscuits.

o Eggs – these are added to some mixtures to bind the ingredients together.

Biscuits can be made by the same methods as cakes. However, they need to be shaped. This is usually done before baking and can be done by:

o using cutters
o piping the mixture
o putting spoonfuls of mixture on the baking tray.

Biscuits made by the **rubbing-in method** are usually rolled and cut into shapes.

Activities

1. Prepare a batch of biscuits that could be sold for a charity event. Remember that all the biscuits need to be identical in shape and size.

2. A cake manufacturer wants to develop a new range of cake products that:

o are attractive to schoolchildren
o include fruit
o are suitable for a packed lunch box.

(a) Working in small groups, each group using a different method of cake making, design and make a range of products that will fit the specification.

(b) Evaluate your products against the specification and carry out a sensory analysis of the cakes. Suggest any further improvements that could be made to the cakes.

3. How could you develop creamed cake mixture or all-in-one cake mixture to:

o modify the fat content (total fat content or type of fat content)?
o reduce the sugar content?
o increase the fibre content?

Exam practice questions

1. Explain the functions of the following ingredients in a creamed cake mixture:

(a) self-raising flour   **[4 marks]**
(b) butter   **[4 marks]**
(c) caster sugar   **[4 marks]**
(d) eggs.   **[4 marks]**

Stretch yourself

1. Using a nutritional software program, compare the nutritional profile of each of the different methods of cake making.

Suggest how the recipes could be adapted to improve their nutritional profile.

2. Explain what happens to the following cake mixtures when they are put into the oven:

(a) creamed cake mixture
(b) whisked cake mixture
(c) melted cake mixture, for example, gingerbread
(d) rubbed-in mixture, for example, scones

Key terms

Proportions – relative quantities of ingredients in a recipe, expressed in numbers

Rubbing-in method – this is when the fat is rubbed into the flour until it resembles breadcrumbs; it is used in pastry, cake and biscuit making

Creaming – the fat and sugar are beaten together using either a wooden spoon or a mixer. This helps to add air to the mixture. Cakes and biscuits can be made by this method

Whisked – when sugar and eggs are whisked together, adding air to the mixture – used when making a whisked sponge

4.2 Pastry

There is a wide variety of pastry products available in shops, and they can be purchased from many different sections of a supermarket, such as:

○ the chiller cabinet
○ the delicatessen
○ the bakery section
○ the freezer.

Pastry products can also be served on many different occasions during the day.

Pastry products are often high in calories.

Ingredients and types of pastry

The main ingredients in all types of pastry are:

○ flour
○ fat
○ water
○ salt.

If we now look at three types of pastry in more detail, you will see that similar ingredients are combined in different ratios by different methods to produce a variety of textures and finishes.

Eggs, sugar and other ingredients such as cheese and herbs can be added to some pastries for extra flavour. The ingredients are used in different ratios and are mixed in different ways to produce a variety of textures and flavours.

△ **Figure 4.2** Ingredients used in pastry making

85

Ingredient	Shortcrust	Flaky	Choux
Flour	Soft plain flour – low gluten content to produce short crumb texture	Strong plain flour – high gluten content to produce crispy, flaky layers	Strong plain flour – high gluten content which stretches to hold the expanding steam and air
Fat	Mixture of white fat and margarine or butter – fat coats the flour granules to reduce the water mixing with the gluten.	Mixture of white fat and margarine – when placed as small pieces on the dough, the fat traps air between the layers of dough	Butter or margarine for flavour
Water	Binds the rubbed-in fat and flour	Combines with gluten to form stretchy, elastic dough – lemon juice is added to strengthen the gluten	Boiled to 100 °C so the heat causes the starch in the flour to gelatinise; mixes with flour to develop the gluten
Salt	Helps develop flavour	Helps develop flavour and strengthen gluten	
Egg			Helps to hold air in the starch mixture – gives a smooth, glossy finish and aids piping of the mixture

△ **Table 4.3** Function of ingredients used in pastry making

Type of pastry	Basic recipe	Ratio of fat to flour	How fat is incorporated	Texture required
Short crust	200 g plain flour 100 g fat (mixture of margarine and white fat) water	1:2	Fat rubbed into flour	Light texture, crisp, short
Flaky/rough puff	200 g strong plain flour 150 g fat (mixture of margarine and white fat) 2 tsp lemon juice water	3:4	A ¼ of the fat is rubbed into the flour, then water added; pastry is rolled and folded, adding a ¼ of the fat each time	Layers of crisp pastry

△ **Table 4.4** Information about the main types of pastry   *Cont.*

Type of pastry	Basic recipe	Ratio of fat to flour	How fat is incorporated	Texture required
Choux	75 g plain flour 25 g butter 2 eggs 125 ml water	1:3	Fat is melted in the water	Hollow inside, well risen, with a crisp texture
Suet	200 g self-raising flour 100 g suet water	1:2	Pre-grated suet is stirred in	Light, soft; this pastry can be steamed as well as being baked in an oven

△ **Table 4.4** Information about the main types of pastry

Making good-quality pastry

When preparing pastry (except for choux pastry) it is important to keep everything cool.

Rolling out pastry

Rolling out the pastry has to be done carefully so that it is not spoilt.

The pastry needs to be as cool as possible. It should be of a firm consistency. You should roll out on a lightly floured work surface with a floured rolling pin. The pastry should be rolled with short, even strokes. Once you have rolled across the pastry, turn it through a quarter turn and continue rolling. You should not turn the pastry over.

Choux pastry is not rolled out – it is usually piped or spooned into the desired shapes.

Avoiding common faults

If pastry is not prepared in the correct way, or ingredients not measured carefully, you will not achieve a successful product. Table 4.5 shows some common faults in pastry.

Other types of pastry

You can also get the following types of pastry:

o Filo pastry – this originally came from Greece. When it is cooked it becomes very crisp.

△ **Figure 4.3** Tips for making good shortcrust, flaky, suet and puff pastry

The fat content in filo pastry is much lower than in other pastries. It can be purchased fresh or as a frozen product.

o Puff pastry – similar to flaky pastry. Many people buy this as either a chilled or frozen product as it is quick to use and saves a lot of preparation time.

o Hot water crust pastry – this is used for pork pies and is not made very often in the home.

87

It is possible to buy shortcrust, puff and filo pastry as a standard component. Many people choose to do this because:

o it saves time
o they do not have the skills to make the pastry
o it saves buying lots of separate ingredients they might not use at a later date.

Controlled assessment link
Figure 14.12 on page 237 shows development ideas for a pie, which includes using different types of pastry.

Knowledge link
For more information on standard components, see Chapter 3.

Fault	Cause
Pastry is soft and sticky and difficult to handle	o Too much liquid was added o A soft fat was used o The mixture has been over-handled
Cooked pastry is dry and crumbly	o Not enough liquid was added
Cooked pastry is hard and tough	o Too much water was added and the gluten in the pastry was over-developed o Pastry was handled too much o Too little fat was used o Pastry was over-rolled
Pastry is soft and oily when cooked	o Temperature of the oven was too low
Pastry shrinks when it is cooking	o The pastry was stretched
Pastry is soft and crumbly	o Too much fat was used o Not much water was used o Too much baking powder, if this ingredient has been used
Pastry blisters	o Fat not rubbed in sufficiently o Too much water was used
Pastry is very pale	o Not baked for long enough o Oven temperature was not hot enough
Pastry too dark	o Cooked too long o Oven temperature was too high

△ **Table 4.5** Common faults in pastry

Activities

1. (a) Investigate the nutritional values of the different types of pastry.

(b) Record your findings and discuss how you could possibly adapt the basic recipe, reduce or change the types of pastry used in traditional dishes.

2. (a) Produce a web/spider diagram to show how you could investigate making the following improvements to the nutritional aspects of shortcrust pastry:

o reducing the saturated fat content
o increasing the fibre content.

(b) In groups, make up small samples of the suggested pastry developments. Produce a sensory analysis chart to show your results.

Exam practice questions

1. Sketch and annotate **two** different design ideas for a savoury snack pastry product. You must annotate your sketches to explain how your ideas meet each of the criteria below.

    o It must be a savoury pastry product.
    o It must be hand-held.
    o It must appeal to teenagers.
    o It must contribute to the 5-a-day of the person who eats it.   **[10 marks]**

2. The manufacturer of the hand-held pastry product has chosen to purchase the pastry as a standard component. Give **four** reasons why the manufacturer might have chosen to do this.   **[4 marks]**

3. Many people choose to purchase pastry as a standard component from the supermarket. Give **three** advantages and **three** disadvantages of this.   **[6 marks]**

4.3 Bread making

There is a large variety of breads made with a wide range of flours. Many types of bread are traditional to different parts of this country and to different parts of the world. They can also be made from a wide variety of different flours.

△ **Figure 4.4** Different types of bread

The main ingredients in bread are:

o strong plain flour
o yeast – fresh or dried
o salt.

△ **Figure 4.5** Ingredients used to make bread

Other ingredients can be added to the bread to give variety to the taste and texture of the product.

Making good-quality bread

To successfully make bread, the following are important to note:

○ Use strong plain flour. This contains gluten (the protein in flour), which will provide the structure to the cooked bread.
○ Salt helps to improve the mixture and adds flavour.

○ Yeast is the raising agent. When the warm (25–35 °C) liquid is added to the dry ingredients and yeast it must not be too hot, as this will kill the yeast and the bread will not rise.
○ Kneading the bread helps to develop the gluten, which stretches to hold the carbon dioxide bubbles produced by the yeast.

When making bread, if you do not follow the recipe carefully faults may occur. Table 4.6 shows the common faults that can occur in bread making.

Fault	Cause
Bread has a dense texture	○ Ordinary plain flour was used, which does not have a high enough gluten content ○ The yeast was killed before the bread was baked ○ Too much salt was used in the mixture ○ The dough was too dry, which meant it was too dry to allow the expansion ○ The dough was not left to prove for long enough
Bread has not risen well and is coarse in texture	○ The dough was over-fermented/left to prove for too long ○ The yeast was killed before the bread was baked
Bread has uneven texture and large holes	○ Bread was not kneaded enough after the first proving
Dough collapses when being baked	○ The mixture was left to prove for too long

△ **Table 4.6** Faults in bread making

Exam practice questions

1. Describe different ways in which white bread can be made more appealing to different consumer groups. **[8 marks]**
2. Explain why breads from different countries are becoming more popular. **[2 marks]**
3. Which type of flour is most suitable for making a loaf of bread? Give reasons for your choice. **[2 marks]**

Stretch yourself

1. Investigate what happens to each of the ingredients used in bread making, from the stage when they are mixed together until they come out of the oven.

2. Investigate how a bakery would manufacture bread. You may find it useful to visit the website http://activekidsgetcooking.org.uk. If you go to 'Secondary Awards' and then 'Product Case Studies', you can click on the 'Bread' arrow to find some useful information.

Activities

1. Research the different types of bread available in a supermarket. Produce a chart or poster to show where they originate from and the types of flour used in them.

2. A bakery wants to develop a hand-held snack bread product. The specification for the product is:
   - can be eaten 'on the go'
   - suitable for a wide range of consumers
   - costs under £1 per portion
   - attractive
   - contains either fruit or vegetables
   - includes a variety of textures.

   (a) Using a basic bread recipe, design a product that meets this specification.

   (b) List the ingredients and their costs.

   (c) Explain how your design meets the specification.

   (d) Produce a plan of how to make the product.

   (e) Evaluate the product against the specification and suggest any improvements.

3. (a) In groups, make small amounts of bread dough (100 g flour) using different types of flour, for example, plain flour, strong plain flour, wholewheat flour, half strong plain and half wholewheat.

   (b) Copy and complete the chart below to show your results.

Flour	Amount of water added	Colour of dough before baking	Colour of dough after baking	Texture of the baked bread	Flavour of the bread

   (c) Explain which type of flour you would use to make bread.

   (d) Explain why you would not use the other flours.

   (e) Give detailed reasons for your answers.

4.4 Sauce making for sweet and savoury products

There are many different types of sauces used in a wide variety of dishes. In this section we are going to focus on starch-based sauces.

The different starches that are often used to thicken sauces are:
- flour
- cornflour
- arrowroot.

Depending on the proportions of the ingredient used, the thickness of the sauce varies.

Knowledge link

Chapter 2 explains in detail what happens to sauce mixtures when they are cooked (see page 60).

Methods of making sauces

Sauces can be made by three different methods:

○ roux
○ blended
○ all-in-one.

Roux

This is the traditional method of making a sauce. The fat is melted and the flour stirred in and cooked on a medium heat. The liquid is added gradually. The sauce is returned to the heat and brought back to the boil, stirring all the time.

Blended

This is often used for cornflour- and arrowroot-based sauces. A little of the liquid is blended with the cornflour. The remaining liquid is heated. The hot liquid is poured onto the cornflour mixture, stirring carefully. The sauce is returned to the pan and brought back to the boil, stirring all the time.

All-in-one

All the ingredients are placed in the pan and brought to the boil. Stirring or whisking is required all the time to prevent the sauce from going lumpy.

Controlled assessment link

Figure 14.12 on page 237 shows development ideas for a pie, which includes using different sauces.

Activities

1. In groups, prepare a cheese sauce by the three different methods detailed on page 93, and also prepare one using a packet mix.

2. Compare the results of making the sauce for:

   ○ ease of making
   ○ time it took to make
   ○ quality of the finished sauce
   ○ cost
   ○ nutritional value.

3. Use the sauce to make a savoury dish of your choice.

Type of sauce	Proportions of ingredients	Description of sauce	Example of dish
Pouring	250 ml milk 15 g fat 15 g flour	Pours freely	Custard
Coating	250 ml milk 25 g fat 25 g flour	Coats the back of a spoon	Cauliflower cheese
Binding	250 ml flour 50 g fat 50 g flour	Very thick sauce that can bind ingredients	Fishcakes

△ **Table 4.7** Proportions of ingredients used in sauces

1. List the **three** main methods of making sauces. **[3 marks]**

2. Suggest **three** different ingredients that could be used to flavour a savoury white sauce. **[3 marks]**

3. Give **two** reasons why it is important to stir a sauce when it is being cooked. **[2 marks]**

4. These are the ingredients used in a plain white sauce:

   ○ 25 g flour
   ○ 25 g fat
   ○ 250 ml milk

   Explain what happens to the ingredients when they are heated. **[4 marks]**

4.5 Fruit and vegetable preparation

Fruits and vegetables need to be prepared carefully to maintain their nutritional profile. They must also be stored correctly before they are prepared, to help retain their nutritional value. This can be done by:

○ storing in a cool, dry place
○ handling carefully – bruising will reduce the vitamin C content
○ removing any damaged fruit or vegetables

△ **Figure 4.6** There is a wide variety of fruits and vegetables to choose from

○ checking the storage instructions on the products
○ keeping salad ingredients in the salad drawer.

Preparing fruits and vegetables

When preparing fruits and vegetables:

○ wash to remove dirt
○ remove any blemishes or outer leaves
○ peel if necessary, however, many fruits and vegetables can be eaten with their skin on, and peeling them will reduce the nutrient content as many of the nutrients are stored just below the surface of the skin
○ prepare vegetables just before cooking to prevent loss of vitamins by the action of enzymes and **oxidisation**
○ do not soak them in water as this will result in the loss of water-soluble vitamins (vitamins B and C)
○ some fruits and vegetables will go brown once they are peeled and cut, for example, apples, potatoes, pears. This is called **enzymic browning**. This can be reduced by:
  ○ blanching vegetables in boiling water
  ○ dipping fruit into lemon juice
  ○ cooking the foods as soon as they have been prepared
○ handle delicate fruits and vegetables carefully so they do not get bruised.

Most fruits can be eaten raw and should be washed before they are eaten. Fruits are sometimes cooked, for instance, stewing apples or poaching pears.

Key terms

Oxidisation – occurs when fruit and vegetables are cut and the cells are exposed to the air

Enzymic browning – a reaction between a food product and oxygen, resulting in the food becoming brown

Key points

- o Fruits and vegetables need to be carefully prepared so that vitamins are not lost.
- o It is important that fruits and vegetables are prepared correctly. This will often involve using a sharp knife. Figure 4.7 shows the correct ways to hold vegetables when chopping and slicing them.

Activities

Soups can be a nutritious snack product.

1. Design a soup, using seasonal vegetables, that would be attractive to teenagers.
2. Calculate the nutritional value and the cost per portion of your soup.
3. Compare your product with different types of soup already on the market.

Exam practice questions

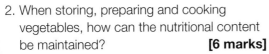

1. Why is it important to wash fruits before they are eaten? **[2 marks]**
2. When storing, preparing and cooking vegetables, how can the nutritional content be maintained? **[6 marks]**

△ **Figure 4.7** Bridge and claw grip used when preparing fruits and vegetables

4.6 Preparation of meat

A wide variety of meat, poultry and offal can be used in cooking. There are also many products made for consumers to cook at home, such as sausages and beefburgers.

△ **Figure 4.8** Butcher's window display

Today most people buy their meat ready prepared and do not joint or bone pieces of meat. The meat will come cut into portions or joints, and may also be chopped or minced.

Cooking methods

It is important that meat is cooked in an appropriate way so that it is tender to eat. Usually, lean, tender cuts of meat are suitable for dry methods of cooking, and tougher cuts of meat require long, slow methods of cooking, such as stewing and braising.

Safety

Meat is classed as a high-risk food (because it contains protein and is moist), so it is important that it is processed, stored, handled and cooked correctly so that it is safe to eat.

The following is good practice:

- o Wash your hands before and after touching any type of raw meat.
- o Keep raw meat separate from other foods. Cover and store the meat at the bottom of the fridge so that it cannot touch any other foods.

o Raw meat contains harmful bacteria that can spread to anything it touches, so it is important to clean surfaces and equipment thoroughly after preparing meat.

o Raw meat should be stored at temperatures below 5 °C.

o Any bacteria present in the meat will be destroyed by heat. It is therefore important to check that the meat is thoroughly cooked. This can be done with a food probe or meat thermometer. The food probe should be inserted into the centre of the food to a depth of about 2 cm. Record the reading. Make sure you clean the probe thoroughly after each use.

△ **Figure 4.9** Checking the temperature of meat

 Controlled assessment link
Figure 14.9 on page 234 shows a student practical write-up for a chicken and chorizo casserole. Food safety checks for meat have been identified.

Exam practice questions

1. Explain why it is important to store raw meat away from other foods. **[2 marks]**

Activities

Minced beef is used in many meat dishes. You have been challenged to develop a traditional minced beef dish (for example, shepherd's pie, lasagne, spaghetti bolognaise) into a new dish that could be promoted in a supermarket or butcher's.

You will need to:

1. Make your product to check that it works.

2. Produce a promotional recipe card that includes:

o details of the nutritional information for the product

o a list of ingredients needed to make the dish

o the instructions for how to make the product.

4.7 Preparation of fish

Most people buy fish ready-prepared, from supermarkets. There are fewer independent fishmongers today. Fish can be bought fresh, frozen or canned. Fresh fish is usually sold as whole fish, or cut into steaks or fillets.

△ **Figure 4.10** The fish counter

Safety

When choosing fresh fish:

o   it should have a sea-fresh smell
o   the flesh of the fish should be moist and firm
o   the scales on the fish should be shiny.

Fish, like meat, is a high-risk food, and therefore the same good practices that are used when preparing meat need to be applied when preparing fish. It is also wise to thoroughly wrap fish so that the smell does not pass to other foods.

Activities

We are being encouraged to eat at least two portions of fish a week.

1. Produce a fish dish that would appeal to either young children or teenagers.

2. Explain why your dish would appeal your target group.

Key points

o   Fish is a high-risk food.
o   It needs to be stored and cooked correctly.
o   It should be eaten as soon as possible after purchase.

4.8 Preparation of alternative protein foods

There is a wide range of alternative protein foods available. These include products made from soya beans, such as **textured vegetable protein** (TVP) tofu, and mycoprotein, such as Quorn®. These products can be bought in a variety of forms. The products will either simply need cooking or will require other ingredients to be added to them to make a dish or product.

△ **Figure 4.11** Soya products

Cooking and storage

The cooking instructions must be followed carefully for all these products. Soya beans can be bought frozen, tinned or dried. Quorn® is sold as a variety of ready-to-eat products, but can also be bought as mince, chunks or fillets. These are sold from either the chiller cabinet or the freezer.

Tofu is purchased as a solid curd. It is usually sold from the chiller cabinet. It can be frozen, but must be cooked when it has been defrosted. It can be grilled or stir-fried.

When purchasing alternative protein foods as frozen or chilled products you must remember to treat these as high-risk foods.

Activities

1. In pairs, adapt a dish that usually uses meat and make two versions of the dish, using an alternative protein food and meat.

2. Compare the sensory qualities of the dish.

Stretch yourself

For the dishes that were made for the activity above, compare the:

○ cost
○ nutritional profile of the dishes.

Key term

Textured vegetable protein – protein produced from soya beans used as an alternative to protein or as a meat extender; it is either extruded or formed into chunks

Controlled assessment link

The content of this chapter will also help improve your understanding of practical work situations.

chapter 5

Design and market influences – factors affecting people's choice of food

Learning objectives

By the end of this chapter you should have developed a knowledge and understanding of the health, dietary, socio-economic, cultural and religious factors that affect people's choice of food, including:

- ○ availability, cost, personal preferences, storage, cooking facilities, and the effects of advertising, promotions and food scares
- ○ how cultural preferences, religion, lifestyle, health and multicultural factors have influenced food production
- ○ the implications that sustainability, food miles, seasonality, local food, genetically modified foods, organic and free-range foods, Fairtrade and Farm Assured have for the environment.

Introduction

Most people make a choice of food at least two or three times a day. The availability of a wide range of foods makes it easier to choose foods that are nutritionally good for us, but we are all influenced by a variety of other factors.

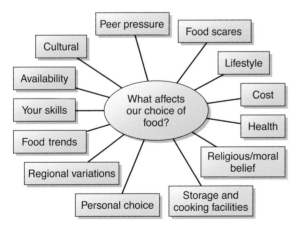

△ **Figure 5.1** The factors affecting food choice

5.1 **Factors affecting your choice of foods**

A range of factors affect your choice of foods. These include the foods available, costs, personal preferences, storage and cooking facilities, the effect of advertising, promotions and food scares.

Availability

Choice depends on the type of food available in the country and place where you live. In developing countries, such as in parts of Africa, there is very little choice and often insufficient food available, and they may not be able to grow produce because of climate, or because they cannot afford expensive agricultural equipment.

In the UK there is a wide variety of food because of technological developments and improvements in the growth, transport, preservation and storage of food. Food technologists have also created many new foods, such as Quorn®. We can import foods that we cannot grow ourselves. In the UK we can go to the supermarket at any time of the year and buy whatever food we want, as long as we are prepared to pay for it.

98

△ **Figure 5.2** Modern transportation has improved consumer choice

Cost

One of the most important influences on food choice is what people can afford to spend. People have to think of ways they can save money on their food bill, for example:

- using cheaper protein foods, for example, eggs, cheese and pulses
- buying locally grown vegetables or even growing your own
- buying special offers, such as 'buy one get one free'
- using a variety of supermarkets and planning meals around their special offers
- buying foods with a short shelf life that have been reduced in price
- not wasting foods – the average family in the UK throws away £600 worth of food in a year
- following the advice of the eatwell plate and using more carbohydrates (which are cheaper) in meals
- adapting recipes by swapping expensive ingredients for cheaper ones, for example, yoghurt instead of cream
- planning meals and shopping carefully
- using 'own-brand' economy-range products
- buying loose produce, which is often cheaper than the pre-packaged varieties
- using economical methods of cooking.

Better-off people tend to buy more protein foods, so their starch and fibre intake tends to decrease, while those on lower incomes tend to buy less fruit and vegetables, thus having a lower intake of vitamins and minerals.

Controlled assessment link
Figure 14.6 on page 232 shows that cost is an important factor to consider in your design specification.

Personal preferences

We all have our personal likes and dislikes and are influenced by our senses. We use all of our five senses when we eat. These give us information about the food.

The five senses are:

- *Sight* – the appearance (aesthetics) of food can make it look more or less appetising. Aspects such as colour, size, shape, age, texture, garnish and decoration will all affect how you feel about the product.

◁ **Figure 5.3** Sight

- *Sound* – some food products make sounds during preparation, cooking, serving or eating. For instance, the crackle of popcorn, the sizzle of bacon, the crunch of crisps and raw carrot.

◁ **Figure 5.4** Sound

- *Smell* – you can detect the aroma of foods, such as ripeness and freshness of apples and cabbage. Aroma stimulates the digestive juices and makes the food seem more appetising.

Areas of taste

△ **Figure 5.8** Areas of the tongue

◁ **Figure 5.5** Smell

o *Taste* – taste buds detect four groups of flavours: bitter, sweet, sour and salt. Flavour develops when the food is combined through chewing and mixing with saliva.

◁ **Figure 5.6** Taste

o *Touch* – the surface of the tongue is sensitive to different sensations, such as moist, dry, soft, sticky, gritty, crumbly, mushy. As we bite and chew food we can feel how hard or soft it is through our teeth and jaw. These qualities are known as 'mouthfeel'; if they are missing, food is considered to be unpalatable.

◁ **Figure 5.7** Touch

Key points

o The characteristics of food that affect our organs are known as **organoleptic** qualities.
o Smell and taste work together to develop the flavour of food.
o The sensitivity of the tongue is reduced when the food is either very hot or very cold.

Key term

Organoleptic – qualities of food associated with the senses

Activities

1. Use the internet to compare the prices in three different supermarkets of:

o 12 eggs
o 250 g soft margarine
o 1.5 kg self-raising flour
o 500 g castor sugar
o 500 g cooking apples
o 500 g Cheddar cheese.

2. You could choose your own ingredients list to make a comparison.

3. Make a list of the ways that supermarkets try to help people on low incomes.

4. Choose a recipe for a dessert and modify it to meet a low-budget specification.

5. Carry out a survey of 20 of your school friends to find out their likes and dislikes when choosing foods. Analyse your results and present your findings as a letter to a food company advising them of teenage food preferences.

Knowledge link

See Chapter 6 for help with writing a questionnaire (page 113).

Storage and cooking facilities

Food technologists are continually developing new food products that require little preparation and are easy to store and cook.

Most households have a microwave to reheat convenience foods. A refrigerator is considered an essential item of equipment to ensure food safety – if you do not have a refrigerator, your choice is restricted to canned and dried foods. Many households have a freezer, which means that that they can shop weekly.

If you do not have the skills to prepare ingredients, you can buy them ready-prepared, such as frozen vegetables. Students at university and the elderly, for instance, often have limited cooking facilities. However, these can be expanded through the purchase of a wide range of cooking equipment that will perform different tasks, including low-fat grilling machines, electric woks and electric barbecues.

Advertising and promotions

We are strongly influenced by our peer group and by the media. Manufacturers spend many millions every year on advertising, especially on chocolate, crisps, snacks and sweets. Also, manufacturers may promote the product by special offers, free gifts and competitions.

△ **Figure 5.9** Lots of new equipment is available

Ways of advertising and promoting food products include:

- advertisements on the television and the internet, in cinemas, newspapers and magazines, and on posters and flyers
- displays in supermarkets and shop windows
- special money offers, such as 'buy one get one free' (bogof) or money-off coupons
- celebrity endorsements by sports or pop stars
- competitions
- free samples or tasting in supermarkets
- free gifts
- eye-catching, attractive packaging.

△ **Figure 5.10** A selection of products targeted at children

We watch chefs on the television and see advertising all around us. This influences our choice of food.

Advertising must be legal, decent, honest and truthful, and this is monitored by the Office of Fair Trading.

Food scares

Food scares in the media have a dramatic influence on food choice and sometimes result in product sales dropping so dramatically that the company involved ceases to exist. Recent food scares include:

- salmonella in eggs
- hazelnut yoghurts
- listeria in chilled foods
- dioxins in Coke (in 1999)
- E. coli in meat products
- food contamination during production, for example, metals, insects, glass, fabric
- BSE.

Exam practice questions

1. Explain why advertising and promotion are important when a manufacturer makes a new product.

    [6 marks]

2. Explain why there are standards and controls on advertising to children.

    [6 marks]

3. Explain, using examples, why consumers are influenced by food scares. **[4 marks]**

Stretch yourself

1. Discuss the influence that the media has had on school lunches.

2. Explain why there are now more ready meals available in the supermarkets than there used to be.

Activities

1. Consider your family's lifestyle. How are eating patterns affected by the work and social activities of the family members? Are there any ways that you could improve the eating habits of any one in your family?

2. Research a range of different cooking equipment. For each piece of equipment consider:

    - What is its function?
    - How much does it cost?
    - Who would benefit from using the equipment?

3. Collect two different advertisements for food products. Consider their suitability for the target market.

    (a) What is it describing?

    (b) Who is the product aimed at?

    (c) What is the message?

    (d) Is it a good or a bad advert?

    (e) Would you buy the product?

5.2 **Cultural, moral and social influences**

Culture

The word culture is used to describe our way of life. A cultural group is a group of people who share the same norms, beliefs and values.

We adopt the eating patterns of our parents from infancy; we learn to like the foods that our families like. Styles of eating and cooking tend to be determined by the availability of cheap, locally grown food products. Rice is the staple crop in India, China and Japan, the potato in Britain and yams in parts of Africa.

Wheat is grown in many countries, but is used in a variety of ways. Look at Figure 5.11. Can you name the wheat products and their country of origin?

△ **Figure 5.11** Wheat is the basis for staple foods across the world

Controlled assessment link

Multicultural society is one of the design contexts for the Controlled Assessment. The Malaysia chicken curry produced by a student in Figure 14.10 on page 235 considers cultural influences.

In some cultures and religions certain foods are not permitted because they are considered 'dirty' or 'unclean' or sacred. Manufacturers are influenced by cultures – if there is a demand for a certain type of food they will respond.

Certain foods have become an important part of celebrations in many cultures, such as:

○ special events in the year, for example, Christmas, Divali
○ birthdays
○ weddings
○ retirements
○ special achievements
○ celebrating someone's life.

There are many more.

Religious and moral issues

Religious beliefs influence eating habits, as religions often have laws related to foods.

Hinduism

The cow is sacred to Hindus, so they will not eat beef or any product from slaughtered cows. They avoid foods that may have caused an animal pain, so are usually vegetarians and have many days of fasting.

Sikhism

Sikhs have similar eating habits to Hindus. Again, many are vegetarian. Some do not drink alcohol, tea or coffee.

Islam

Muslims have a set of dietary rules. The pig is considered unclean, so Muslims do not eat pork or any pork products. Other meats and poultry must be slaughtered in a particular way so that no blood remains. This is called Halal meat. Unlawful foods are called 'haram' and include alcohol and caffeine.

Judaism

Food is an important part of the Jewish religion. Kosher food is food that Jews are allowed to eat.

Meat must be specially slaughtered, soaked and then treated with kosher salt. Jews do not eat pork. Meat and dairy produce must not be eaten at the same meal.

Rastafarianism

Rastafarians eat food that is natural and clean. They do not eat pork and only eat fish that is longer than 30 cm. They cook with coconut oil and do not drink alcohol, milk or coffee.

Buddhism

Most Buddhists are vegetarian.

Lifestyle

Eating habits have been affected by social changes within households during the past 30 years. Changes in lifestyle due to both parents working and the consequent increase in income (two wages) have resulted in people spending less time in the kitchen preparing food from raw ingredients, choosing to buy more foods that are ready to eat or just need reheating, and an increase in eating out. In some homes, due to different members of the family eating at different times, some of the traditional mealtimes of breakfast, lunch and dinner are being replaced by snack meals and takeaway dinners.

Lifestyle factors that affect eating habits include:

○ More mothers are employed outside the home.
○ More people live alone.
○ People travel greater distances to work.
○ People have social activities outside the home.
○ The use of convenience foods and ready meals, and the availability of takeaways allow people to have more flexible lifestyles.
○ There has been an increase in snack foods available.
○ There is a wide variety of foods available to choose from.
○ There are many types of restaurants in most cities.
○ There is less emphasis on the family meal, and family members eat when they want to (grazing).

△ **Figure 5.12** Shopping has become a family occasion, with everyone choosing food

Health

The nutritional needs of individuals and groups of people are affected by their health. Eating for health means making small changes to the meals that we already eat.

We should all choose foods carefully:

○ Overweight people should choose low-calorie, low-fat foods.
○ People recovering from an injury or illness should choose high-protein foods.

△ **Figure 5.13** The NHS is spending valuable funds on helping people with diet-related disorders

- Someone recovering from a heart attack should choose products lower in fat.
- Anyone suffering from high blood pressure is usually advised to have a diet lower in salt.

Many people are in hospital because of diet-related conditions. We do not have deficiency diseases in the UK, but there is a problem because of people eating the wrong foods.

Activities

1. Make a list of all the celebrations that we have in the UK during one year. Which ones do supermarkets sell special food for? Name a special food served. For example: special event in the year = Christmas; special food = mince pies.

2. Make a list of celebrations from different cultures and find out what special foods are served.

Exam practice questions

1. Explain why some people choose to buy ready meals. **[4 marks]**

2. Give **four** reasons why the range of multicultural vegetables and fruit available in supermarkets has increased. **[4 marks]**

3. There is an increasing range of bread products for sale in shops. Discuss the reasons for this increase. **[6 marks]**

5.3 Sustainability issues

Your choice of food products affects the environment. This includes moral issues, seasonality, local food, **organic** and free-range foods, **genetically modified** foods, **sustainable** design, food miles, **Fairtrade** foods and **Farm Assured** foods.

Moral issues

Some people may make moral decisions, for example, vegetarians who decide that it is morally wrong to kill animals to eat their flesh. Other current moral issues affecting food production include: intensive farming, genetically modified foods, animal welfare, factory farming, selective breeding.

Factory-farmed animals are often kept in very distressing conditions – cramped, with limited lighting and no room for the animals to move or exercise.

Free-range animals are allowed to live and grow in natural surroundings. Products from these animals will cost the consumer more because the farmer will not produce as much.

△ **Figure 5.14** Free-range hens

Selective breeding has resulted in egg-laying hens that will produce 300 eggs a year. A broiler chicken, reared for meat rather than eggs, will reach its slaughter weight in about 40 days.

Seasonality

This relates to the availability and use of products when they are in season. We have become accustomed to going into supermarkets and buying anything at any time, but the production of crops in the UK is limited to short seasons during the year. The range of products and ingredients available for us to buy is a result of **globalisation**. This has been made possible by improved storage, preservation and transportation of foods. Our food products travel many miles to reach our table. Think about the effect on the environment of the miles that food travels. This is called the **carbon footprint** of the product, or food miles.

△ **Figure 5.15** Factory-farmed egg production

Key terms

Organic – grown or reared without the use of artificial aids/fertilisers/pesticides/antibiotics

Genetically modified – describes crops in which the genetic structure of the cells has been changed

Sustainability – this means reducing the impact of a product on the environment

Fairtrade – guarantees that disadvantaged producers get a fair deal

Farm Assured – guarantees the highest standards of food safety and hygiene, animal welfare and environmental protection

Globalisation – process by which different parts of the globe become interconnected by economic, social, cultural and political means

Carbon footprint – the amount of carbon emissions produced in the growing, processing and distribution of our food

Local food

Using local products means that you are getting quality products with a low carbon footprint. We can eat with the seasons.

January	February	March	April
Cabbage Kale Parsnips Swede	Artichokes Spring greens Watercress	Cauliflower Purple sprouting broccoli	Greenhouse lettuce Spring greens Salad onions
May	**June**	**July**	**August**
Asparagus Tomatoes Spring cabbage	Finger carrots Gooseberries Broad beans Lettuce Spinach Strawberries	Cherries Cauliflower Mange tout/peas Raspberries Salad potatoes	Charlotte potatoes Courgettes Discovery apples French beans Romaine lettuce

△ **Table 5.1** Fruit and vegetables grown in the UK   *Cont.*

September	October	November	December
Beetroot Pears Apples Runner beans	Celery Pumpkin Turnips Squash	Chinese leaves Green cabbage Brussels sprouts	Brussels sprouts on a stalk Leeks Savoy cabbage Chantenay carrots

△ **Table 5.1** Fruit and vegetables grown in the UK

A new trend is for households to have boxes of organic local produce delivered to the door.

△ **Figure 5.16** Local organic fruits and vegetables delivered to your door

Organic foods

Most farming relies heavily on artificial chemical fertilisers and pesticides. Around 350 pesticides are permitted in the UK, and it is estimated that 4.5 billion litres of them are used annually. There can be concerns about their long-term effect on us and they can harm the environment too, for example, chemicals in pesticides leach into rivers and pollute the water.

◁ **Figure 5.17** The Soil Association organic logo

Organic agriculture is carried out to a set of legally defined standards. Producers then pay to have their produce monitored and certified by one of several organic organisations, of which the Soil Association is the largest in the UK.

The Soil Association was founded in 1946 by a group of farmers, scientists and nutritionists who observed a direct connection between the health of the soil, food, people and the environment. Today the Soil Association is the UK's leading organic organisation, with over 200 staff based in Bristol and Edinburgh. It is an educational charity with some 27,000 members and its certification subsidiary, Soil Association Certification Ltd, certifies over 80 per cent of organic farming and food processing in the UK. For more information see www.soilassociation.org.

Organic farming strictly limits the use of artificial chemical fertilisers or pesticides. Antibiotics for animals are kept to an absolute minimum. Genetically modified crops are forbidden. Organic bodies also demand more space for animals and higher welfare standards.

In Brazil thousands of children pick oranges to be made into concentrate and processed into juice. They are often exposed to high levels of pesticide and may be paid as little as 13p an hour (www.sustain.co.uk).

So, what does organic mean?

○ All food sold as organic must be approved by organic certification bodies and produced according to stringent EC laws.
○ It is produced by farmers who grow, handle and process crops without synthetic fertilisers, pesticides and herbicides or any other artificial ingredient.
○ It will not contain any genetically engineered ingredients.

○ Organic meat, poultry, eggs and dairy products come from animals that are given no antibiotics or growth hormones.

○ Organic producers can only use natural fertilisers, not synthetic ones.

Organic foods are considered to taste nicer, avoid the risk of a combination of chemicals and respect soil structure and wildlife.

△ **Figure 5.18** Organic crops grown on a local allotment

Genetically modified foods

The use of new technology in the food industry is controversial, especially products made by modifying or engineering the genetic make-up of food. It might improve the quality of the food, for instance, blackcurrants can be modified to make them higher in vitamin C, tomatoes can be modified to improve their flavour or keeping qualities. Advantages of genetically modified (GM) foods are:

○ improvements to quantity and quality of food
○ can grow in adverse conditions, for example, drought
○ herbicide and insect-resistant, therefore thrive better
○ high nutritional quality
○ cheaper to produce.

The concerns about GM foods include:

○ long-term safety is unknown
○ environmental effects, as the pollen from GM crops does not stop in one place

△ **Figure 5.19** Genetically modified crops

○ ethics – we need adequate labelling: if a product has over 1 per cent of GM food this must be stated on the label; if it is under 1 per cent it does not need to be stated.

Sustainable design

The choices we make as consumers and designers have an impact on other people, especially elsewhere in the world. If we buy chocolate, coffee or tea in the supermarket there are consequences for the people in Kenya, Sri Lanka, Nicaragua and many other places. These consequences extend to their families, schools, communities, and so on. We have a moral dilemma whether to buy British or support developing countries in some way. By eating food out of season and from far away we are using up the world's resources.

Eco footprint

More people are stopping to consider the impact that our food has on the environment. 'Eco footprint' is the term used to refer to the measurement of our actions on the environment. As a designer you must consider the effect of your product on the environment from the first stages of your design ideas through to the final making and eventual disposal or recycling of your product.

Figure 5.20 Carbon footprint logo

Food miles

The distance food travels from field to plate is a way of indicating the environmental impact of the food we eat. Half the vegetables and 95 per cent of the fruit eaten in the UK comes from beyond our shores. Food is transported across the world because we want to buy foods out of season. Asparagus is only in season for May and June in the UK, but we want to buy it all year. It comes from Italy or Spain for a few months and the rest of the year it comes from Peru!

Planes are powered by fossil fuel oil. When the oil is burnt it gives off carbon dioxide gas emissions which contribute hugely to global warming. You can offset this by planting trees to absorb the CO_2 given off. This is called carbon offsetting. If we reduced the amount of packaging used in products, it might reduce costs and save energy in terms of fuel and transportation.

△ Figure 5.21 Transportation by aeroplane

What can we do? Buy local! This means supporting local growers. It is much better for the environment if you grow and/or buy local organic produce.

What is Fairtrade?

Fairtrade is about better prices, decent working conditions, local sustainability and fair terms of trade for farmers and workers in the developing world. By requiring companies to pay sustainable prices (which must never fall lower than the market price), Fairtrade addresses the injustices of conventional trade, which traditionally discriminates against the poorest, weakest producers.

®

◁ Figure 5.22
The FAIRTRADE Mark

The Fairtrade Foundation has licensed over 3,000 Fairtrade certified products for sale through retail and catering outlets in the UK. The UK market is doubling in value every two years. The UK is one of the world's leading Fairtrade markets, with more products and more awareness of Fairtrade than anywhere else. Around 20 per cent of roast and ground coffee sold in the UK retail market is Fairtrade. Stable prices mean that coffee farmers can plan for the future.

Fairtrade food products include:
○ bananas
○ cocoa
○ coffee
○ dried fruit
○ fresh fruit and fresh vegetables
○ honey
○ nuts/oil seeds
○ rice
○ spices
○ sugar
○ tea.

Controlled assessment link
Fairtrade is one of the contexts for the Controlled Assessment.

Organisations such as Traidcraft use only ethically produced materials and ingredients, which helps both the producers and the manufacturers in developing countries. Adriano Kalilii, a tea plucker from Kibena in Tanzania, can afford iron sheets to roof his house thanks to Fairtrade.

△ **Figure 5.23** Tea in Tanzania (Traidcraft photo)

Farm Assured

We all want quality food that is affordable and safe to eat. The Red Tractor is an independent mark of quality that guarantees that the food we are buying comes from farms and food companies that meet high standards of food safety and hygiene, animal welfare and environmental protection. Look for the Red Tractor Assurance logo.

△ **Figure 5.24** The Red Tractor Assurance logo

Key points

o The Fairtrade mark is an independent consumer label that appears on products as a guarantee that disadvantaged producers are getting a better deal. It guarantees that farmers in developing countries get a fair price for their products, which covers their costs.
o Organic foods avoid health risks associated with a combination of chemicals used as pesticides and herbicides.

Activities

1. Design and make a product using seasonal foods.
2. Produce monthly posters of seasonal foods with recipes.
3. Investigate the range of organic products in the supermarket. Compare prices with non-organic products.
4. Discuss the reasons why a family might choose to buy organic foods.
5. Carry out research to find out what common foods contain GM ingredients.
6. Investigate the different symbols that may be found on products to show their eco footprints.
7. Look at the ingredients in a ready meal and work out the food miles in the product. Use the internet to help. Type in 'food miles'.
8. Calculate the food miles of your Sunday dinner.
9. We can grow apples in the UK. Have a look in your local supermarket and see where the fruit is imported from. Record on a map where all the fruit has come from.
10. Look on the Fairtrade website and produce a leaflet that encourages people to buy ethically produced ingredients.

Exam practice questions

1. State what is meant by organic vegetables. Explain why organic vegetables have become increasingly popular. **[5 marks]**

2. The poultry sold at a farm shop is described as free-range. Explain what is meant by free-range. **[4 marks]**

3. Give **two** reasons why a consumer would choose to buy free-range products. **[2 marks]**

4. Many farmers are selling local produce from farm shops. Give **three** reasons why consumers choose to buy foods from farm shops. **[3 marks]**

5. Give **three** reasons why consumers might choose to buy products from other cultures. **[3 marks]**

6. Explain why we should consider our carbon footprint when choosing food products. **[4 marks]**

Stretch yourself

Discuss the factors other than nutritional needs that affect an individual's choice of food.

Learning objectives

By the end of this chapter you should have developed a knowledge and understanding of how to:

o find out customer views and preferences for a range of different products using an appropriate range of methods including ICT (for example, interview, questionnaire, product analysis)

o identify physical, nutritional and sensory characteristics in existing products in order to develop design criteria and generate your own ideas

o use product analysis to compare a range of existing packaged products to determine how the types, proportions and functions of ingredients have contributed to a product's overall characteristics and its ability to meet a specific need.

Introduction

Products should be developed according to what people want. These people will become your customer group or your intended target market. For example, some food products are developed specifically for people on a special diet, such as Weight Watchers®, others for people living on their own, for example, single-portion products, others for a specific age group, such as children. Your first step is to carry out market research to identify a need for a new product.

△ **Figure 6.1** You must identify your user group

6.1 Finding out customer views and preferences

Consideration of food trends, consumer preference, and socio-economic issues

Consumers change their ideas about the products they want to buy as they are influenced by a changing economic, technological and social environment. In order for your product to be successful you must identify changing consumer needs and new trends, and develop products to meet these. This can be done by adapting an existing product or by developing a completely new and original product.

There are many different issues affecting people's choice of food. They include:

o Current dietary trends – low in fat, sugar and salt, high in fibre.

o Social issues – cost remains the top priority for some people. However, other people have more money to spend on food products. Consequently, there has been an increase in the number of luxury products available.

o Environmental issues – using locally grown ingredients, using recycled materials for packaging.

- o Ethical issues – deciding whether to use genetically modified foods, organic foods.
- o Cultural issues – religious beliefs prevent some people eating certain products.
- o Media influence – advertising is very powerful in encouraging consumers to try new products.

Knowledge link
For more information on factor's affecting people's food choices, see Chapter 5 (page 98).

Controlled assessment link
Figure 14.1 on page 224 shows an analysis of a design brief, with the user group clearly identified.

Initial research

You will need to carry out some initial market **research** to gain as much information as possible to help you develop your **design criteria** (list of points from which you can develop different design ideas).

- o Primary research material is your own information that you have obtained from interviews, **questionnaires** and observations or from sensory testing.
- o Secondary research material is information that has been collected by other people, for instance, from books or newspapers.

Key terms
Research – the use of a variety of sources to find relevant information

Design criteria – a list of general points from which a range of different ideas can be made

Questionnaire – a set of questions asked to a range of people; results can be used to form ideas

Questionnaires and interviews

A questionnaire and/or interview should be designed so that it helps you to extract specific information from people about the qualities they would like to see in a new product. When you design your questionnaire, start with an introduction. This will allow the public to:

- o focus clearly on the theme of the questionnaire/interview
- o feel involved from the start, so a more satisfactory response is given
- o understand the purpose of the questionnaire/ interview.

The questions need to be clear and easy to understand and answer. It should be easy for you to collate the results using graphs, tables, tally charts, pie charts, and so on, before analysing the results and coming to your conclusions.

The questionnaire/interview must not be too long or people will become irritated and often will not think about their response but will just give the first response that comes to them.

△ **Figure 6.2** Carrying out an interview

Different types of questions can be used.

- o *Closed* – can be a very quick way of finding out specific information, for example, Do you like the flavour of chocolate? Yes ☐ No ☐

- ○ *Multiple choice* – offers a range of responses for the respondents to choose from, for example, Which flavour do you prefer?
  Chocolate ☐   Lemon ☐
  Coffee ☐   Ginger ☐

- ○ *Ordered choice* – sometimes it is useful for the respondent to rank a set of options by numbering them in order; for example, Place in order of preference the following flavourings. Indicate by numbering from 1 to 4 in order, where 1 is the most preferred.
  Chocolate ☐   Lemon ☐   Coffee ☐   Ginger ☐

- ○ *Open-ended* questions can produce a wide variety of responses that take a long time to interpret and put into categories. They are useful for finding out about attitudes and opinions, for example,

  1. What do you like about biscuits?

     _____

  2. What flavour would you like the biscuit to be and why?

     _____

Designing the correct questions can be time-consuming. You should always check questions before you use the questionnaire. Make sure that each one will lead to a useful answer, for instance, do you really need to know the respondent's age/gender or which supermarket they shop at?

ICT can be used to design the questionnaire, analyse and compare data and present results (as shown in Figure 6.3).

When you have obtained the results from your questionnaire or interview you should **summarise** your findings as this will help you to determine the design criteria for your product (see Figure 6.4).

Controlled assessment link

Figure 14.3 on page 227 shows an example of a student's questionnaire and an analysis of the results.

Key term

Summarise – give a concise account of the main points

Market research – the study of consumers' needs, preferences and lifestyles

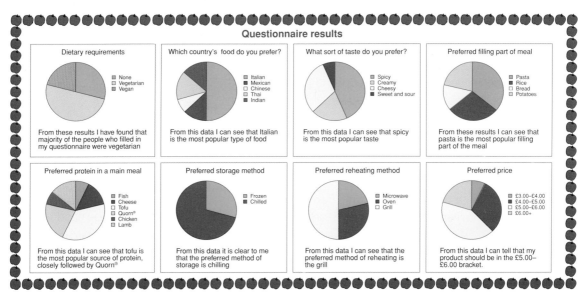

Questionnaire results

Dietary requirements — None / Vegetarian / Vegan
From these results I have found that majority of the people who filled in my questionnaire were vegetarian

Which country's food do you prefer? — Italian / Mexican / Chinese / Thai / Indian
From this data I can see that Italian is the most popular type of food

What sort of taste do you prefer? — Spicy / Creamy / Cheesy / Sweet and sour
From this data I can see that spicy is the most popular taste

Preferred filling part of meal — Pasta / Rice / Bread / Potatoes
From these results I can see that pasta is the most popular filling part of the meal

Preferred protein in a main meal — Fish / Cheese / Tofu / Quorn® / Chicken / Lamb
From this data I can see that tofu is the most popular source of protein, closely followed by Quorn®

Preferred storage method — Frozen / Chilled
From this data it is clear to me that the preferred method of storage is chilling

Preferred reheating method — Microwave / Oven / Grill
From this data I can see that the preferred method of reheating is the grill

Preferred price — £3.00–£4.00 / £4.00–£5.00 / £5.00–£6.00 / £6.00+
From this data I can tell that my product should be in the £5.00–£6.00 bracket.

△ **Figure 6.3** A student uses a questionnaire to find out more about the target group; from the analysis of the results the student can list the identified needs

Analysis of questionnaire

I have collected data by creating a questionnaire and asking members of the public to complete it.

From the results of the questionnaire I can see that my main meal product should be suitable for vegetarians, as the majority of people who filled in my questionnaire were vegetarian, and I feel there is definitely a gap in the market for vegetarian main meals.

From my data I have found that the most popular type of cuisine is Italian, closely followed by Indian, Mexican and Thai. This shows me that when I am deciding on recipes I should consider this and choose dishes in the style of this country's cuisine. The flavours that came out most popular are spicy, cheesy and creamy. This is a very good outcome because these flavours compliment the styles of food that came out most popular, that is, Italian, Indian, Mexican and Thai).

From my results I have also found that most people prefer pasta as the filling part of the meal, although potatoes and rice also scored highly. This is also a very good outcome as these complement the style of food that came out most popular. The most popular source of protein came out as tofu, closely followed by Quorn® and cheese. So, when choosing recipes I shall have to take this into account and make sure my recipes contain at least one of the three.

The price bracket that came out most popular was the £5.00–£6.00 bracket. This is a great outcome because it gives me quite a bit of money to work with so I can choose good ingredients.

The preferred storage method came out as chilling and the preferred reheating method as either oven or grill. This means my dish must be suitable for chilling, putting in the oven or the grill.

Identified needs

- My main meal needs to be suitable for vegetarians.
- My dish should be in an Italian style.
- My recipes should have creamy, cheesy or spicy flavours.
- The filling part of my meal should be pasta, potatoes or rice.
- For the protein part of my meal I should use tofu or Quorn®.
- The optimum price for my meal is between £5.00 and £6.00.
- My meal should be suitable for chilling.
- My meal should be suitable to be reheated in the grill or oven.
- My main meal must feed two people, that is, have two portions.
- My main meal should be suitable for batch production.

△ **Figure 6.4** The identified needs of the target group

Exam practice questions

1. Initial research is carried out to identify a need and to find out the qualities people require in a new product. List **two** methods that can be used to carry out research. **[2 marks]**

2. Explain why it is important to carry out initial research. **[4 marks]**

3. How can findings from research be recorded? Give **two** ways. **[2 marks]**

Key term

Brief – a clear statement of design intention

Activities

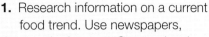

1. Research information on a current food trend. Use newspapers, magazines or the internet. Summarise the information you find and identify a need (product type and user group).

2. Design a questionnaire to find out the qualities teenagers would like to see in a new snack product.

3. Ask ten teenagers to complete the questionnaire, then draw conclusions from the results. Using your conclusions, develop a design specification.

4. Find a range of labels for food products. Suggest the target group for each product and give reasons for your answer.

Stretch yourself

Explain why it is important for a manufacturer to know the target group for a product.

Key points

- Lifestyles and technology are changing our food choices.
- Research findings should be analysed and used.
- A design **brief** is a short statement outlining the design problem to be solved.

6.2 Using sensory analysis

Evaluation of existing products

Evaluating existing products allows you to see what products are already available and to identify how these meet identified needs, that is, the qualities identified from the analysis of results from your questionnaire/interview. You could taste some products and carry out sensory analysis in order to evaluate how existing products meet identified **sensory qualities**, such as texture, taste and appearance. Sensory analysis is part of product analysis.

Carrying out this type of research may also give you some ideas when designing food products. The products you choose to evaluate should be relevant to your **consumer** group.

> **Controlled assessment link**
> Figures 14.3 and 14.4 on page 227 show students' analysis of existing products as part of their Controlled Assessment.

> **Key terms**
>
> **Evaluating** – summarising information, drawing conclusions and making judgements
>
> **Sensory qualities** – the look, smell, taste, feel and sound of products
>
> **Aesthetic qualities** – the properties that make a product attractive to look at or experience. The look, smell, taste, feel and sound of products
>
> **Consumer** – a person who buys or uses products or services

Sensory analysis

To enable the qualities to be monitored and recorded during the design and production of a new product, sensory analysis tests (tasting the foods) are carried out. This enables modifications (changes) to be made at each stage of the **development** of

the product so that the end result is successful. This prevents money from being wasted. It also allows a food manufacturer to check that the product matches the specification, is what the consumer likes/wants and has the required shelf life.

Checks can be made throughout production to maintain consistently high standards, and the products can be compared with those of competitors.

> **Key terms**
>
> **Development** – when changes are made to a product that affects its characteristics
>
> **Sensory analysis** – tests that identify the sensory characteristics of products, that is, taste, texture, appearance, mouth feel, colour
>
> **Organoleptic** – describes the sensory qualities (texture, flavour, aroma, appearance) of a food product

Sensory analysis tests

Sensory analysis is used to gather information on food products to establish their most important characteristics. These qualities are called **organoleptic** qualities. There are several types of test, which meet British Standard BS5929.

Food-tasting tests

These tests would be used to evaluate product acceptability by finding out the opinions, likes and dislikes of the consumer.

Ratings test – testers give their opinion of one or more samples of food, from 'extreme like' to 'extreme dislike'.

Sample	1. Dislike very much	2. Dislike	3. Neither like nor dislike	4. Like	5. Like very much	Comments
X						
XX						
XXX						
XXXX						

△ **Table 6.1** Ratings test

Difference testing – These tests are used to see whether people can tell the difference between samples, for instance, when an ingredient or quantity of ingredient is changed and when manufacturers are copying another brand, such as brands of cheese and onion crisps or a veggie burger and a beefburger. Triangle testing is an example of this.

Triangle test – Three samples are given to the tester. Two samples are the same and the tester is asked to identify the 'odd one out'. This test is useful if you have made small changes to a product, for instance, made a lasagne low in fat or used more economical ingredients.

Ranking test – This is used to sort a variety of foods into order, for example, different-flavoured crisps made by one manufacturer. A set of coded samples is presented to the tester. The tester has to rank the samples in order of either:

o a specific attribute, for example, sweetness, saltiness

o a preference on a hedonic (enjoyment) scale or ranking.

Key term

Ranking test – a method of putting in order the intensity of a particular characteristic of a product

o **Ranking test with descriptor** – This is used to place a variety of one type of food into order, for example, the flavour of cream

Taste the samples and put them in the order you like best		
Sample code	Order	Comments
◆		
○		
□		
★		

△ **Table 6.2** Ranking test

Ranking according to flavour	
Sample code	Creaminess choice
◆	2nd
○	1st
□	4th
★	3rd

△ **Table 6.3** Ranking test with descriptor

of tomato soups processed by different methods.

Profiling tests

This test can be used to find out what people particularly like about a food product, to help build up a **profile** of it according to a range of sensory qualities, such as saltiness, smoothness, crispness, flavour. Ask testers to give a score out

Tasting words	Votes by tasting panel (1 = poor, 2 = average, 3 = good, 4 = very good, 5 = excellent)					Total	Average
Flavour	4	4	5	3	4	20	4
Thickness	1	1	2	1	2	7	1.4
Colour	3	4	1	5	2	15	3
Smoothness	3	2	1	2	3	11	2.2

△ **Table 6.4** Profile of a fruit mousse

of five (where one is the least and five is the best). The scores for each quality are added up and divided by the number of testers. This will give average scores. The results can be presented in a table, as shown in Table 6.4.

Star profile

This type of test asks testers to describe the appearance, taste and texture of a food product on a star chart. When the food is tasted, the taster assesses the identified areas and marks the star diagram as required. The marks on each point are joined together to identify them clearly.

Controlled assessment link
Figure 14.9 on page 234 shows examples of a student's use of star profiles for sensory analysis testing.

Carrying out sensory analysis

It is important to use correct procedures when carrying out sensory analysis testing:

o Set up a quiet area where people will not be disturbed (do not allow testers to communicate with each other).
o Give the testers a drink of lemon-flavoured water or a piece of apple to clear the palate.
o Use small quantities of food on plain and identically sized plates/dishes.
o Use some garnish or decoration.
o Try not to give too many samples at once.
o Serve at the correct temperature for the product that is being tested.
o Use clean spoons or forks each time. Do

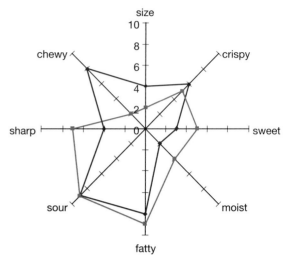

△ **Figure 6.5** Profile of a citrus cookie

NOT allow people to put dirty spoons into your dish.
o Use codes for the products to prevent the testers being influenced by the name of the product (this is known as testing blind).
o Have any charts ready before you begin testing.
o Make sure the testers know how to fill in the charts you are using.

When you carry out sensory analysis of your product this will involve you:

o looking at the product
o smelling the product
o tasting the product.

Results from sensory analysis will be used as evidence when evaluating the product against the design specification and in product development.

	Tester 1	Tester 2	Tester 3	Tester 4	Tester 5	Average
Meaty	3	3	3	3	4	3.2
Square	4	4	4	4	4	4
Tasty	3	3	3	3	3	3

△ **Table 6.5** A rating chart for pasties and the suggested improvements from five tasters   *Cont.*

	Tester 1	Tester 2	Tester 3	Tester 4	Tester 5	Average
Attractive	3	3	3	2	3	2.8
Crisp texture	2	2	3	2	3	2.4
Small	1	2	3	2	4	2.4

△ **Table 6.5** A rating chart for pasties and the suggested improvements from five tasters *continued*

Key	Poor = 1, Good = 2, Very Good = 3, Excellent = 4
Improvements	Taster 1 – make slightly larger so more filling can be added
	Taster 2 – glaze the pasties so they are golden brown
	Taster 3 – add herbs to give a little more flavour
	Taster 4 – make the pasties larger
	Taster 5 – add another vegetable for extra taste

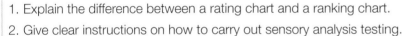

Exam practice questions

1. Explain the difference between a rating chart and a ranking chart.   **[4 marks]**
2. Give clear instructions on how to carry out sensory analysis testing.   **[4 marks]**
3. The chart in Table 6.6 shows the taste test results for a new chicken pasta bake.

Characteristics	Tester 1	Tester 2	Tester 3	Tester 4	Tester 5
Portion size	2	2	1	1	2
Amount of chicken	4	4	3	4	4
Creamy cheese sauce	4	3	4	4	3
Crispiness of topping	1	1	2	1	2
Tomato flavour	4	4	4	4	4
Well seasoned	2	1	1	2	2

△ **Table 6.6** Taste test results for a new chicken pasta bake

a) From the results shown, identify **two** characteristics that need to be improved.   **[2 marks]**

b) Explain how this could be done.   **[4 marks]**

Key
Poor = 1, Good = 2, Very good = 3, Excellent = 4

Key terms

Profiling test – sensory evaluation test to identify specific characteristics of a product

Activities

1. Create a table like Table 6.7, which shows the qualities (identified needs) that a student found through analysis of a questionnaire for a chilled dessert that is to be aimed at 11 to 19-year-olds.

2. Choose three chilled desserts and evaluate them against the identified needs.

3. Write a conclusion from your findings.

4. Choose one of the desserts and evaluate it in detail against the criteria.

Stretch yourself

Explain how the results of sensory testing are used by manufacturers.

6.3 Product analysis

Product analysis consists of looking at all aspects of a product in detail, including how products meet the health, dietary, socio-economic and cultural/religious needs of different groups.

It is one of the responsibilities of a product development team to carry out product analysis of existing products. Product analysis is carried out at the research stage to investigate the ingredients used and how the product is made.

Guidelines for carrying out product analysis

○ Who is the product aimed at and why?
○ What is the purpose of the product? When, where, why and how will it be eaten?
○ What ingredients, components and additives have been used in the product, and why?
○ What processes have been used in making it?
○ How has it been made safe to eat?
○ How does it fit into the eatwell plate?
○ Does it meet the nutritional needs of the **target group**?
○ How well does it meet the identified needs of the target group?
○ How does the product compare with similar products available?
○ Has the manufacturer considered the environment?
○ Are there any moral, cultural and sustainability issues related to the product?

Name of product	Lower in sugar: no more than 5 g/100 g	Aimed at 11 to 19-year-olds	Sold chilled	4+ portions	Attractive	Colourful	Tasty	Good portion size

△ **Table 6.7** Supermarket survey

How can you find out the answers?

- Sensory testing looking at the taste, texture, aroma and appearance, using the opinions of the **user group**.
- What about the packaging? How has the product been made safe to eat? Is it chilled/frozen/canned/bottled/ambient? What essential information is included? You will be able to obtain the ingredients list and the nutritional data from here. What material has been used for the packaging and why?
- What is the cost of the product? Is it in the correct price range for the user?
- How is the product promoted? Does it have any special claims, such as being low in fat? How has it been made to appeal to the target group?
- Is the portion size adequate for the user?
- Use the product. Reheat it and, before you taste/test it, examine how it has been made (disassemble it). Decide what processes have been used to make the product.
- Can you work out the carbon footprint of the product? How many miles have the ingredients travelled?

△ **Figure 6.6** Apple pie

Understand the types, functions and proportions of ingredients used to make the product

By taking a product apart you can see exactly how it has been made. Most products are a variation of an existing product, so taking a product apart may also give you ideas for new products.

Let us look at an apple pie:

- What are the stages in making the pie?
- What is the cost of the pie?
- Has the pie got a base? Why?
- What ingredients have been used in the pastry? Explain why they have been used.
- How much sugar has been used in the apple?
- How could the amount of sugar in the apple be reduced?
- How could the quantity of pastry be reduced?
- Could pastry be higher in fibre?
- How much waste was there from the apples? Could skins be left on?
- Have any additives or colourings been used? Why?
- How could the design be improved to meet healthy eating guidelines?
- How much energy has been used in making this product?

When examining a product you should not only consider who is going to eat it and how it has been made, but also think about where the ingredients have come from, how the workers were paid and treated and what effect this product will have on the environment. So let us look at our apple pie and consider the socio-economic issues.

Key terms

Target group – the specific group of people at which you are aiming the product

User group (or the intended target group) – the person or group of people who will use the product

Ingredient	Socio-economic issues
Pastry	
Flour	Is it a high-fat/high-sugar product? Does it need a top and a bottom? Could the amount of pastry be reduced? Could it be made with gluten-free flour? Is it wholemeal flour? High-fibre? Where was the wheat grown? How far has it been transported? How much was the farmer paid for the grain? Where was it ground and packaged? Were pesticides used?
Fat	What type of fat has been used? Is it a trans-fat (hydrogenated)? Is it morally right to use trans-fats when we know they cause heart disease? Is it vegetable fat for a vegan? Where has it been transported from?
Water	If the pastry has been made in the UK we know that it will have been made with clean water. Is it fluoridated?
Salt	Could it be made without salt?
Filling and topping	
Apple	Are the apples grown in the UK? Not very likely. Where were they grown? How much were the pickers paid? Were pesticides used? How far have they been transported? What is the carbon footprint?
Sugar	Do we need so much sugar in a product when there is such a problem of obesity in the UK? Is it Fair Trade sugar?
Egg glaze	How were the hens reared? Were they free-range? Not likely in such a product. What were the hens fed on?
Dish	Does the container need to be foil? Metal uses up the world's resources. Could it have been put in a cardboard container made from either recycled card or card made from sustainable trees? It is difficult to recycle foil dishes in some areas. We probably use more petrol taking it to a recycle centre. Cardboard could easily be recycled. Does it have other layers of packaging? Is it recyclable?
Cooking/chilling	How much energy has been used in the ingredients/manufacture/chilling and storage of this product? Has it used fossil fuels?

△ **Table 6.8** Ingredients and socio-economic issues

Using the results of product analysis to develop design criteria

△ **Figure 6.7** An improved lower-fat apple pie

Controlled assessment link
In Figure 14.5 on page 230 a student has completed product analysis of snack and meal products.

Activities
1. Carry out a product analysis of a food product. Choose your own or use one of the following:
   o cereal bar for a child's packed lunch
   o fruit-flavoured yoghurt for an 18-month-old
   o pasta main course for a teenager
   o single-portion meal for a senior citizen
   o family-sized dessert, for example, apple pie
   o savoury snack for a meal 'on the go'.
2. Produce a chart similar to Table 6.8 to record your findings.
3. Develop a new idea for the product. Draw a new design for your chosen product. Show how it meets the needs of the target group.

Exam practice questions

1. Explain **two** ways a manufacturer could use the internet when designing a new hand-held snack for a teenager. **[2 × 2 marks]**
2. Name **one** research method to find out consumer views on orange drinks. Describe how this research is carried out. **[4 marks]**
3. A food manufacturer wants to develop a new range of seasonal soups. Write **five** questions that they could use to ask consumers their opinions. **[5 marks]**

Stretch yourself
Explain why it is important for a food manufacturer to carry out product analysis when developing a new product.

Key points
o Remember that you need to have a target group and know their needs to be able to decide on a product's suitability.
o Product analysis is examining a food product to find out the ingredients, packaging characteristics and properties.

Controlled assessment link
You should be prepared to use the skills covered in this chapter in your controlled assessment.

7.1 Investigating a design opportunity

Learning objectives
By the end of this section you should have developed a knowledge and understanding of how to:
- analyse a design brief
- carry out research that will lead to design criteria.

Introduction

In Chapter 6 we looked at how to use questionnaires and interviews to identify a target market from your **design task** and find out about the **consumers'** specific needs. The design brief needs to be analysed to allow other areas of research to be identified. By carrying out further research and evaluating existing products you will be able to develop **a design specification** for a new product.

Key terms

Design task – a statement that provides the situation for your designing and making

Consumer – a person who buys or uses products and services

Design specification – a clear statement of the general criteria of the product to be developed

Analysing the brief – identifying the keywords and any other points that are important in the brief

Analysing a design brief

Once you decide on your design brief, you need to analyse it carefully. Contained within the brief will be certain keywords – it is important that you

identify these. You need to pick out the keywords and any other points that you think are important in the brief. This is called **analysing the brief**.

Figure 7.1 shows how a spider diagram has been used to pick out the keywords and other relevant points from the brief that need to be researched

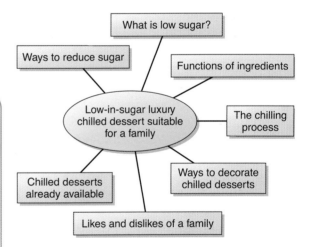

△ **Figure 7.1** Example of the analysis of a design brief

Controlled assessment link
Figure 14.1 on page 224 shows a student's analysis of a design brief as part of their Controlled Assessment.

Further research

By analysing the brief you will be able to identify further research you can undertake to help you in the design and development of a new food product.

You need to think carefully about the amount of research you do and how you will present it.

Remember that:

- projects have to be completed within a certain number of hours
- research is only part of the process
- information can be presented in a number of ways, such as text, diagrams, charts, bulleted lists
- information should be presented clearly and concisely in your own words
- all information should be relevant to your design brief.

Collecting, analysing and applying relevant data allows you to show an understanding of technological knowledge when designing and developing food products. For example, through research the different ways of reducing fat content can be identified. This knowledge can then be applied during the designing and development of a successful food product. Remember that research is carried out at intervals throughout the design process, not just at the start.

You can get research information from:

- the internet (remember that you must give the details of the website)
- newspaper articles
- magazine articles
- official data
- leaflets/posters in supermarkets
- television programmes
- textbooks
- library books
- by evaluating existing products (see Chapter 6, page 116).

> ### Controlled assessment link
> Figures 14.3 and 14.4 on page 227 show analysis of existing products.

Developing design criteria

Once you have carried out all your research, a design specification (**design criteria**) for a new product can be written. It is usually written as a

△ **Figure 7.2** Analysis of existing products

series of bullet points or a numbered list. It may be divided into what are essential criteria and what are the desirable criteria for the product.

Key term

Design criteria – a list of general points from which a range of different ideas can be developed

A design specification is important because it clearly states the general details (criteria) of the product that is to be developed. It is also a checklist for evaluation throughout the development of the new product.

How to produce the design criteria

First you must look back at your design brief and your analysis. You need to make a list of the main points identified when you analysed your brief. You should look back over your research, particularly the analysis of your questionnaire/interviews.

An example of design criteria for a pastry product aimed at adults might be:

- suitable for a packed lunch
- must be eaten cold
- meat-flavoured
- new, creative product
- crisp-textured
- eaten hand-held
- stored chilled
- tasty and attractive
- sold in packs of four
- cost between £1.00 and £1.50 per portion
- contains one of the '5 a day'.

Note that the type of pastry, specific flavours, shape and product have not actually been stated, leaving plenty of opportunity for a wide range of practical skills.

Exam practice questions

1. Explain **two** different ways research can be carried out.

   [4 marks]

2. Explain why design criteria are important when developing new products.

   [4 marks]

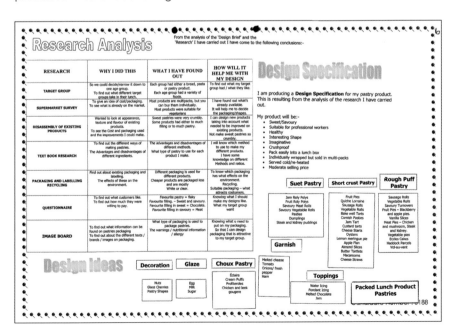

△ **Figure 7.3** Analysis of research

Activities

1. (a) Find a newspaper article reporting examples of the results of unhealthy eating, such as:

- increasing percentage of schoolchildren who are overweight or obese
- consequences of eating a high-fat diet
- increased numbers of adults suffering from diabetes.

    (b) Analyse the report and write a summary that will give you some points for the design criteria.

2. (a) Design a questionnaire to find out the qualities teenagers would like to see in a new snack product. Ask ten teenagers to complete the questionnaire.

    (b) Draw conclusions from the results and use these to develop design criteria.

3. Create a table like Table 7.1, which shows the qualities (identified needs) that a student found through analysis of a questionnaire for a chilled dessert for 11–19 year olds.

    (a) Choose three dessert products and evaluate them against the identified needs.

    (b) Write a conclusion from your findings.

Name of product	Lower in sugar (no more than 5–100 g)	Aimed at 11–19 year olds	Sold chilled	4+ portions	Attractive	Colourful	Tasty	Good portion size

7.2 Development of design proposals

Learning objectives

By the end of this section you should have developed a knowledge and understanding of how to:

- generate, record and make design ideas
- evaluate a design idea by carrying out sensory analysis, including rating/ranking, and how to record results in appropriate ways (star profiles and charts)
- evaluate design ideas against design criteria
- develop a product specification.

Introduction

Generating, recording and making of design ideas will allow a number of products to be adapted and trialled. Through sensory analysis testing, qualities can be monitored and improvements identified. Evaluating ideas against the criteria in your design specification will inform you of how each idea has met the specification.

Design ideas

The design ideas you choose to trial should allow you to demonstrate a range of practical skills appropriate to your brief, for example, peeling, chopping, grating, meat preparation, shaping, rolling, sauce making (roux, blended, all-in-one), kneading, cake and pastry making, piping. You could list the ideas you find to give you time to think and make decisions as to which products you will trial.

You must always ensure that the design ideas you choose to trial are fully explained. You can do this by:

○ drawing your design idea
○ listing ingredients

○ describing the modifications/adaptations (recipe engineering) to each recipe, such as different shape, flavour, texture, ingredients, assembly, presentation/finishing techniques
○ giving reasons for modifications/adaptations
○ carrying out nutritional analysis
○ modelling ideas, which means making your designed practical ideas
○ using sensory analysis to give **sensory descriptors** to help evaluate the ideas
○ suggesting any improvements to the products
○ evaluating products against each of the criteria in the design specification.

Where can I find ideas?

You can find ideas from a variety of sources, including:

○ recipe books
○ analysis of research information
○ existing products
○ websites
○ magazines.

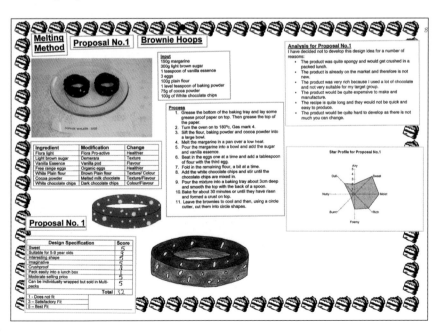

△ **Figure 7.4** Initial ideas to meet the design criteria

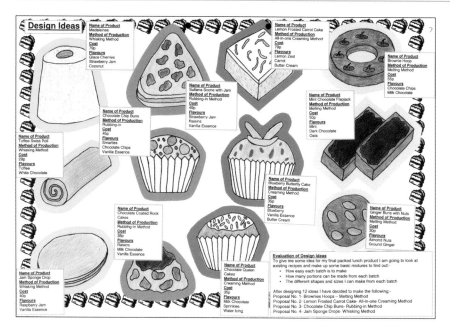

△ **Figure 7.5** Design drawings

How can I communicate my design ideas?

You can use a variety of different methods to **communicate** your ideas, including:

○ word-processed documents
○ **annotated** sketches
○ mood boards
○ analysing nutritional computer printouts – you must use the information that it provides
○ sensory analysis charts
○ photographs of your practical products.

Key terms

Sensory descriptors – words that describe taste, smell, texture and flavour

Communicate – pass on information, ideas and thoughts

Annotated – with explanatory notes added to it, for example, to a sketch

△ **Figure 7.6** Communicating ideas through photographs

Recipe engineering to meet the needs of the user group

Ingredients can be substituted to alter recipes, and proportions can be varied to alter the nutritional content of a product. The shape, finishing techniques and the way the product is assembled can also be changed. Assembling means fitting together the different parts of a food product, for instance, meat sauce, pasta sheets, cheese sauce and grated cheese when making a lasagne.

When changes are made, the colour, flavour, texture and nutritional value of the finished product will be altered.

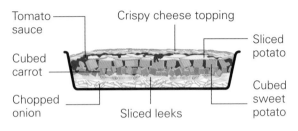

△ **Figure 7.7** Annotated sketch for a spicy vegetable layer pie

Reducing fat	Reducing sugar	Reducing salt
Less moist Less flavour Product will stale more rapidly Paler colour	Less flavour Paler colour Poorer keeping quality Capacity to rise may be reduced	Less flavour May reduce keeping qualities Bread may not rise as well
Increasing fat	**Increasing sugar**	**Adding water**
Result may be greasy Flavour may be improved Darker colour	Baked mixtures become soft during baking, then hard on cooling Increased cooking time Darker colour	May make baked products hard Creates bulk Encourages mould growth

△ **Table 7.1** What happens when the proportions in a recipe are altered

Lower-in-sugar cream-filled eclairs		
Typical value	Per 100g	Per Serving
Energy	1695 kJ 405 kcal	559 kJ 125 kcal
Protein	5.97 g	1.97 g
Carbohydrate of which sugars	18.4 g 5.18 g	6.07 g 1.52 g
Fat of which saturates	34.6 g 16.4 g	11.4 g 5.41 g
Fibre (NSP)	0.56 g	0.19 g
Sodium	0.27 g	0.09 g

Nutrition information – pizza		
	Typical Values	
	Per 100g	Per serving 32 g
Energy	1,168 kJ 279 kcal	374 kJ 89.3 kcal
Protein	12 g	3.84 g
Carbohydrate	49.2 g	15.7 g
Fat	5.16 g	1.65 g

△ **Figure 7.8** Nutritional printouts for eclairs and pizza lower in fat

Controlled assessment link
Figure 14.12 on page 229 shows examples of how recipes can be engineered as part of your development work in the Controlled Assessment.

whether the design idea is appealing and whether any improvements are required.

Knowledge link
Sensory analysis testing is explained in Chapter 6 Sensory Analysis testing (page 115).

Evaluation of design ideas

Evaluation is an ongoing process throughout the designing and making of new food products. Evaluation allows judgements to be made about a product, thereby enabling improvements to be made at each stage. As each design idea is trialled you will need to find out:

○ whether it appeals to your user group or your intended target market
○ whether it meets your design criteria
○ any improvements that need to be made.

Sensory analysis testing

Sensory analysis testing, using tasters from your user group, with the results being presented in tables or star diagrams, should inform you

Evaluating design ideas against design criteria

Evaluating against each criterion in your design specification will inform you how each design idea meets the specification. Results from nutritional analysis and sensory analysis testing should be used as evidence.

Evaluating each idea against the design criteria helps to identify which idea should be taken forward to product development.

Controlled assessment link
Figure 14.8 on page 240 shows how design ideas can be evaluated against design criteria.

△ **Figure 7.9** Evaluating design ideas

During development the product is refined through trialling and testing, taking account of users' views, until a desired outcome is achieved. At this stage, costing of the product should be considered.

Costing food products

Costing is an important part of the development process. As you modify/change your product you will be able to see the effect this has on the cost of the product. Changing ingredients to reduce the cost can sometimes be detrimental to the successful making of the product. However, you could reduce the cost by:

○ making slightly smaller portions
○ changing an expensive ingredient to a cheaper one, for example, substituting meat with vegetables
○ mixing meat with an alternative protein food, for example, textured vegetable protein
○ increasing the carbohydrate content and reducing, for example, the protein content of the product
○ using flavourings and colourings instead of fresh ingredients such as fresh fruits
○ drizzling chocolate/glacé icing instead of spreading on top of a product.

Product specification

Once a number of products have been trialled, you have to decide which product to take forward for product development. Looking back at your evaluations of design ideas will help you make a decision.

You need to explain clearly why you have chosen this product and why you have rejected the other ideas. Details of your chosen design idea must be written as a **product specification**.

Controlled assessment link
Figure 14.6 on page 232 shows an example of a student's design specification.

Key term
Product specification – a list of features/characteristics/properties that a food product must meet. It also identifies what cannot be changed (essential criteria) and those that can be changed (desirable criteria)

Developing a product specification

A product specification does not provide general points like the design criteria. Instead, it describes very specific characteristics that a product must have, so the product can be produced in identical batches. It is written before the development work is completed.

The product specification will:

○ give success criteria when evaluating the final product
○ be written to help you achieve the desired outcome in your development work
○ give exact and precise details of the product so that a final prototype can be produced.

You will need to look at your design criteria and your development work to produce your product specification, which should include a labelled sketch of your final product.

Writing a product specification

Your product specification should include:

○ the name of the target group that the product is going to be manufactured for, for example, teenagers
○ any nutritional claims or important information for the label, for example, lower in fat (the actual amount of fat content needs to be given per 100 g)
○ details of any special dietary claims, for example, vegetarian
○ specific descriptions of the ingredients, for example, flaked/ground almonds, block/soft margarine, diced/sliced carrots
○ sensory qualities of the actual final product

- how it is to be assembled, or the shape and size, for example, layers of…, round shape
- finishing techniques, for example, brushed with an egg glaze before baking, garnished with two slices of tomato and one small sprig of parsley, decorated with…
- portion size, for example, will serve four people
- preparation and serving details
- cost of the product
- storage requirements, for example, chilled/ frozen.

Key points

- Recipes need adapting for design work.
- Sensory analysis testing is used to test the quality of existing products and evaluate design ideas.
- Evaluation is an ongoing process throughout the designing and making of new food products.
- Evaluation enables products to be improved.

Exam practice questions

1. Show **three** ways of communicating thoughts when generating ideas. **[3 marks]**

2. Suggest **four** different flavourings that could be added to each of the following products:
   (a) shortbread biscuits
   (b) bread
   (c) scones. **[3 × 4 marks]**

3. Complete a nutritional analysis for a pizza and eclairs, or use the ones shown in Figure 7.8. Look at the nutrition information for the pizza. How much fat per 100 g does the pizza contain? **[1 mark]**

4. How does this compare with the eclairs? **[2 marks]**

5. What would be the effect of reducing the fat content in the lower-in-sugar cream-filled eclairs? **[2 marks]**

6. Give **two** reasons why evaluation takes place when trialling design ideas. **[2 marks]**

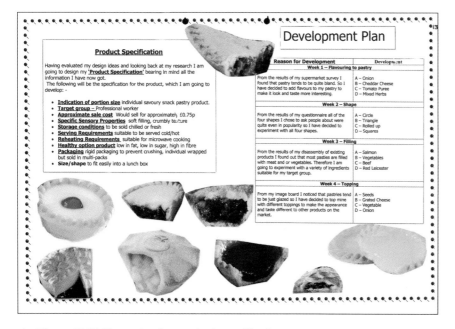

△ **Figure 7.10** Example of a product specification

Activities

1. Draw an annotated sketch of a layered luxury dessert.

2. Select a recipe for a main meal product and show ways that the recipe could be adapted to meet the requirements of the eatwell plate.

3. Sketch a design idea for the new salad. Use notes and labels to explain how the idea meets the design criteria.

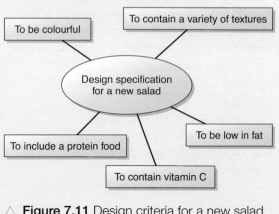

△ **Figure 7.11** Design criteria for a new salad

7.3 Product development

Learning objectives

By the end of this section you should have developed a knowledge and understanding of how to:

○ identify ways in which a product could be developed

○ carry out modification and reformulation by changing the type, ratio and proportion of ingredients

○ use investigations on small quantities to trial different developments to understand the relevance of function and aesthetics (sensory and functional considerations during the modification of ideas, that is, taste, texture and appearance)

○ write a manufacturing specification.

Introduction

Development is all about changing, testing or modifying all or parts of your product until a desired outcome is achieved. It is more complex than adapting recipes to meet the needs of your user group.

You will need to carry out modifications to the type, ratio and proportions of the ingredients to meet the nutritional and sensory aspects of the specification.

Development gives you the opportunity to try out changes on small quantities of your design,

to find out the effect that the functions of the ingredients have on the finished result.

Evaluation enables you to make appropriate decisions. Simple notes, charts or diagrams with comments are adequate ways of recording your results.

Key term

Evaluation – summarising information and forming conclusions/judgements

Ways that a product could be developed

There are many ways that you could develop a product:

○ to improve the nutritional content
○ to change the flavour/sensory appeal
○ to alter the texture
○ to alter the shape
○ to alter the colour
○ to alter the size
○ to improve the final appearance
○ to consider the cost
○ to consider different storage methods (chilling/freezing/reheating)
○ to consider how the product is going to be reheated.

> **Controlled assessment link**
> Figures 14.12 and 14.13 on pages 229 and 232 show ideas for development in the Controlled Assessment.

Modifying and reformulating a product

Some examples of ways that modifications can be made to a product are:

○ the ingredients used – Are the ingredients available? Could you use seasonal foods?
○ varying the proportions of ingredients used
○ the method of combining the ingredients – Could you use different equipment?
○ changing the method of cooking
○ the finishing techniques used
○ how the product is assembled, for example, layering differently.

The key to product development is that the product must be developed according to the needs of your user group or your intended target market, so their views must be considered as the product develops. You are aiming to produce a high-quality outcome which meets the product specification.

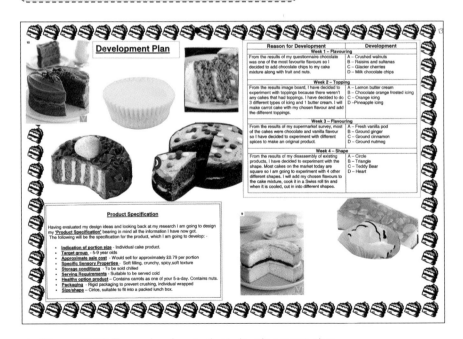

△ **Figure 7.12** Example of a student development plan

Investigating on small quantities to trial different developments

You will need to consider the functions of the ingredients that you are using. For example, what ingredients will improve the crunchiness of biscuits?

You must always ensure that your development work is fully explained. You can do this by:

- listing and costing ingredients
- describing the modifications/changes
- giving reasons for modifications/changes
- carrying out nutritional analysis if this is relevant to the product specification
- using sensory analysis to evaluate each development
- evaluating each development, showing how effective the modifications/changes have been and any further improvements that need to be made.

Manufacturing specification

When you have completed your development you must write a manufacturing specification, including all the details a manufacturer would need to produce the product in quantity.

This will be more detailed than your product specification and will include the results from your development work

△ **Figure 7.13** Developing the flavour of a biscuit

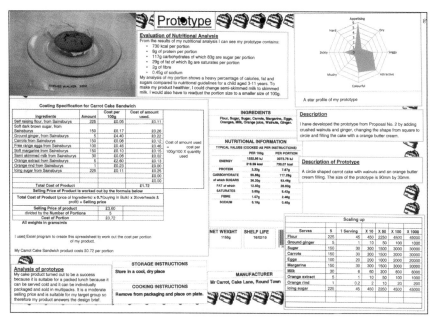

△ **Figure 7.14** Example of a manufacturing specification for a prototype

Exam practice questions

1. Traditional plain scones are made by using the following ingredients and shaped by using a round, fluted cutter:

   200 g self-raising flour
   50 g margarine
   50 g sugar
   1 egg
   125 ml (¼ pt) milk

   (a) Give details, using notes or sketches, of **three** adaptations you could make to the scones.

   (b) Give reasons for these adaptations. **[9 marks]**

2. Below is a recipe for spaghetti bolognese:

1 small onion	25 g margarine
1 small carrot	225 g minced beef
tin chopped tomatoes	1 stock cube
4 tomatoes	salt and pepper
200 g spaghetti	

   (a) Give **two** ways in which the fat content can be reduced. **[2 marks]**

   (b) Give **two** ways in which the fibre content can be increased. **[2 marks]**

   Cont.

Exam practice questions *continued*

3. The ingredients used in a spicy burger product are listed below:

250g minced lamb   25g breadcrumbs
10g coriander – fresh   2 cloves garlic
75g finely chopped onion   3g ground cumin
3g paprika   10ml lemon juice
5g mild curry powder   15g tomato purée
1 small egg   salt and pepper

The rating chart shown in Table 7.2 shows the results from the tasting and testing of the spicy burger product.

	Taster 1	Taster 2	Taster 3
Evenly browned	3	5	5
Round shape	2	2	1
Excellent aroma	5	5	4
Consistent size	5	5	4
Correct level of spiciness	1	2	2
Even texture	2	2	3

△ **Table 7.2** Results from the tasting and testing of the spicy burger product

(a) Consider the results shown in the rating chart. Discuss the implications to the product development team of these results. **[4 marks]**

(b) State **two** ways in which the cost of the spicy burger can be reduced. **[2 marks]**

4. Explain the difference between a design specification and a product specification. **[4 marks]**

7.4 **Product planning and evaluation**

Learning objectives

By the end of this section you should have developed a knowledge and understanding of how to:

○ produce a production plan for the prototype in a test kitchen
○ identify **quality control** checks
○ consider the use of standard components in your product
○ develop critical evaluation skills.

Introduction

When product development has been completed, planning for the final product can take place. This involves making reasoned decisions about the functions of the ingredients you are going to use and the cost of the ingredients, and producing a plan of action for making the final product. You must also consider whether you could use standard components in your final product. (See Chapter 3, page 78.) For example, will you use frozen, ready-made pastry?

When you have completed your product development work you will be ready to plan for your final product. Your plans will need to show:

- choice and functions of your final ingredients
- costing of the final ingredients
- nutritional analysis
- quality control checks (see chapter 11, page 192).

Controlled assessment link

In Figure 14.9 on page 234 the student has identified quality control checks.

Producing a plan

You will need to plan your making activities. Time management is a very important part of this.

The presentation of the plan for a practical product may be in many different forms. A **flow chart** is a diagrammatical way to show a plan of work. A good place to start is to read the original method for the product you are making and then change this to match your new product, adding further detail. A flow chart uses the standard symbols shown in Figure 7.16. It is important to identify quality control checks in your production plan.

Key terms

Quality control – steps taken to check a product at various stages of making to ensure that a consistent and high-quality outcome is achieved

Standard components – pre-prepared ingredients used in the production of another product

Flowchart – a diagram that shows a sequence of events

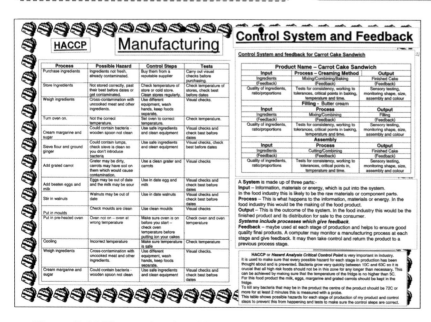

△ **Figure 7.15** The student has identified quality control checks

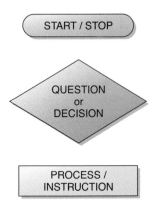

△ **Figure 7.16** Standard flow chart symbols

Alternatively, you could present your plan as a chart, as shown in Table 7.3.

Health and safety	Process	Quality checks

△ **Table 7.3** Presenting your plan as a chart

Evaluation at different stages of development

Evaluation is all about making judgements. It is a very important part of designing and making and should be done at all stages so that you can make the right decisions for the next step in the process. Evaluation takes place:

○ during research – evaluating existing products
○ while generating and trialling ideas – sensory analysis and evaluating ideas against the design specification/criteria
○ during product development – sensory analysis and evaluating the effectiveness of modifications/changes made to the product as it is developed
○ after production of the final product – sensory analysis and evaluating against the product specification.

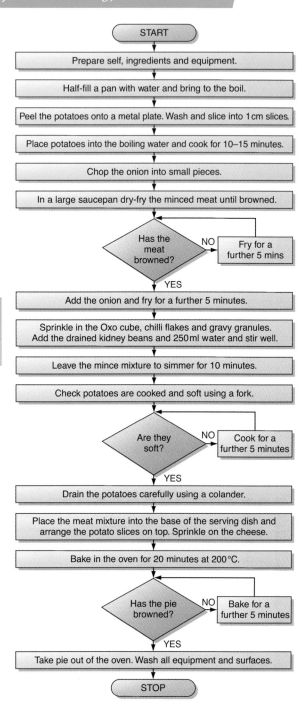

△ **Figure 7.17** Example of a flow chart for a spicy pie

By evaluating throughout the whole process you should be able to make a final product that meets your original design brief.

Evaluation of the final product

The first stage of your evaluation will be to carry out sensory analysis testing with your user group or your intended target market, for instance, using a tasting chart or star profile.

When evaluating your final product, your comments need to show:

○ how successful you have been in terms of your product specification and your design brief

○ suggestions for further modifications.

Comments from your user group or your intended target market can support your views, and they can be given as evidence when you offer conclusions for your work. To achieve a high level you must produce a critical evaluation.

Controlled assessment link
Figure 14.11 on page 236 shows an example of an evaluation.

Activities

1. The flow chart for a spicy pie has clear steps that can be followed when making the pie.

For a product that you will be making, design a detailed flow chart for the production of the product.

2. Produce a product specification for a product you will be making. Ask three people to carry out sensory analysis testing of the product. Critically evaluate the product against your product specification, giving results from your sensory analysis testing as evidence. Suggest further modifications that could be made to your product, giving reasons for these modifications

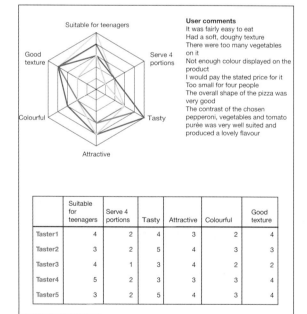

User comments
It was fairly easy to eat
Had a soft, doughy texture
There were too many vegetables on it
Not enough colour displayed on the product
I would pay the stated price for it
Too small for four people
The overall shape of the pizza was very good
The contrast of the chosen pepperoni, vegetables and tomato purée was very well suited and produced a lovely flavour

	Suitable for teenagers	Serve 4 portions	Tasty	Attractive	Colourful	Good texture
Taster1	4	2	4	3	2	4
Taster2	3	2	5	4	3	3
Taster3	4	1	3	4	2	2
Taster4	5	2	3	3	3	4
Taster5	3	2	5	4	3	4

△ **Figure 7.18** Sensory testing for a low-fat pizza

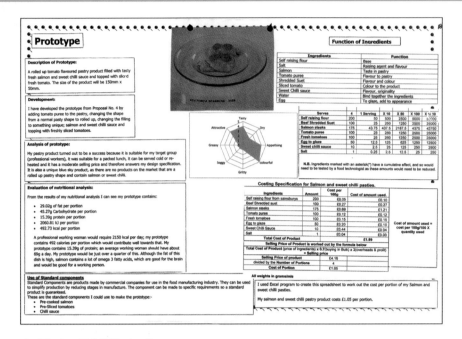

△ **Figure 7.19** Evaluation

chapter 8
Design and market influences – labelling, packaging, product information and codes of practice

Learning objectives

By the end of this section you should have developed a knowledge and understanding of:

○ using current labelling requirements and information on packaging and food labels and applying these to your own products
○ the legislation governing statutory and non-statutory content and layout for food labels
○ the requirements for conveying product information to the consumer, including, where necessary, information about accompaniments
○ the use of nutritional software to analyse the nutritional content of your final prototype
○ why food may be packaged in different forms to extend shelf life
○ packaging materials used within food production and their impact on cost and the environment.

Introduction

Nearly all the food we buy today is packaged in some way. Food packaging and the design of the packaging are important because of the range of products on sale in supermarkets. Over the years, the materials and methods of packaging have changed as new technology has been introduced.

8.1 Food labelling

△ **Figure 8.1** Supermarket shopping today

Reasons why food is packaged

Packaging has a number of important functions. Food is packaged for the following reasons:

○ It contains the product so it is easy to transport, store and display.
○ It identifies the product by providing information and attracting customers.
○ Labelling information is required by law to describe and inform consumers about products.
○ It protects the product from damage, so reduces food waste. It is protected from:
   ○ physical damage, for example, crushing
   ○ contamination from chemicals, micro-organisms, insects
   ○ atmospheric conditions, for example, warm conditions may cause fruit to over-ripen.
○ It increases the shelf life of the product.

Food packaging legislation states that food packaging must not:

○ be hazardous to human health
○ cause the food to deteriorate
○ cause unacceptable changes in the substance or quality of the product.

Food labelling requirements

The Food Regulations 1996 describe the information that must be on a food label. By law a food label must contain the information listed in Table 8.1.

Information	Reason
Product name	Inform the consumer what the product is, for example, cornflakes, apricot jam. Differences between similar products must be clearly identified, for example, fruit-flavoured yoghurt and raspberry yoghurt. Any pictures used must not be misleading, for example, strawberry-flavoured ice cream must not show pictures of strawberries on the packaging.
List of ingredients	To inform consumers exactly what ingredients are contained in the product. All ingredients must be listed in descending order of weight, with the largest amount of ingredient first. Food additives and water must be included.
Storage instructions	Informs the consumer how to store the product in order to prevent food spoilage. Temperature guidelines are important, for example, keep refrigerated, suitable for home freezing.
Date marking	Informs the consumer of the length of time the product can be kept, that is, for example, the shelf life. '**Use by date**' for high-risk foods, for example, raw and cooked meat, chilled foods (perishable foods). The date and month will be shown; after this date the food may not look or taste different, but it will be unsafe to eat and it should be thrown away. '**Best before date**' for low-risk foods, for example, biscuits, crisps or foods that are processed and packaged to have a long shelf life, for example, UHT milk. The date, month and year will be shown. After this date the food will start to deteriorate in terms of flavour, colour, texture or taste. '**Display until/sell by date**' informs the retailer when to remove the product from the shelves or chill/freezer cabinets. This date is usually a few days before the 'use by date', so the consumer has a number of days to use the product. **This is not a legal requirement**.
Manufacturer's name and address	So that a product can be returned if faulty, or a letter of complaint can be made in writing.

△ **Table 8.1** Legal requirements of food labels *Cont.*

Information	Reason
Weight or volume	Most pre-packed food is required to show the net weight or volume, within a few grams of the weight. If not sold pre-packed, most foods have to be sold either by quantity or number. Some foods are sold in standard amounts. This allows consumers to compare products in terms of value for money. A large **e** placed alongside the amount shows that it is an average quantity. **e 190g**
Product description	It may not be clear from the product name what the product is. A description is required to inform the consumer.
Instructions for use	Preparation, cooking and heating instructions inform the consumer as to how the product should be used.
Place of origin	Informs the consumer the place the food has come from, for example, 'Product of Spain'.
Allergies	Informs the customer about any ingredients that may cause reactions in people with allergies.

△ **Table 8.1** Legal requirements of food labels

Key terms

Date marking – used on manufactured food to ensure that it is safe to eat

Use by date – used on perishable foods; if stored correctly foods will keep until this date. This required by law.

Best before date – the date up to which the food will remain in peak condition. This is required by law.

Display until/Sell by date – used by some shops to help staff know when they need to take food products off the shelves, but they must also have either a 'use by' or 'best before' date. This is not required by law.

Sensory analysis and shelf life

Food technologists and microbiologists work together to ensure that food products are of a high quality and safe to eat. The shelf life, that is, 'use by' and 'best before' (safety and quality), is determined through a range of testing.

○ Microbiologists examine the growth of bacteria in foods and identify a safe shelf life.
○ Food technologists examine by taste testing, with advice from the microbiologists, how long the product maintains its sensory qualities.

Information	Reason
Bar code	A way of identifying the product. Helps the retailer with stock control. An electronic scanner at the checkout reads the bar code; the price of the product is recorded and displayed and details are recorded for stocktaking.
Nutritional information	Consumers know what nutrients are in the product, so informed choices can be made. This allows consumers to select foods that have a specific nutrient content, for example, low in sugar. Consumers can compare the nutrient content of one product with another. Many manufacturers put nutritional information on food product labels, although they are not required to do so unless a special claim is made about the product, for example, low in fat.
Serving instructions	Gives consumers ideas of what could be served with a product.
Cost	The consumer can compare the price of different products.

△ **Table 8.2** Other information found on food packaging

Nutrition labels

The Food Labelling Regulations specify labelling requirements for nutritional information. Nutritional information is voluntary unless a nutrition claim is made.

Nutrients are shown as amounts in every 100 g or 100 ml of a food.

Nutrition labelling may be given two formats:

○ Group 1 – the 'Big 4'

Nutrition information	Typical values per 100 g
Energy	kJ or kcal
Protein	g
Carbohydrate	g
Fat	g

△ **Table 8.3** Group 1 – the 'Big 4'

○ Group 2 – 'Big 4 + Little 4' or 4 + 4.

Nutrition information	Typical values per 100 g
Energy	kJ or kcal
Protein	g
Carbohydrate	g
of which sugars	g
Fat	g
of which saturates	g
Fibre	g
Sodium	g

△ **Table 8.4** Group 2 – 'Big 4 + Little 4' or 4 + 4

The government recommends that Group 2 information is given on all foods on a voluntary basis, as this gives consumers more information so they can make informed choices.

Some manufacturers are using a traffic light colour system on the front of packaging.

This helps you to see at a glance if the food has low, medium or high amounts of fat, sugar and salt.

○ Green = low
○ Amber = medium
○ Red = high

Many foods have a mixture of greens, ambers and reds. If you want to make a healthier choice, try to go for products with more greens and ambers and fewer reds.

LOW Fat — 7.7g Per serve
LOW Sat Fat — 2.0g Per serve
HIGH Sugars — 42.2g Per serve
MED Salt — 2.0g Per serve

△ **Figure 8.2** The Food Standards Agency traffic light labelling system (Source: Food Standards Agency)

Nutrition claims on food labels

The Food Labelling Regulations 1999 impose conditions for making nutrition claims. If manufacturers make a nutritional claim, such as low fat or high fibre, they must provide nutritional information.

The Food Standards Agency is working on new rules to make it easier for people to trust some of the claims they see on labels. At the moment you need to check the claims yourself by looking at the nutrition information. Symbols or words, 'flashes', may be printed on the label to give information about:

○ dietary group, for example, suitable for vegetarians
○ storage, for example, suitable for home freezing
○ ingredients, for example, this product contains traces of nuts
○ cooking, for example, suitable for microwave
○ special features, for example, medium hot curry
○ serving suggestions, for example, 'serve with boiled rice'.

The following figures show examples of a range of symbols used on food packaging.

◁ **Figure 8.3** Cooking instructions

◁ **Figure 8.4** Suitable for microwaving

◁ **Figure 8.5** Suitable for recycling

◁ **Figure 8.6** Vegetarian

◁ **Figure 8.7** Suitable for freezing

KEEP BRITAIN TIDY ◁ **Figure 8.8** Keep Britain Tidy

Labelling can help prevent food poisoning:

○ Looking at the list of ingredients will allow consumers to identify any high-risk foods.
○ Correct storage conditions are given which the consumer should follow in order to keep food safe, that is, where the food should be stored (for example, fridge) and for how long.
○ Best before/use by dates inform the consumer for how long the food will be safe to eat.

△ **Figure 8.9** Part of a food label showing storage information and display until and best before dates

Cooking instructions tell the consumer how the food should be cooked and at what temperatures it is safe to eat.

△ **Figure 8.10** Part of a food label showing cooking instructions

Controlled assessment link
Figure 14.4 on page 227 shows a student's analysis of existing products, which includes nutrition labelling and symbols.

The manufacturer's choice of food packaging is important with regard to preventing food poisoning:

o packaging protects the product from damage/contamination
o choice of material should suit the cooking method/storage
o impermeable materials should be used for some foods, and some foods need to be packaged so they are airtight
o some foods, need to be packaged using MAP (modified atmosphere packaging)
o some materials can extend the shelf life of the product, such as foods that are heat processed, for example, pasteurised milk is packaged in glass; metal is used during the canning process
o plastics can prevent contamination when sealed.

Exam practice questions

1. A chilli con carne product is purchased from the freezer section in a supermarket. Information on the packaging informs the consumer:

   o that the product should be eaten on the day of purchase if it is not kept frozen
   o not to refreeze it after thawing.

   Explain why the consumer should follow these instructions. **[6 marks]**

2. Give **two** benefits to the consumer of having nutritional information on food packaging. **[2 marks]**

Activities

1. Find a food label and stick it onto plain paper.

   Draw arrows to show where the information required by law can be found on your label.

Using your food label, answer the following questions.

(a) Who is the product aimed at? Explain why you have come to this conclusion.

(b) Which ingredient represents the highest proportion by weight?

(c) How should the product be stored?

(d) What type of date marking is used on your label? Why is this type of date mark used?

(e) What preparation and cooking instructions are given on your label?

(f) Are there any special claims (information) given on your label? What are they?

(g) Does the nutritional information on your label comply with government regulations? How?

(h) How does the manufacturer describe the product?

(i) Do you think your label is attractive? Why?

(j) How could the manufacturer improve the label?

(k) What materials are used for your packaging/label? Why have these materials been used?

2. Find and draw the symbol that tells the consumer a product is gluten-free.

3. Cook a product of your choice and then produce all the information that you would need on a packaging label. Include the nutritional analysis. Can you make any special claims for this product?

Stretch yourself

1. Find out the legal requirements for the following claims:

   o low in fat
   o lower in fat
   o low in sugar.

2. Research the different ingredients that are listed as allergies/food intolerances on food products.

3. Discuss how nutritional information on packaging can help consumers make informed choices when buying food products.

8.2 Different forms of packaging

Materials

A variety of materials can be used to package food products. Some food products are packaged in a mixture of materials.

Packaging material	Benefits/advantages	Limitations/ disadvantages	Examples of food
Glass	Can be moulded into a variety of shapes Transparent, so the product can be seen Withstands high temperatures Strong **Recyclable** Cheap to produce	Brittle and will often break easily Heavy	 △ Jam, sauces, pickles
Metals, including foil and cans	Strong Withstands high temperatures Lightweight Available in different thicknesses Recyclable Can be moulded into a variety of shapes Easy to store	Cannot see the food Cannot be used in the microwave	 △ Canned foods, for example, fruit, soup, meat, fish, ready meals
Plastic	Cheap to produce Can be moulded into a variety of shapes Available in different thicknesses Can be used in the microwave Easy to print on Lightweight Some are **biodegradable** (these plastics can be expensive) Most do not react with foods Transparent, so the product can be seen Can withstand high temperatures	Can be difficult to dispose of Made initially from oil A lot is still not recyclable	 △ Yogurts, cheese, bread, fruit, vegetables, ready meals, biscuits

△ **Table 8.5** Types of materials used in food packaging

Cont.

Packaging material	Benefits/advantages	Limitations/ disadvantages	Examples of food
Paper/card	Cheap to produce Available in different thicknesses Easy to open Recyclable Easy to print on Can be laminated Lightweight Variety of shapes Used in sheets for flexible wrapping Biodegradable Can be made from recycled material	Can tear easily Not waterproof unless it is laminated Product could be easily crushed and damaged	 △ Cereals, eggs, flour, sugar, baked products, for example, cakes, biscuits, pizza
Ovenable paperboard	Used in the oven and microwave Easy to print on Lightweight	Loses its shape and strength when soggy Can easily be crushed, so damaging the product	Frozen and chilled meals

△ **Table 8.5** Types of materials used in food packages *continued*

Key terms

Recyclable – made from materials that can be used again, such as glass, paper, card

Biodegradable – with time, the material, such as paper, will break down

Tamper-proof packaging – guarantees that the product has not been opened

○ plastic collars on sauce bottles
○ film overwraps on cardboard boxes
○ tear-away strips around the top of plastic bottles
○ tin foil seals in pourable boxes, for example, fruit juices.

If these are broken you should not buy the product.

Tamper-evident packaging

Many manufacturers use **tamper-proof packaging** techniques on their products. These techniques make it easy to see if the packaging has been opened, so reducing the risk of the food becoming contaminated if it is opened by mistake and then re-closed. Examples include:

◁ **Figure 8.11** An example of tamper-evident packaging

Exam practice questions

1. Suggest a material that a manufacturer could use to package the following foods for sale in a supermarket. Give **two** benefits and **one** limitation of using each material:

- ○ pickled onions
- ○ chilled sandwich
- ○ cornflakes
- ○ baked beans in tomato sauce.

Present your answers in a chart like Table 8.6. **[4 × 2 marks]**

Food	Material	Benefits	Limitation
Pickled onions			
Chilled sandwich			
Cornflakes			
Baked beans in tomato sauce			

△ **Table 8.6** Benefits and limitations chart

2. Tin foil is sometimes used to package food products. Explain the benefits of using tin foil in the packaging of food products. **[3 marks]**

3. How would a ready-to-eat lasagne that is to be reheated in a microwave be packaged? **[2 marks]**

4. Explain why food manufacturers are using tamper-proof techniques when packaging their food products. **[4 marks]**

Activities

1. Using a packaged food product of your choice, explain how the packaging:

- ○ contains the food product
- ○ identifies the food product
- ○ protects the food product
- ○ increases the shelf life of the food product.

2. Create a mood board or image board to show the different types of packaging materials and tamper-proof techniques used to package food products. To create the mood board you could use pictures, photographs, sketches, text from magazines, leaflets, packaging, images from the internet, and so on.

Stretch yourself

Discuss how manufacturers ensure that the packaging they use is environmentally friendly and supports sustainable resources.

8.3 **Packaging and the environment**

Many people are concerned about the environment. Food packaging can cause a number of environmental problems because:

○ it uses up natural resources, for example, oil, trees, metal ore
○ it can cause air, land or water pollution
○ it cannot always be recycled and is not biodegradable. It has to be disposed of in landfill sites.

We are constantly being told to consider sustainable design. Climate change is now accepted as the biggest threat to all people and all other species on our planet. We should consider, when designing packaging for products, whether all environmental impacts have been reduced. Have we considered:

○ where the raw material comes from?
○ whether the raw material can be replaced as fast as we use it (sustainability)?
○ if it causes any air or water pollution?
○ how much energy is used?
○ what happens to the waste products?
○ how the packaging is disposed of?
○ whether the packaging can be reused?

To encourage us to create more sustainable designs and be more environmentally aware in our way of life, we are advised to:

○ rethink the way we use materials
○ reduce waste materials
○ refuse unnecessary packaging
○ recycle whenever we can
○ reuse materials to make other products
○ repair instead of buying new.

Recycling

Everything we dispose of goes somewhere, although once the container or bag of rubbish is out of our hands and out of our houses we forget it instantly. Our consumer lifestyle is rapidly filling up landfill sites all over the world. When designing and making a new product, designers

and manufacturers need to consider how their product can be recycled at the end of its **life cycle**.

> ## Key terms
>
> **Life cycle** – the stages a new product goes through from conception to eventual decomposition
>
> **Recycle** – to reuse or reprocess a product

△ **Figure 8.12** Recycling logo

Packaging made from glass, metal, card and paper can all be recycled. Some plastics may also be recycled. It is difficult to **recycle** packaging made from mixed materials, for example, layers of foil, plastic or card bonded together. Manufacturers should also use materials that are formed from recycled material. It is up to us, the consumer, to make sure that we recycle the packaging that we have. Packaging used for food is often difficult to recycle. However, biodegradable packaging is now being developed. Most people associate recycling with packaging.

○ We wash out tins and bottles ready to be collected or to take to a recycling centre.
○ More than half of food packaging is plastic. This is made from a non-renewable source and is the most difficult to recycle.
○ There are mixed materials used in packaging such as Tetra Pak. These are difficult to recycle because of the mixture of different materials.

o The average family gets through 4 glass jars or bottles, 13 cans, 3 plastic bottles and 5 kg of paper each week.

Reducing the environmental impact of packaging

Consumers can reduce environmental impact by:

o buying reusable containers, for example, bags, jars, egg cartons
o reusing carrier bags, for example, plastic or thick paper
o taking waste packaging to recycling centres, for example, glass, cans, paper
o buying minimum packaging, for example, single-wrapped rather than double-wrapped products
o selecting biodegradable materials wherever possible.

Manufacturers can reduce environmental impact waste by:

o reducing the amount of packaging
o using paper or card that has come from sustainable forests
o avoiding harmful processes, such as bleaching wood pulp with chemicals
o using materials that the consumer can recycle
o printing symbols on the packaging that informs consumers, for example, recycling logos, plastic identification symbols, anti-litter symbols
o providing information about the packaging materials.

Key points

When manufacturers are packaging food products they need to consider:

o the type of packaging material used
o where the materials come from
o how the packaging can be disposed of
o the effects this might have on the environment.

△ **Figure 8.13** Recycling plastic, metal, glass and paper

△ **Figure 8.14** Consumers can sort their waste at home

△ **Figure 8.15** shopping bags made from recycled drinks cartons

Reuse

Some products can be reused either for the same purpose or as a new product. Britain throws away £20 billion worth of unused food every year – enough to lift 150 million people out of starvation. When food waste cannot be reused it ends up in landfill sites, it rots and produces methane, which is a powerful greenhouse gas. Food containers can sometimes be reused.

Refuse

Buy products with little or no packaging. If you do not need it or if it is environmentally or socially unsustainable, you can choose not to use it.

Plastic packaging and carrier bags are made from oil, although occasionally they are made from recycled plastics. They can take up to 500 years to decay in a landfill site. We could use paper and card, but they are much heavier and therefore use more fuel to transport them to the shop, and they break easily when they become wet. For shopping we could use a reusable bag, made from organically sourced Fairtrade hemp or cotton, but what can we do about the actual packaging on food products? We could choose to shop at a local market stall, farmer's shop or local small business, where the products may be sold without packaging. Do bananas really need to be wrapped in plastic?

Rethink

Manufacturers are encouraged to think about their designs and so should you, both in the workshop and at home.

On average a person in the UK throws away each year:

- ○ 450 kg of waste
- ○ 149 kg of paper and card (570 magazines!)
- ○ 90 kg of organic material (2,000 banana skins!)
- ○ 50 kg plastic (900 fizzy drinks bottles!)
- ○ 32 kg metal (6,320 baked beans tins!).

Eco footprint

Knowledge link
This is described in Chapter 5, page 108.

Food and packaging is the largest single factor affecting our **eco footprint**. Packaging, processing and transport use huge amounts of energy, and discarded packaging creates massive waste. Throwaway drinks containers have become very popular. Stop and think where they end up. Usually in landfill! This is a waste of materials, and even if they were recycled the process would take up energy and cause pollution.

Key term

Eco footprint – the term used to refer to the measurement of the effects of our actions on the environment

Key points

- ○ Food manufacturers have to consider carefully the materials they choose to package food products in.
- ○ Processing, manufacturing, packaging and transport of our products use huge amounts of energy and can create lots of waste.

Activities

1. There are many different recycling logos. Using the internet and existing products, record the different logos you have found and say what types of products they are used on.

2. Create a leaflet or fact sheet on the environmental problems caused by food packaging and how waste can be reduced by both the manufacturer and the consumer. The leaflet/fact sheet should contain images as well as text.

3. Make two lists of foods and ingredients. In the first one list foods and ingredients that could be sold without any packaging, and in the second list foods and ingredients for which packaging is essential. Discuss your lists with a partner and then put an action plan together to send to a supermarket giving advice on how they could reduce food packaging.

4. Select three different processed products and carry out an analysis of each one to show the processes carried out. What is the effect of these products on the environment?

5. Working in groups, look at the packaging of a variety of food products, such as:

   microwave meal
   can of Coke
   Easter egg/box of chocolates

   pack of fresh fruit
   ready-to-cook pizza
   pack of fresh cakes.

   You could choose your own selection of food products.

6. Discuss and consider what you have bought recently and why. Did you really need it?

7. Investigate the different symbols that may be found on products to show eco footprints.

8. Discuss how you could refuse to have the packaging but still buy the product.

   What materials are used? How much of the packaging can be recycled? How?

9. In one of your practical lessons, wash and save all the packaging that is used by your class. In the next lesson, look at the packaging and look at all the sustainability issues. Decide what could be recycled or reused. Could less packaging be used?

10. Look at a range of products and complete a chart like the one in Table 8.7.

Product	Packaging material	Can the material be recycled?	What could it be recycled into?
Chocolate bar	Paper Foil	Yes	Recycled paper, for example, writing paper Metal product

△ **Table 8.7** Recycling possibilities

Exam practice questions

1. What does the term 'recycling' mean? **[3 marks]**

2. List **three** products that can be recycled. What can they be recycled into? **[6 marks]**

3. Name a material made from recycled products. **[1 mark]**

4. Explain how methods of transportation can harm the environment. **[4 marks]**

5. Suggest ways a family can reduce the carbon footprint of the foods they buy. **[4 marks]**

6. Describe **two** ways that packaging for a product could be more sustainable. **[2 × 2 marks]**

Stretch yourself

1. Explain why processed foods have a bigger environmental impact than fresh produce.

2. Cardboard used in packaging states that it comes from sustainable sources. Explain what this means.

chapter 9
The use, need and effect of additives

> ## Learning objectives
>
> By the end of this chapter you should have developed a knowledge and understanding of:
>
> ○ why additives are used in food manufacture
> ○ different types of additives and why they are used
> ○ how and why some foods are fortified.

Introduction

Additives are substances that are added to foods during manufacturing or processing to improve their:

○ **keeping properties**
○ flavour
○ colour
○ texture
○ appearance
○ stability.

Additives are used in a large range of food products today. The main groups of food additives are:

○ **antioxidants**
○ **colours**
○ **flavour enhancers**
○ **sweeteners**
○ **emulsifiers and stabilisers**
○ **preservatives.**

Over 300 additives are allowed in the UK. Flavourings are not included in this figure. More than 3,000 flavourings are used in many different combinations. All additives have to be checked for safety before they can be used in any foods. Additives that manufacturers are allowed to use are given a number. Some are also given an 'E' if they have been accepted as safe for use within the European Union. All additives also have a chemical name. Table 9.1 shows you how the E numbers are allocated.

9.1 Why are additives used?

Additives are used for the following reasons:

○ They can help make food safe for longer.
○ They can make food more attractive or taste better.
○ They can help to keep the price of food competitive.
○ They can give food an improved nutritional profile (higher in vitamins or lower in fat).

Additives may be:

○ natural – obtained from natural sources, for instance, red colouring made from beetroot juice (E162) is used in making ice cream, sweets and liquorice

Colours	E100–E180
Preservatives	E200–E299
Antioxidants	E300–E322
Emulsifiers and stabilisers	E400–E495

△ **Table 9.1** Classification of E numbers

○ nature identical (synthetic) – made in a laboratory to be chemically the same as certain natural materials, such as vanillin, which is found naturally in vanilla pods
○ artificial – synthetic compounds that do not occur in nature, such as saccharin (E954), a low-calorie sweetener.

△ **Figure 9.1** Colourings used in sweets

Many consumers prefer food products to contain additives obtained from natural sources. Many manufacturers now try to use fewer synthetic additives. For example, a cake manufacturer may use additives from natural sources and will then advertise the range of cakes as 'homestyle baking'.

Artificial additives are used a lot by the food manufacturing industry. Their use is controlled by government departments. The long-term effects of additives are not known.

The additives must be listed on the label by their:

○ type
○ chemical name or number.

They must appear on the label in descending order of quantity (greatest amount first).

Advantages of using additives for the manufacturer

○ Used in a wide range of food products to meet consumer needs, for example, quick, easy, convenient meals, such as Pot Noodles, instant whipped desserts and instant mash.
○ To improve a specific characteristic of a food, for example, vanilla-flavoured ice cream, orange-flavoured soft centres in chocolates, coffee liqueur-flavoured hot chocolate drinks.
○ To produce the expected qualities in foods, such as colour and flavour, for example, soft-centred chocolates with pink colouring and strawberry flavouring.
○ To produce a product range by using different additives in the basic food, for example, potato crisps flavoured with salt and vinegar, cheese and onion, smoky bacon, etc.
○ To help maintain product consistency in large-scale production, for example, the use of emulsifiers to prevent salad cream separating.
○ To restore original characteristics of a food after processing, for example, adding colour to processed vegetables such as canned peas
○ To prevent food spoilage, to preserve foods and give them a longer shelf life, for example, bread, cakes and biscuits.
○ To disguise inferior ingredients. This can help to reduce the cost of food products.

Disadvantages of using additives for the manufacturer

Some people may have an allergy to additives and therefore may choose not to purchase the product. It is often difficult to find out which additive is causing the allergic reaction. Examples of allergies caused by food additives include asthma attacks, skin rashes and hyperactivity in children.

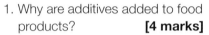

Controlled assessment link

The existing products analysed as part of the Controlled Assessment in Figures 14.3 and 14.4 on page 227 are likely to contain additives.

Activities

1. Look at a variety of different food labels and see if you can recognise the different types of additives used.

2. Working in groups, carry out the following task and prepare a short presentation to give to the rest of your class.

Two different manufacturers are trying to persuade a major supermarket to sell their new pasta bake. Manufacturer A does not use any additives in his product; manufacturer B uses additives.

o Decide whether you are going to be manufacturer A or B.
o Prepare a presentation to persuade the supermarket to take your product.

Exam practice questions

1. Why are additives added to food products? **[4 marks]**

2. Explain why some people have concerns over the use of some additives in food products. **[6 marks – this is a banded response question where you will be assessed on the quality of your written communication]**

9.2 Types of food additives and their functions

Colours

Colours are added to make foods look more attractive. They are used in manufacturing to:

o replace colour lost during heat treatment, for example, in canned peas
o boost colours already in foods, for example, strawberry yoghurt
o maintain consistency between different batch productions as they are added in precise quantities, for example, yellow colouring in tinned custard
o make foods that are normally colourless look attractive, for example, carbonated drinks.

Manufacturers are not allowed to add colours to baby foods.

Stretch yourself

Some consumers believe that the use of colour additives is not necessary for foods to taste good. What are the arguments for and against using artificial colours from the consumer's and the manufacturer's perspective?

△ **Figure 9.2** Colourings added to yogurt to make it more appealing to the consumer

Preservatives

Preservatives help to keep food safe for longer. They are added to foods to:

○ extend shelf life, which means that consumers do not need to go shopping as often
○ prevent the growth of micro-organisms, which can cause food spoilage and lead to poisoning.

Preservatives are found in:

○ many processed foods with a long shelf life
○ cured meats, such as bacon, ham, corned beef
○ dried fruit, such as sultanas, raisins.

Sugar, salt and vinegar are still used to preserve some foods, but most people tend to think of preservatives as chemicals. Some additives used for preservation have been used for a long time, for instance:

○ sugar to make jam and marmalade
○ vinegar to make pickles, for example, pickled cabbage, eggs and onions
○ salt in meat and fish
○ alcohol, for example, peaches in brandy.

Sweeteners

There are two types of sweeteners, intense sweeteners and bulk sweeteners.

Intense sweeteners

Intense sweeteners are aspartame and saccharin. They are:

○ approximately 300 times sweeter than sugar and only in very small amounts
○ very low in energy
○ used in low-calorie drinks and reduced-sugar products, and are also available as sweetening tablets
○ useful for consumers who want to reduce the amount of sugar in their diet.

However, they:

○ lack the bulk that is needed in recipes that normally use sugar cane or beet
○ do not have the same characteristics as sugar for cooking
○ may leave a bitter aftertaste.

Bulk sweeteners

Bulk sweeteners are hydrogenated glucose syrup, sorbital (E420) and sucralose. They are:

○ similar to sugar in levels of sweetness
○ used in similar amounts to sugar
○ used in sugar-free confectionery and preserves for diabetics.

There have been developments in half-sugar products recently. Ordinary sugar has a small amount of aspartame added to it, which makes it twice as sweet and means half the calories. This means that half the amount of sugar is needed.

Activities

1. Investigate how successfully half-sugar can be used in traditional, sweet, baked products such as Victoria sandwich cake, scones or biscuits.

2. Produce a chart to show how the products differ when cooked with half-sugar rather than normal sugar.

Stretch yourself

For the activity above compare the nutritional value of the products.

Emulsifiers, stabilisers, gelling agents and thickeners

These help to improve the consistency of food during processing and storage. Emulsifiers and stabilisers help mix together ingredients like oil and water that would normally separate, for instance, when a salad dressing is left to stand the oil rises to the top. Lecithin is a natural emulsifier found in eggs, and is used to make mayonnaise, low-fat spreads, salad dressings, and so on.

△ **Figure 9.3** Oil and water do not mix

Thickeners are often used in thick and creamy desserts and in low-fat products such as low-fat spreads, which often have a high percentage of water.

There are occasions in food preparation when a product needs the assistance of a gelling agent in order to produce the correct consistency. Some uses of gelling agents are:

○ to create a smooth, set texture, for example, in a cheesecake
○ for setting meat and fish in savoury jelly
○ as a stabiliser to stop separation, for example, yoghurt
○ as a stabiliser to ensure smooth texture
○ to give set liquid a pliable texture, for example, marshmallows.

Gelling agents are often extracted from foods such as beans, seaweed and plants.

Flavourings and flavour enhancers

○ Flavourings and flavour enhancers must meet the requirements of the Food Safety Act 1990 and all other flavouring regulations.
○ They are used widely in savoury foods to make the existing flavour in the food stronger. Monosodium glutamate (MSG) is an example of a flavour enhancer. It is often used in Chinese foods. Some consumers may be allergic to MSG, causing them sickness and dizziness.
○ They replace flavours lost during the processing of the food.
○ Flavourings can also be natural flavourings, for example, vanilla, and herbs and spices.

Activity

Prepare a dish that showcases the use of herbs and/or spices.

△ **Figure 9.4** A variety of spices.

Antioxidants

Most foods containing fats and oils, such as pies, cakes, biscuits, dried soups, preserved meat and fish products and cheese spreads, are likely to contain antioxidants. Some antioxidants are natural, such as vitamins C and E.

These are used to:

○ help prevent fat-soluble vitamins (A and D), oils and fats from combining with oxygen and making the product rancid. Rancid fats have an unpleasant smell and taste

○ prevent some foods from going brown, for example, apples and pears when they are exposed to air.

Fortification of foods

In the UK there is a range of fortified foods. Some are fortified by law, such as white and brown flour with calcium. Today there are many foods that are voluntarily fortified, as food manufacturers seek to promote foods that are linked to healthy lifestyles; for instance, fruit juices and the majority of breakfast cereals have added vitamins and other nutrients.

△ **Figure 9.5** Examples of foods that have been fortified

Why are food products fortified?

○ To increase the nutrient content, especially when added to staple foods such as bread. When wheat is processed, iron, thiamine and niacin are removed with the bran. These nutrients have to be replaced in white and brown flour by law in the UK.

○ Where there is nutrient deficiency in a country, fortification can help to reduce the deficiency.

○ Manufacturers may see it as an advantage in helping them to sell more of their product, as it can be marketed as containing the nutrient or having added nutrients.

○ The addition of some nutrients may help with other aspects of the product. Vitamin C is an antioxidant; it will therefore reduce the rate of spoilage in some products.

- To replace the nutrients lost during the processing of the food. This is very important if the food was a good source of the nutrient before it was processed.
- To produce a product that is similar to another. By law, margarine has to have vitamins A and D added to similar levels as in butter. Manufacturers of some soya-based drinks add calcium, as the drinks are sold as a substitute for milk.
- Sometimes manufacturers choose to voluntarily fortify foods. Some examples of voluntary fortification are given below:
  - Fruit juices made from concentrate are often fortified with vitamin C so that they have the same nutritional profile as freshly squeezed fruit juice.
  - Textured vegetable protein, when used for savoury products, is fortified with iron and the vitamin B complex so that its nutritional profile is similar to meat.
  - Low-fat spreads often have vitamins A and D added to them so they are similar to margarine and butter.
  - Many breakfast cereal products are fortified. These are clearly labelled on the packet.

Activity

Look at a variety of fortified food ingredient labels and complete Table 9.2 to show how they have been fortified and the function of the nutrient added.

Key points

- Some foods are fortified by law.
- Safety and technical considerations are taken into account when deciding which foods to fortify and to what level.
- Fortified foods make an important contribution to diets in the UK.

Exam practice questions

1. Explain why flour is fortified.
   [2 marks]
2. Manufacturers sometimes choose to fortify foods. Give **three** reasons why they may choose to do this. **[3 marks]**

Stretch yourself

Investigate how fortified foods can make a contribution to the nutritional intake of consumers in the UK.

Product	Ingredient added	Function of the nutrient in the diet

△ **Table 9.2** Fortified food ingredients and their function

chapter 10
Using tools and equipment

Introduction

You need to choose suitable equipment to prepare ingredients efficiently and safely.

Using the correct equipment is essential for producing the required result in food preparation. Electrical equipment, such as mixers and processors, can take some of the hard work out of mixing, slicing and chopping, while also saving time. They cannot entirely replace handheld equipment for efficiency, particularly for working quickly with small amounts of ingredients. During your practical sessions you need to demonstrate the correct use of equipment and look for opportunities to use a range of equipment, including labour- and time-saving items. Always read recipes carefully to ensure that you are using the correct piece of equipment for the job.

◁ **Figure 10.3** Balance scales

◁ **Figure 10.4** Spring scales

10.1 Equipment

Measuring

For measuring, scales, cups, jugs or spoons may be used.

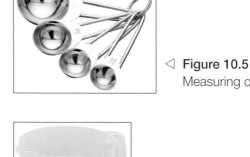

◁ **Figure 10.5** Measuring cups

◁ **Figure 10.1** Tablespoon

Figure 10.2 Teaspoon ▷

◁ **Figure 10.6** Measuring jug

Cutting and chopping

Knives of various types and styles are used to cut and chop. They vary in size and blade type, depending on what they are to be used for.

Graters are used for preparing cheese or vegetables and they can be round or box shaped or, for more safety, the rotary type.

Ceramic or nylon chopping boards are more hygienic than wood. In the catering industry different-coloured boards are used for different tasks.

Red = raw meat
Blue = raw fish
Yellow = cooked meat
White = vegetables
Green = salad/fruit

△ **Figure 10.7**
Vegetable knife

△ **Figure 10.8**
Bread knife

△ **Figure 10.9** Cook's knife

△ **Figure 10.10**
Box grater

△ **Figure 10.11**
Rotary or mouli grater

Whisking

Whisks can be used for adding air to a mixture. They can be operated by hand or electricity. Hand whisks can be balloon-shaped, coil or rotary. Electric mixers are often used when making cake products.

△ **Figure 10.12**
Coil whisk

△ **Figure 10.13**
Balloon whisk

△ **Figure 10.14**
Electric whisk

△ **Figure 10.15**
Rotary whisk

Spreading and lifting

For this a variety of equipment is available. Examples include spatulas (which are used for scraping out bowls), fish slices and palette knives (which can be used for lifting food).

△ **Figure 10.16**
Fish slice

△ **Figure 10.17**
Spatula

△ **Figure 10.18**
Palette knife

Other equipment

More specialist equipment can be used for fruit and vegetable preparation, to save waste and make tasks easier, for example, vegetable peelers and corers.

Sieves can be used for aerating flour, and strainers for separating solids from liquids.

△ **Figure 10.19**
Peeler

△ **Figure 10.20**
Apple corer

△ **Figure 10.21**
Fileting knife

△ **Figure 10.22**
Zester

△ **Figure 10.23** Sieve

Controlled assessment link
You will need to use a range of tools and equipment when making products as part of your Controlled Assessment.

10.2 Food preparation

When food is prepared it often undergoes one or more of three manipulative processes:

o mixing (for example, beating an egg white)
o cutting (for example, grating cheese)
o forming and shaping (for example, rolling pastry).

All tools and equipment used in the preparation of food will fulfil one or more of these functions. The correct tool must be selected to:

o complete the task safely, hygienically and efficiently

o achieve a consistency of finish
o achieve a quality outcome.

Mixing

There are many ways of combining foods, such as stirring, whisking, kneading and rubbing in. Sometimes personal preference determines the piece of equipment used. At other times choosing the right tool is important, for instance, using a metal spoon when folding flour into a whisked sponge – it has a thinner edge, cuts through the mixture cleanly and destroys fewer air bubbles so when baked it has a light texture. A wooden spoon is needed when creaming mixtures for example, margarine and sugar.

Cutting

Different cutting tools and equipment give varying results. For instance, a knife would not be a good choice for a consistent finish for cheese – results would be irregular, slices varying in thickness, shape and length. A cheese slicer will produce more consistent results and therefore would be more cost-effective.

Forming and shaping

Items for shaping include pastry cutters, piping bag and nozzles, rolling pin, mould (jelly, dariole), cake tin, sausage maker, mincer, pasta maker, burger press. Some give a more decorative finish which can look more professional, for example, piping potatoes on the top of a shepherd's pie rather than forking.

Electrical equipment (labour-saving devices)

Machines can perform tasks efficiently, accurately, safely and with a consistency of outcome. They can save time and effort. In industry, labour-saving equipment is very important when large quantities of food need to be produced within a specified time. Catering outlets use machines to achieve uniformity of appearance, taste and texture.

Alternative ways of carrying out processes

You may choose to prepare ingredients by hand or use equipment such as food processors and electric whisks. You could test different ways of carrying out a particular process to see which gives you the best result.

Process	Hand method	Using machinery
Cutting, peeling, chopping	Using a range of knives for meat and vegetable preparation Pastry cutters, for example, for jam tarts Peeler to remove skins from potatoes, fruit, and so on	Food processor – chopping blade, used to chop food very finely; slicing blade for cucumber, carrot Electric knife can also be used, for example, slicing meat Automatic peeler to remove skins
Whisking	Rotary, balloon or coil whisk to beat cream or egg whites, as in meringue	Electric whisk can do the same jobs but will save time and effort
Mixing	Mixing doughs, for example, rubbing fat into flour using the fingertips and mixing in water with a round-bladed knife to create the dough, for example, shortcrust pastry Kneading bread dough	Food processor will carry out the rubbing-in and mixing process during pastry making Large food mixer will knead bread by means of a dough hook
Purée	Puréeing fruit/vegetables using a sieve	Blender/smoothie maker will purée fruit/vegetables much more quickly and the result will often be smoother
Shaping	Shaping beefburgers	Using a beefburger press
Grating	Box, flat or mouli grater	Food processor has a grater attachment

△ **Table 10.1** Hand method versus machinery

Large-scale equipment

The equipment used in the food industry will be different from that used in a domestic setting. Table 10.2 shows a comparison of equipment used in a domestic setting and equipment used in industry.

Small-scale	Large-scale
Weighing ingredients using scales	Computer-controlled weighing or measuring into the hopper
Slicing vegetables using a knife and chopping board	Automatic slicer fed from the hopper
Peeling potatoes with a peeler	Mechanical peeler with specially lined drum
Rolling out with a rolling pin	Dough is sheeted using rollers
Cutting dough with tart cutters	Dough is cut using rollers with blades
Puréeing in a liquidiser	Enormous liquidiser used
Cooking in a saucepan	Large bratt pans are used
Cooking in an oven	Computer-controlled travelling or tunnel ovens or rotary ovens are used
Cooling on a wire tray	Blast-chilled in cooling tunnels
Cutting dough into portions using a knife	Automatic cutting
Portion controlled with a spoon measure	Squeezed out with an extruder
Using a food probe for temperature control	Sensors are computer-controlled
Mixing in a bowl or processor	Giant mixing systems are used
Piping bag for cream	An injector or extruder is used
Piping bag for biscuits	A depositing machine is used

△ **Table 10.2** Equipment used in a domestic setting versus equipment used in industry

Activities

1. Find a recipe for each of the following food products:

o shepherd's pie
o vegetable soup
o cheesecake (with a biscuit base).

Draw a chart like Table 10.3. Using the recipes you have found, plus your knowledge of making practical products, write down the processes involved in making each food product. List the equipment required to carry out each process.

You can suggest hand and any alternative equipment if this is appropriate.

Name of product	Processes	Equipment if made in school	Equipment if made in industry
Shepherd's pie			
Vegetable soup			
Cheesecake (biscuit base)			

△ **Table 10.3** Processes and equipment

2. Look at the making instructions for a food dish. Create a chart like Table 10.4 to show:

o the list of equipment you will be using
o the reason for using each piece of equipment.

List of equipment	Reason for using

△ **Table 10.4** Instructions for a food dish

Key point

Choose equipment appropriate to the task.

Stretch yourself

Evaluate the efficiency of using a food processor to carry out various practical tasks.

What are the advantages and disadvantages of using a food processor?

10.3 Selecting the most appropriate method of cooking

Learning objectives

By the end of this section you should have developed a knowledge and understanding of:

o heat transference through the different methods of cooking: boiling, baking, grilling, microwaving, steaming, frying and roasting
o the effect of heat on different foods
o the most appropriate equipment and healthier cooking methods for food outcomes.

Introduction

When preparing foods to eat, there are many different processes and skills involved. It is essential that preparation is carried out correctly so that food is safe to eat and is presented in a way that is appealing and appetising.

Heat

Heat is a type of energy. When it is applied to foods, the foods will change. The most noticeable changes in foods are:

o colour
o texture.

The nutritional content of the food may also change and this needs to be considered when deciding on the method of cooking.

Cooking methods

The choice of method of cooking will depend on the following:

o the type of food that is being cooked
o the facilities that are available
o how much time is available
o the needs of the individual, for example, special dietary requirements
o choice of the consumer, for example, healthy diet
o skill of the cook.

There are three basic methods of heat transference:

o conduction
o convection
o radiation.

Key terms

Conduction – where heat is transferred from one molecule to another

Convection – where warm molecules rise and the cooler molecules fall closer to the source of heat

Radiation – where heat is passed by electromagnetic waves from one place to another

The different methods of cooking available use at least one of these methods of heat transference. Table 10.5 shows the different methods of heat transference for the most common methods of cooking foods.

Cooking methods are classified as either dry or moist, depending on whether water is involved.

o Moist-heat cooking methods include boiling, simmering and steaming.
o Dry-heat cooking methods include baking, roasting, deep-fat frying, sautéing and stir-frying.

Conduction	Radiation	Convection
Boiling, baking, frying, microwaving, roasting	Barbecuing, grilling, microwaving	Baking, boiling, frying, roasting, steaming
Heat is transferred by contact with heat.	Direct rays pass from the heat source to the food.	Heat moves through the convection currents. The hot air rises and cool air falls.

△ **Table 10.5** Different methods of heat conduction

Moist methods of cooking

These use fairly low temperatures to cook foods. The liquid used to cook the food can vary, for example, fruit juice, milk and stock.

Boiling

Boiling is probably the most popular of the moist-heat cooking methods. Boiling uses large amounts of rapidly bubbling liquid (100 °C) to cook foods. Examples of foods cooked by this method are rice, pasta and potatoes. When boiling foods water-soluble vitamins (vitamins C and B) are lost into the water.

Simmering

Simmering is one of the most widely used moist-heat cooking methods. Properly simmered foods should be moist and tender. The foods are cooked in hot liquid (85–99 °C), but require gentler treatment than boiling, for example, to prevent food such as fish or meat from toughening or vegetables from disintegrating.

Poaching

The temperature of the liquid is just below simmering. Foods that are often poached include eggs, fish and fruit. These foods do not need a long cooking time.

Steaming

The food does not come into contact with the boiling water, but is cooked by the steam that which is rising from the boiling water. This means that the water-soluble vitamins are not lost. Steaming can be carried out in a variety of ways, as shown in Figures 10.24–10.27.

In a tiered steamer it is also possible to cook several foods at once, such as potatoes in the base and various vegetables in the different layers of the steamer. This can help to reduce energy costs.

△ **Figure 10.24** Plate method

△ **Figure 10.25** Saucepan method

△ **Figure 10.26** Tiered steamer

△ **Figure 10.27** Electric Steamer

The types of foods suitable for steaming include:

o puddings – suet, sponge
o fish
o vegetables.

Dry methods of cooking

Higher temperatures are used in dry methods of cooking compared with moist methods.

Baking

When food is baked it mainly uses dry heat. The temperature used varies depending on the type of food product being cooked – a very low temperature is used to cook meringues so that they will dry out and have a crisp texture, while Yorkshire puddings are cooked at a high temperature so that steam is produced in the mixture to cause the batter to rise. On some occasions moisture may be added to help develop certain textures in a food, for instance, placing egg custards in a bath of water to prevent them from curdling. Baking is regarded as a healthy way of cooking as fat is not usually involved.

Grilling

This is a quick method of cooking. The source of heat can come from above and/or below the food. Suitable foods for grilling are tender cuts of meat, such as chops and chicken breast, plus sausages, beefburgers, mushrooms, tomatoes and bread. When the foods are cooked, the surface is quickly sealed due to the dry heat. The food must be turned often to ensure even cooking. It is recommended that foods which are to be grilled are no more than 3.5 cm thick. Grilling is considered to be a healthy way of cooking foods as no fat is added and the fat drains away below the foods. With the trend for healthier ways of cooking foods, manufacturers have also developed electric griddles, which cook food from both the top and the bottom and have ridges on the heat plates so that the fat drains away from the food.

△ **Figure 10.28** Example of an electric griddle

Roasting

Food is cooked by dry heat. A small amount of fat is also used to prevent the food from drying out and to develop the flavour. Foods that are commonly roasted include vegetables and meat.

Frying

This is still a popular method of cooking, although we are being encouraged to reduce the amount of fried food we consume. There are four different types of frying:

o dry-frying
o stir-frying
o shallow-frying
o deep-frying.

When frying, it is important that the correct type of fat is used. A low-fat spread is unsuitable for frying due to its high water content. The water causes the fat to split and separate when it is heated. The fat used must be suitable to heat to a temperature of 200 °C without it burning or changing in taste. The most common type of fat for frying is vegetable oil, although in the past lard was often used.

Dry-frying

Some foods can be fried without any fat being added to the pan. These foods have to have a fairly high fat content, such as in sausages and bacon. Non-stick frying pans are the best as they help to prevent the food from sticking. It is possible to purchase fat sprays which can be used to put a very thin layer of oil onto a frying pan. See Figure 10.29 for an example of a spray.

△ **Figure 10.29** Example of a spray which can be used when frying

Stir-frying

This method of frying originated in East Asia. Small pieces of finely chopped food are cooked in a wok. The temperature of the oil is high and the food is constantly moved around the pan. This is becoming a popular method of cooking foods as:

o it is a quick method of cooking
o it is an energy-saving method of cooking

o it is a relatively healthy method of cooking food as very little fat or oil is added to the wok
o very few nutrients are destroyed by this method.

△ **Figure 10.30** Example of stir-frying

Shallow-frying

This is when foods are cooked in a shallow layer of hot fat or oil. The fat comes about half-way up the food. As this is a very quick method of cooking it is not suitable for tough cuts of meat and poultry. The following are suitable foods for shallow-frying:

o eggs – omelettes, fried eggs, pancakes, crepes
o fish (fresh/frozen) – various cuts, fillets, small whole fish

△ **Figure 10.31** Example of shallow-frying

o   meat and poultry – prime cuts, for example, filet steak, chicken breast
o   fishcakes
o   sausages
o   bacon.

Deep-frying

Figure 10.32 shows a commercial deep-fat fryer, which is commonly seen in fish and chip shops and commercial kitchens. When food is deep-fried it is totally covered in fat during the frying process. The types of foods suitable for deep-fat frying include:

o   chips
o   doughnuts
o   small poultry joints
o   fish
o   Scotch eggs.

It is recommended that we reduce the amount of deep-fried foods we consume.

△ **Figure 10.32** Example of commercial deep-fat frying

> ### Activity
> Make a list of the types of foods that are commonly fried. Suggest an alternative way each food could be cooked to reduce the amount of fat in the product.

Microwaving

Microwaves are in common use in many homes – statistics from the Expenditure and Food Survey carried out by the Office for National

Statistics showed that 91 per cent of households had a microwave in 2006. They are widely used in catering kitchens, shops, offices and work canteens.

They are popular because foods can be defrosted, cooked and reheated quickly. They are also continually being developed to include extra features, such as:

o   child locks
o   weight sensors
o   different cooking modes, for example, cooking vegetables, meat, fish, pasta
o   defrost modes
o   turbo reheat
o   auto-sensor cooking.

Microwave ovens work by the microwaves penetrating into the food and causing the molecules in the food to vibrate. As the molecules vibrate against each other this causes friction, which produces heat. Standing time is part of the cooking process. When food comes out of the oven, the water molecules continue to vibrate, which generates the heat, allowing the cooking process to be completed. During this time the centre of the food will gain rather than lose temperature. Standing times given on food labels should always be followed.

Microwave ovens should have a label on the front, as shown below.

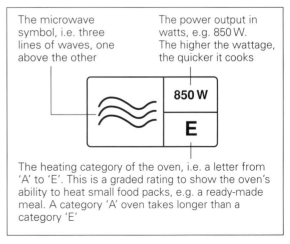

△ **Figure 10.33** A microwave oven label

There are many different types of microwaves available today, as Table 10.6 illustrates.

Type of microwave	Example	Uses
Standard		To defrost, reheat and cook foods
Standard with grill		All the features of a standard microwave oven, plus an internal grill; this can be used as a stand-alone grill or for browning or crisping food, in conjunction with the microwave
Combination		A combined microwave, grill and convection (hot-air) oven, gives more flexibility; the functions can be used independently or together, and some combination ovens offer a steaming function

△ **Table 10.6** Different types of microwave

When deciding which method of cooking to use there are always advantages and disadvantages to each method. Table 10.7 shows some of these.

Method of cooking	Advantages	Disadvantages
Boiling	○ A quick method of cooking as the transfer of heat is quite quick ○ Food is not likely to burn ○ A simple method of cooking	○ Food may disintegrate if it is not carefully timed ○ Water-soluble vitamins (B and C) may be lost ○ Some flavour from the foods will leach into the water

△ **Table 10.7** Advantages and disadvantages of different methods of cooking   *Cont.*

Method of cooking	Advantages	Disadvantages
Steaming	○ As the food does not come into contact with the liquid, the loss of water-soluble nutrients is reduced ○ Food cooked by this method is usually light in texture and therefore easy to digest ○ Different foods can be cooked in the different tiers of a steamer, therefore reducing energy costs	○ Depending on the product being cooked, it can take a long time to cook, for example, a steamed pudding ○ Care with timings must be taken so that delicate foods such as fish are not overcooked
Grilling	○ A quick method of cooking food, therefore reduces the energy costs ○ No added fat, therefore it is a healthier method than frying – as the food cooks, fat drains off the grilling rack ○ It is possible to trim excess fat off some meats, for example, bacon, before grilling	○ Not suitable for tough cuts of meat ○ Careful timing of cooking is needed so that foods are not overcooked
Frying	○ A quick method of cooking food ○ Food is usually attractive in colour – golden brown ○ Soluble nutrients are not lost	○ Heat-sensitive nutrients are destroyed ○ We are being encouraged to reduce the consumption of fats – this method of cooking does not assist this ○ Fats need straining and changing regularly ○ Fried food is more difficult to digest ○ Great care has to be taken from a safety perspective when frying food
Microwave	○ Food is cooked very quickly – saves energy ○ Useful for people who have busy lifestyles ○ Less destruction of heat-sensitive nutrients as the cooking time is short ○ Less loss of water-soluble vitamins when cooking vegetables ○ The bright colour of vegetables is retained as cooking time is short ○ Very useful for defrosting frozen foods	○ Careful timing is required as foods can easily be overcooked ○ As the food is cooked so quickly the flavours may not develop in the food ○ The colour of the food may be pale if it is cooked in a standard microwave

△ **Table 10.7** Advantages and disadvantages of different methods of cooking

Controlled assessment link

Your design proposals will need to show a wide range of cooking processes (see, for example Figure 7.4 on page 128).

Activities

1 Cook a variety of different vegetables in different ways and compare the end results in terms of colour, flavour and texture. Which method of cooking would you recommend for each vegetable you have cooked?

2 Produce a chart to show the advantages and disadvantages of the different methods of cooking vegetables.

3 Microwaves are often used to cook foods. Compare cooking the following foods in the traditional way with cooking them in a microwave:

○ Victoria sandwich cake
○ steamed pudding
○ jacket potato.

Produce a chart to compare the length of cooking time and the sensory qualities of the products.

Stretch yourself

Many consumers are trying to reduce the amount of fat they consume. Produce a fact sheet to help inform consumers of which methods of cooking will help them in achieving this goal.

Exam practice questions

1. We are being encouraged to eat fewer fried foods. Suggest suitable alternative methods to frying for cooking the following foods:

   (a) sausages
   (b) eggs
   (c) beefburgers
   (d) potatoes. **[4 marks]**

2. Explain why we are being encouraged to eat less fried food. **[4 marks]**

3. Explain why stir-frying is considered a healthy method of cooking. **[2 marks]**

4. We are being encouraged to reduce the amount of energy we use when cooking meals. Discuss how this can be done in the home. **[6 marks]**

5. Water-soluble vitamins can be lost when preparing and cooking vegetables. Explain how you can reduce the loss of these nutrients. **[4 marks]**

Controlled assessment link

You should be prepared to use the skills covered in this chapter in your controlled assessment.

chapter 11
Storage of food and food products

Learning objectives

By the end of this chapter you should have developed a knowledge and understanding of:

- the need for different types of equipment and temperature for the storage of food, including:
  - chilling (0 to 5°C)
  - freezing (−18°C)
  - re-heating (72°C)
  - ambient conditions (room temperature)
- critical storage temperatures
- different ways of **monitoring** temperature
- the changes that occur in ingredients and foods during their preparation and storage
- the need for appropriate hygiene and safety procedures from raw material to product outcome
- the need for food safety and hygiene when purchasing, storing, preparing, cooking and serving food
- risk posed by physical, chemical and biological contamination – food poisoning
- the reasons why food may be packaged in different forms to extend shelf life, including the use of new technologies.

11.1 Food spoilage

If food is not preserved it will **deteriorate** and become unfit to eat. Deterioration of food is caused by **micro-organisms** and **enzymes**. Food **preservation** is a way of increasing the **shelf life** of a product and ensuring that it is safe to eat.

Deterioration of food

Fresh foods cannot be stored for very long before changes occur which affect the texture, flavour or colour of the food. Some changes are noticeable, for instance, a banana as it ripens changes from green to yellow, and eventually it will turn black. These changes are due to the action of enzymes. They speed up ripening and natural decay, and because they

are proteins they are destroyed by heat. Some of the changes that occur can often make the foods unfit to eat; this is known as food spoilage. **Enzymic browning** causes slices of apple to go brown.

Micro-organisms and enzymes can cause changes in food. Changes are caused by the following micro-organisms:

- yeasts
- moulds
- **bacteria.**

Key terms

Deteriorate – start to decay and lose freshness

Micro-organisms – tiny living things such as bacteria, yeasts and moulds which cause food spoilage; can only be seen through a microscope

Enzymes – proteins that speed up chemical reactions

Preservation – the protection of perishable foods from deterioration by removing the conditions necessary for the growth of micro-organisms

Enzymic browning – reaction between a food product and oxygen resulting in a brown colour, for example, a sliced apple

Bacteria – single-celled organisms present in the air, soil, on animals and humans

Hygienically – to prepare food in a clean environment to stop food spoilage or poisoning

Monitoring – keeping a constant watch on

Shelf life – how long a food product can be kept safely and remain of high quality

Food spoilage – damage to food caused by the natural decay of food or by contamination by micro-organisms

Food-spoilage bacteria – bacteria that cause a food to go bad but do not usually cause food poisoning

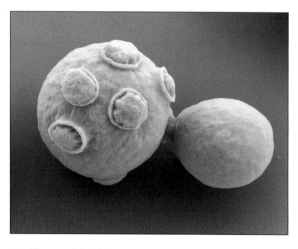

△ **Figure 11.1** Yeast

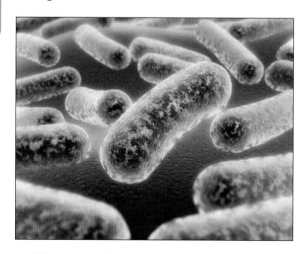

△ **Figure 11.2** Mould

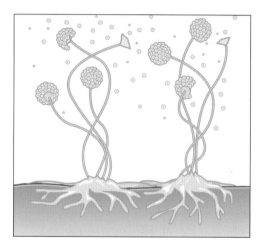

△ **Figure 11.3** Bacteria

Micro-organisms are usually visible only under a microscope. They can be found in water, soil, air and rubbish, as well as on animals, humans and equipment. Some foods may already contain micro-organisms, for example, salmonella in chicken. Other micro-organisms can be transferred to food by poor hygienic practices, by humans, flies and rodents.

Micro-organisms can be harmful and cause food spoilage, but not all micro-organisms are harmful. For example, yeast is used to ferment wine and beer and to make bread, and some bacteria and moulds are used to make cheese.

When foods are described as **contaminated** it means that they are infected with micro-organisms and therefore are not safe to eat. Some micro-organisms, known as **pathogens**, can cause food poisoning, which can result in serious illness or even death. Micro-organisms multiply rapidly in conditions which, when combined, offer warmth, moisture, food and time.

△ **Figure 11.4** Fruit spoilage

Conditions needed for growth

Active in warm, moist conditions with food for growth and reproduction.

Does not need oxygen to grow (**anaerobic** growth).

Moulds
Function

Used in food manufacture to produce specific flavours and textures, for example, the manufacture of blue-veined cheeses such as Danish blue and Stilton. These moulds are considered harmless.

Spoilage

- Visible to the eye. Grow as thread-like filaments, usually on the surface of food, for example, on cheese and bread. They can be black, white or blue.
- Reproduce by producing spores which travel in the air. Spores settle, germinate and multiply into new growths.
- Harmful only when they produce myotoxins, which are poisonous substances.

Key terms

Contaminated – spoilt or dirty

Pathogenic/Pathogens – bacteria causing disease

Fermentation – when yeast produces carbon dioxide

Anaerobic – without oxygen

Yeasts
Function

Through the process of **fermentation** they are used to make breads and alcohol (sugars break down into alcohol and carbon dioxide gas).

Spoilage

Responsible for food spoilage in high-sugar foods such as fruit, jam and fruit yogurts.

△ **Figure 11.5** Mould on a cheese and cucumber sandwich

Conditions needed for growth

○ Grows quickly in moist conditions at temperatures of 20–30 °C. Grows slowly in dry, cold conditions.
○ Grows on food that may be dry, moist, acid, alkaline, or has salt or sugar concentrations.

Bacteria

Function

Used in food manufacture, for example, making cheese and yoghurt. The lactic acid bacteria cultures used in these products are not harmful.

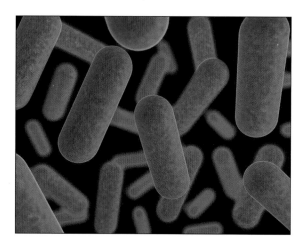

△ **Figure 11.6** E. coli bacteria seen under a microscope

Spoilage

○ Often undetected because the food looks, tastes and smells as it should, but the presence of bacteria makes it potentially very dangerous to eat.
○ Those which cause food poisoning are known as **pathogenic bacteria**, for example, Escherichia coli (E. coli), which can be very harmful, and clostridium found in the soil and in animals.

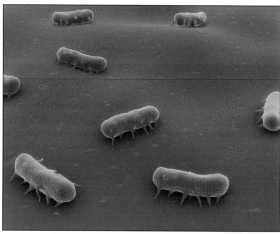

△ **Figure 11.7** Salmonella bacteria seen under a microscope

Conditions needed for growth

○ Active in warmth, moisture, food and oxygen (optimum conditions). These conditions are found in **high-risk foods**.
○ Reproduce rapidly by dividing in two, and in two again in minutes.
○ Able to grow rapidly in neutral **pH** conditions. Most pathogenic bacteria are unable to grow in acid or alkaline conditions, for example, beetroot preserved in vinegar.
○ Most active in a temperature range of 5–65 °C, known as the **danger zone**. Ambient room temperature is usually 20–25 °C. The optimum temperature is 37 °C, that is, the human body temperature. Below 0 °C bacteria will become dormant. Most cannot survive at temperatures of 70 °C or above.

○ Some are able to form spores that can lie dormant. If the right conditions are provided the spores will germinate.

Key terms

Pathogenic bacteria – harmful bacteria which can cause food poisoning

High-risk foods – foods which are the ideal medium for the growth of bacteria or micro-organisms

pH – a measure of alkalinity or acidity

Danger zone – the temperature range (5–63 °C) in which bacteria grow rapidly

Ambient temperature – normal room temperature (20–25 °C)

Low-risk foods – foods which have a long shelf life, such as dried foods

Changes caused by enzymes

Enzymes are found in all foods and can also cause changes in food. They are proteins that speed up chemical reactions.

Function

Enzymes are used in a wide range of manufacturing processes:

○ bread and brewing – enzymes present in yeast are active in the fermentation process
○ cheese – enzymes speed up the ripening stage.

Spoilage

Enzymes can cause 'browning' in certain foods. Enzymatic browning can be reduced by:

○ high temperatures, for example, blanching cut vegetables in boiling water
○ acidic conditions, for example, dipping cut fruit in lemon juice.

Everyone working in the food chain must make sure that food is safe to eat, as food can be infected at any stage of production. This includes farmers, manufacturers and consumers.

In Table 11.1 you can see a selection of high- and **low-risk foods**. High-risk foods are easily contaminated by bacteria. They are often used without further cooking, for example, cooked meats. They need to be kept in the refrigerator. Low-risk foods have a longer shelf life and are not so easily contaminated by bacteria.

High-risk foods	Low-risk foods
(Often have high protein and moisture content.) ○ Raw fish ○ Dairy products ○ Cooked meat and poultry ○ Shellfish and seafood ○ Gravies, sauces, stocks, soups and stews ○ Egg products, for example, raw egg in chilled desserts and mayonnaise ○ Cooked rice ○ Protein-based baby foods	○ High acid content foods, for example, pickles and chutney, fruit juice ○ High sugar content foods, for example, marmalades, jams, fruit packed syrup ○ Sugar based confectionery, for example, sweets, icing ○ Unprocessed raw vegetables, for example, potatoes, carrot ○ Edible oils and fats

△ **Table 11.1** High-risk and low-risk foods

Exam practice questions

1. Explain what you understand about the term 'food spoilage'. **[2 marks]**
2. Draw a chart like the one in Table 11.2 and complete it. **[6 marks]**

Micro-organism	Function	Spoilage
Yeast		
Moulds		
Bacteria		

△ **Table 11.2** Food spoilage

3. State the conditions required for micro-organisms to multiply rapidly. **[4 marks]**
4. Look at the following list of foods and note down which are classed as high-risk:

- cooked rice
- chicken
- cakes
- tomato sauce
- milk
- biscuits
- cabbage
- shellfish. **[4 marks]**

Stretch yourself

Describe how enzymatic browning can be reduced in cut fruits and vegetables. **[6 marks]**

11.2 Storage of food

Food must be stored correctly at all times to prevent spoilage.

Refrigerators

Refrigerators provide safe storage of food with less risk of food poisoning. There are many types of refrigerator units available – some just refrigerate (larder fridges), while others contain both refrigerator and freezer (fridge freezers). Stand-alone freezers are also available. A domestic refrigerator should be between 0 °C and 5 °C.

Sensible use of your fridge

- Avoid opening the door regularly – warm air enters every time you open the door.
- Avoid putting in hot food – this raises the temperature and fills the inside with steam, which condenses on the shelves and lining and so raises the temperature of other foods.
- Cover food.
- Maintain a consistent temperature. Increasing the temperature inside the fridge could lead to bacterial growth.

Freezing

During freezing foods become frozen as the water content in the food becomes solid. The freezer 'star' rating indicates the temperature range of the freezer section in the refrigerator and the length of time you can store foods.

A domestic freezer should be kept at −18 °C.

A freezer box within a fridge cannot be used to store fresh foods – it can only be used to store already frozen foods.

Thawing and refreezing

When food is thawed the structure is damaged and there is sometimes loss of colour, flavour, texture and nutritional value. Food poisoning

Star rating	Temperature °C	Storage times
∗	−6	up to 1 week
∗∗	−12	up to 1 month
∗∗∗	−18	up to 3 months
∗(∗∗∗)		Can be used to freeze fresh foods

△ **Table 11.3** Freezer star rating

bacteria will not multiply in a freezer, but it must be remembered that the bacteria present are not destroyed in the freezer and will multiply when they are sufficiently warm. Frozen foods are therefore transported in temperature-controlled vehicles to keep the foods in a frozen state. On entering the supermarkets, restaurants, and so on, they are quickly packed into large freezers.

You should never refreeze food after it has thawed – bacteria grow quickly in thawed food because the cells have been damaged.

Foods that do not freeze well

Foods that contain a large proportion of water and have a delicate cell structure do not freeze well because ice crystals damage the cell structure, causing it to collapse.

Freezing vegetables

Most vegetables, with the exception of salad, freeze well and can be kept for up to a year. It is important to blanch vegetables before freezing to halt enzyme activity which causes changes in colour, flavour, texture and nutritional value.

Freezer burn

Greyish-white marks appear on the food when it has been packaged badly. The food dehydrates and, although safe to eat, will change colour, texture and flavour.

11.3 Preservation

You have already seen that bacteria, yeasts and mould cause changes in food, which can be harmful. Micro-organisms need food, warmth, moisture and time to multiply. If one of these conditions is removed, the food is preserved and will keep for a longer time. If micro-organisms and enzymes are destroyed or a chemical added (**preservative**) this also allows food to last longer.

Limitations of processed foods

- Can sometimes be more expensive.
- Often contain a lot of fat, sugar and salt.
- Do not contain much fibre (except for canned baked beans and sweetcorn).
- Some nutrients have been lost when the food was processed.

Food	Change that takes place
Baked egg custard	separates
Bananas	turn black
Cream (single)	separates
Jelly	collapses
Salad	becomes limp

△ **Table 11.4** Foods that do not freeze well

185

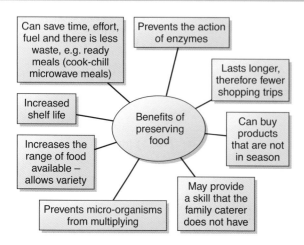

△ **Figure 11.8** The benefits of preserving food

- Additives may need to be added to restore colour, flavour and texture.
- Texture of food may change, for example, canned strawberries are much softer than fresh strawberries.

Food is preserved in many ways so that it keeps longer.

High-temperature methods
Pasteurisation

- Pathogenic micro-organisms are destroyed. The food is heated to 72 °C for 15 seconds.
- Storage of food is extended for a limited time – days not months.
- Used for heat-treating milk, some soups, liquid egg and ice cream.

Sterilisation

- Food is heated for a long period of time at higher temperatures. Heated to 104 °C for 40 minutes.
- Destroys nearly all micro-organisms and enzymes.
- Extends storage period.
- Used for milk and fruit juices.
- Milk is changed to a creamy colour, with a slight caramelisation of the milk sugar content, giving a 'cooked' flavour.

△ **Figure 11.9** Milk is pasteurised

Ultra heat treatment (UHT)

- Uses very high temperatures, up to 130 °C for 1–5 seconds. Destroys all bacteria.
- Extends storage period of milk, up to six months unopened.
- Little colour change.
- Only slight change in taste.
- Little loss of nutrient content.
- Sold in airtight cartons, for example, soups, prepared sauces, such as chilli.

Canning

Canning is a form of sterilisation. Food can be:

- packed in cans and then sterilised
- sterilised and then packed into **aseptic** (sterilised) cans.

The cans are then sealed with a double seam to prevent leakage and to prevent re-**contamination**. Temperature and time vary depending on the food type, but it is crucial to ensure that the sterilisation process is complete and that the food retains its structure and texture. After sterilisation the cans are sprayed with water to prevent the contents overcooking.

- Canning is used for a huge range of foods, for example, soup, vegetables, fruit, meat and fish, to give a long shelf life.
- The texture of some foods may change, for example, strawberries become soft.
- There is some loss of nutrients, especially vitamins B and C.
- Acid foods, for example, grapefruit, are canned in plastic-lined cans to prevent corrosion.

Key terms

Preservative – a substance that extends the shelf life of a food

Pasteurisation – the process of prolonging the keeping quality of products such as milk by heating to destroy harmful bacteria

Sterilisation – heating at 104 °C for 40 minutes to extend the shelf life of a product

Ultra heat treatment (UHT) – the high-temperature, short-time sterilization of milk, known as long-life milk

Contamination – when foods are infected with micro-organisms and therefore are not safe to eat

Aseptic – sterilised; preserves foods without using preservatives or chilling

Low-temperature methods

Bacterial growth is slowed down when the temperature is lowered, and at −18 °C bacteria become dormant.

Chilling and freezing in industry
Cook-chill

Chilling is a short-term way of preserving fresh food.

It is critical that the correct temperature controls are followed at all stages of manufacture, storage and distribution. This is in order to:

- have records of temperature control which can be shown to the Environmental Health Officer
- prevent waste
- avoid bacterial growth
- avoid complaints
- meet the requirements of the Food Safety Regulations
- keep the food at its best (texture/colour/taste/appearance).

Products are transported by refrigerated vans and on delivery to the supermarket are transferred immediately to refrigerated storage rooms. If it goes below 0 °C the product will freeze. It is not possible to detect by looking at the packaging whether a product has been stored at the correct temperature.

Cook-chill products are always sold from the chiller cabinets in shops. Once bought, cook-chill products should be transported home quickly, preferably in a cool bag, and stored at below 5 °C in the refrigerator.

Key term

Cook-chill – food that has been cooked, fast-chilled in 1½ hours and stored at low temperatures

Cook-chill products are often thought to be of a better quality than frozen products. They have a shorter shelf life (usually a few days) but do not need to be defrosted first.

Advantages of cook-chill:

- very little change in nutritional value, flavour, colour, texture or shape
- fresh foods can be kept at maximum quality for a longer time
- the consumer can be offered a much larger range of fresh and convenience foods
- nutrients are not destroyed
- no need to defrost as in frozen products, therefore quicker to cook/reheat
- fewer additives needed during manufacture
- available in single portions

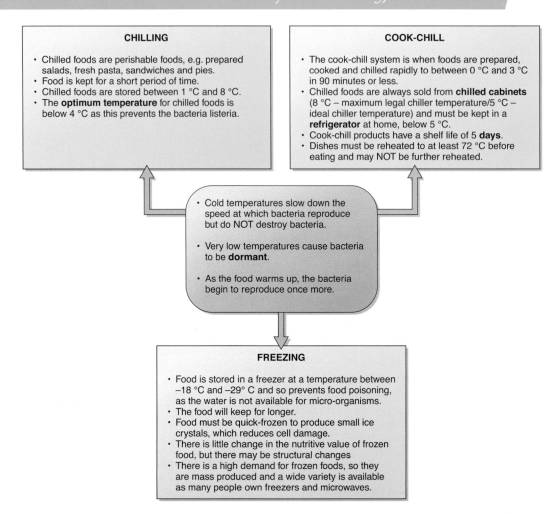

CHILLING

- Chilled foods are perishable foods, e.g. prepared salads, fresh pasta, sandwiches and pies.
- Food is kept for a short period of time.
- Chilled foods are stored between 1 °C and 8 °C.
- The **optimum temperature** for chilled foods is below 4 °C as this prevents the bacteria listeria.

COOK-CHILL

- The cook-chill system is when foods are prepared, cooked and chilled rapidly to between 0 °C and 3 °C in 90 minutes or less.
- Chilled foods are always sold from **chilled cabinets** (8 °C – maximum legal chiller temperature/5 °C – ideal chiller temperature) and must be kept in a **refrigerator** at home, below 5 °C.
- Cook-chill products have a shelf life of 5 **days**.
- Dishes must be reheated to at least 72 °C before eating and may NOT be further reheated.

- Cold temperatures slow down the speed at which bacteria reproduce but do NOT destroy bacteria.
- Very low temperatures cause bacteria to be **dormant**.
- As the food warms up, the bacteria begin to reproduce once more.

FREEZING

- Food is stored in a freezer at a temperature between −18 °C and −29° C and so prevents food poisoning, as the water is not available for micro-organisms.
- The food will keep for longer.
- Food must be quick-frozen to produce small ice crystals, which reduces cell damage.
- There is little change in the nutritive value of frozen food, but there may be structural changes
- There is a high demand for frozen foods, so they are mass produced and a wide variety is available as many people own freezers and microwaves.

△ **Figure 11.10** Low-temperature methods

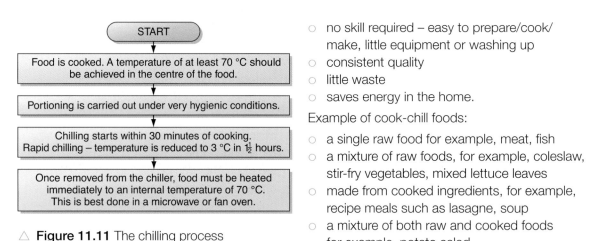

START

Food is cooked. A temperature of at least 70 °C should be achieved in the centre of the food.

Portioning is carried out under very hygienic conditions.

Chilling starts within 30 minutes of cooking. Rapid chilling – temperature is reduced to 3 °C in 1½ hours.

Once removed from the chiller, food must be heated immediately to an internal temperature of 70 °C. This is best done in a microwave or fan oven.

△ **Figure 11.11** The chilling process

- no skill required – easy to prepare/cook/make, little equipment or washing up
- consistent quality
- little waste
- saves energy in the home.

Example of cook-chill foods:

- a single raw food for example, meat, fish
- a mixture of raw foods, for example, coleslaw, stir-fry vegetables, mixed lettuce leaves
- made from cooked ingredients, for example, recipe meals such as lasagne, soup
- a mixture of both raw and cooked foods for example, potato salad.

Blast-freezing

This method is suitable for most foods. Complete meals can also be frozen, provided their maximum thickness is no greater than 4 cm. Air is circulated around a freezing compartment by a fan, reducing the temperature of the food quickly. Food must be kept in storage units at a temperature of between –20 °C and –30 °C after freezing.

Freezing is rapid, so the texture of soft tissue is unchanged. This is not a widely used method because it is expensive. Vacuum chilling is now being used instead of blast-freezing because it is a quicker method of cooling.

Cryogenic freezing

Cryogenic freezing is used for delicate products and fruits, such as raspberries and meringue desserts. The foods are immersed in or sprayed with liquid nitrogen.

Key terms

Blast-freezing – a quick-freezing method; small ice crystals form and there is less damage to the food than in slow freezing

Cryogenic freezing – food is immersed or sprayed with liquid nitrogen

Cook-freeze

Meals are blast-frozen and stored at –20 °C until required. Dishes must be prepared with strict attention to hygiene. Many large catering operators find it convenient to use cook-freeze systems today. Meals are prepared and frozen rapidly. The food can be distributed to branch outlets in the frozen state and heated by microwave or micro-ovens when required for service. (Micro-ovens cook using both microwaves and convected heat.)

Manufacturers have increased their range of frozen foods for the reasons outlined in Figure 11.12.

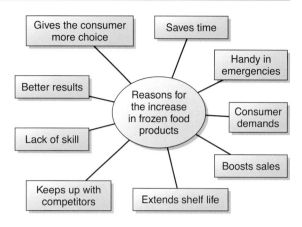

△ **Figure 11.12** Reasons for the increase in frozen food products

Dehydration (drying)

There are various methods of using drying to preserve food, as shown in Figure 11.13. Dried foods are cheaper and easy to transport and store. They have a relatively long shelf life if stored in protective packaging. The flavour, colour, texture and nutritional value of dried foods are affected. They lose vitamin C.

Key term

Dehydration – removal of water from food

Chemicals

Chemical preservation destroys bacteria or prevents them reproducing. The chemicals work by affecting the growth of micro-organisms. Chemicals used for preserving food include the following.

Vinegar

- Acetic acid with a low pH of 3.5 (bacteria cannot survive below 4.5).
- Used for foods such as pickled onions, cabbage and eggs.

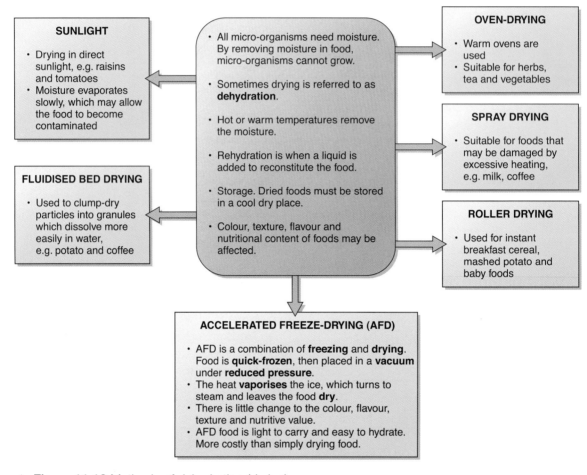

SUNLIGHT

- Drying in direct sunlight, e.g. raisins and tomatoes
- Moisture evaporates slowly, which may allow the food to become contaminated

FLUIDISED BED DRYING

- Used to clump-dry particles into granules which dissolve more easily in water, e.g. potato and coffee

- All micro-organisms need moisture. By removing moisture in food, micro-organisms cannot grow.
- Sometimes drying is referred to as **dehydration**.
- Hot or warm temperatures remove the moisture.
- Rehydration is when a liquid is added to reconstitute the food.
- Storage. Dried foods must be stored in a cool dry place.
- Colour, texture, flavour and nutritional content of foods may be affected.

OVEN-DRYING

- Warm ovens are used
- Suitable for herbs, tea and vegetables

SPRAY DRYING

- Suitable for foods that may be damaged by excessive heating, e.g. milk, coffee

ROLLER DRYING

- Used for instant breakfast cereal, mashed potato and baby foods

ACCELERATED FREEZE-DRYING (AFD)

- AFD is a combination of **freezing** and **drying**. Food is **quick-frozen**, then placed in a **vacuum** under **reduced pressure**.
- The heat **vaporises** the ice, which turns to steam and leaves the food **dry**.
- There is little change to the colour, flavour, texture and nutritive value.
- AFD food is light to carry and easy to hydrate. More costly than simply drying food.

△ **Figure 11.13** Methods of dehydration (drying)

Salt

- ○ Used to coat foods such as ham, bacon and fish, or used in a brine solution (salt and water), such as for tuna and vegetables.
- ○ Reduces moisture content by osmosis.

Sugar

- ○ In high concentrations (60 per cent of final product) it prevents bacteria from growing because it makes the water unavailable.
- ○ Used in jams, marmalades and jellies.
- ○ Strong sugar solutions can also be used for coating candied and crystallised fruit.

△ **Figure 11.14** Preservation using sugar

Physical methods

Physical means of preserving foods include **vacuum packing**, smoking, modified atmosphere packing (MAP) and **irradiation**.

△ **Figure 11.15** Using MAP to package apples

Key terms

Vacuum packing – a method of preserving by removing air

Irradiation – a process involving passing strictly controlled X-rays from a radioactive or electron beam through food

Hermetic – airtight

Accelerated freeze-dried (AFD) – a technique where food is frozen and then dried

Modified atmosphere packaging

MAP involves changing the atmosphere around the food inside some packaging so that growth of micro-organisms is slowed down, so that the product can last longer. Altering the gas in the packet prevents bacteria being able to use the oxygen for growth, which means the product has an increased shelf life. The advantage is that you can see the product. It is used for chilled meats, vegetables and fruits.

The process involves:

○ packaging fresh foods in peak condition; the colour of the food remains the same until the pack is opened, and once opened the food has a normal shelf life

○ replacing the air by 'gas-flushing' a combination of gases around the food; gases used are oxygen, nitrogen and carbon dioxide

○ sealing the plastic bag or plastic lid to a food tray by means of **hermetic** sealing process.

Vacuum packing

○ This is done by removing air and sealing the package. It also prevents bacteria growing. Once opened it has a normal shelf life.

○ The food is kept in anaerobic conditions, that is, there is no oxygen

○ Foods maintain colour and texture.

○ Coffee, once **accelerated freeze-dried (AFD)**, is vacuum packed so that it does not lose taste or flavour.

Irradiation

This process uses radiation to fire gamma rays into food. This kills pests, insects and some micro-organisms. It is used to stop onions and potatoes sprouting, and to kill insects in spices, fruits and vegetables. It is not popular in the UK and many supermarkets refuse to sell irradiated foods.

Nanotechnology

Knowledge link

For information on nanotechnology, see Chapter 13, page 220.

Stretch yourself

Discuss whether irradiation should be widely used as a method of preserving foods.

Exam practice questions

1. Give **four** ways that you can prevent the inside temperature of a fridge from becoming warm. Explain why it is important to prevent this from happening. **[2 × 4 marks]**

2. Explain why it is important to blanch vegetables before freezing them. **[4 marks]**

3. Draw a chart to show **four** benefits and **four** limitations of preserving food. **[8 marks]**

4. Milk is a high-risk food. Give **two** processing methods which increase the shelf life of milk. **[2 marks]**

5. Describe how a sandwich should be packed and stored if it is to be sold in a supermarket. **[4 marks]**

6. Complete statements (a) to (e) with the correct ending to form a complete sentence. **[5 marks]**

(a) Freezing or chilling	moisture is not available for micro-organisms.
(b) Drying food removes	in packaging for other gases.
(c) Freezing turns liquids into solids and therefore	slows down the rate of bacterial reproduction.
(d) Systems are available which exchange air	heated to above 62 °C to reduce bacterial growth.
(e) Food should be cooled below 5 °C or	the water, preventing bacterial growth.

7. Explain why freezing is a popular method of preservation. **[4 marks]**

8. Soup can be manufactured as a dried product. Draw a chart to show two benefits and two limitations to the consumer of using a dried soup. **[4 marks]**

9. State two methods of preserving for each of the following foods: strawberries, peas, fish, onions, milk. **[10 marks]**

Key points

○ Bacteria need warmth, moisture, food and time to multiply.
○ The shelf life of a product is the length of time it will last without deteriorating.
○ Food spoilage will occur if food is not stored correctly or if it has reached the end of its shelf life.
○ Food can be processed in a variety of ways.
○ Preservation is used to prolong the shelf life of products.

11.4 Hygiene and safety procedures from raw material to product outcome

Safe and hygienic practices are essential for the preparation, cooking, transportation and storage of food ingredients and products. The food industry has legislation that protects the consumer, which must be followed when making any food product to sell.

Using tools and equipment safely and effectively

Equipment used in any kitchen should be designed so that it is hygienic and safe. All equipment should be properly maintained, used correctly and regularly disinfected. Particular care should be given to any surface that comes into contact with food.

Key term

Disinfection – cleaning with a chemical (cleaning agent) to kill or reduce micro-organisms to an acceptable level to maintain the highest hygienic standards

Equipment should:

- protect food from contamination
- be made from a material that does not contaminate
- be hard-wearing
- be designed so that it does not trap dirt and bacteria
- be easy to move and disassemble for thorough cleaning and disinfecting.

Equipment selected for industrial use must conform to European Union safety directives. Equipment must carry the CE mark, which indicates that the required safety standards have been met.

Knives

These must be used correctly to avoid accidents and **cross-contamination**.

Key term

Cross-contamination – the transference of bacteria between raw and cooked food

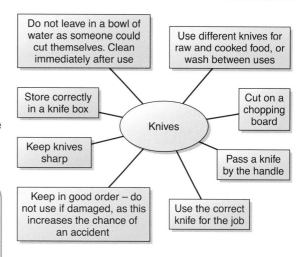

△ **Figure 11.16** The safe use of knives

Electrical equipment

This should be bought from a reputable shop/ manufacturer. Safety rules include the following:

- Set up and use equipment correctly. Always use the correct attachments.
- Do not use near water. Only use with dry hands.
- Check equipment regularly, for example, check for loose, bare, frayed wires.
- Ensure it is in good working order before using it. Check the equipment is not broken/ damaged and that all correct parts are present.
- Plug it in correctly. All equipment should be fitted with the correct plug and fuse.
- Only one person should operate the equipment.
- Keep hands away from moving parts, for example, do not place hands in a bowl with a whisk or dough hook.
- Wash blades from food processors, and so on, carefully.
- Place equipment in a safe place on the worktop, that is, not near the edge.
- Turn off after use.

Safety rules when using a cooker

△ **Figure 11.17** Removing hot dishes safely from the oven

○ Turn saucepan handles inwards. No handles should be placed over rings.
○ Use oven gloves.
○ Do not leave oven doors open or leave a grill unattended.
○ Turn off after use.

○ Do not touch electric rings after use as they take time to cool down.
○ Make sure gas is lit.
○ Reposition oven shelves before heating the oven.
○ Use back rings rather than front rings if these are available.
○ Use the correct size ring for the pan.
○ Do not clean while still hot.
○ Use the correct temperature – not too high.
○ Stir liquids with a wooden spoon rather than metal. Wooden spoon handles will not get hot.
○ Maintain/service cookers regularly.
○ Tie back hair and have no loose clothing which may catch fire.

The importance of safe and hygienic practices

Food is in danger of becoming infected by yeasts/moulds/bacteria at each stage of its production, from the farm to the table. If poor hygiene practices are applied, food can easily become contaminated and this could lead to food poisoning.

Buying food	Buy from a reputable shop that keeps food in safe conditions. Choose food that looks fresh. Check that the food is within the date mark.
Transporting food	Make sure food is appropriately packaged and transported so it does not get damaged in transit. Keep chilled, perishable foods cool, below 8 °C. Quickly transport from one area to another. Insulated lorries are used by food manufacturers. Frozen foods are transported by special freezer lorries. Use cool bags to transport frozen and chilled food from the supermarket.
Storage of food	Store in correct conditions: ○ frozen food in the freezer ○ chilled and perishable foods in the fridge ○ non-perishable foods, for example, dry packaged foods, canned foods, in a cool, dry, well-ventilated cupboard.

△ **Table 11.5** Safe hygiene practices

Cont.

Preparing food	Leave perishable foods in the fridge until ready for use.
	Defrost frozen foods before preparation unless the label says otherwise.
	Clean work surfaces before and after preparation.
	Wash fruits and vegetables before use.
	Take special care when preparing meat and poultry to avoid cross-contamination.
	Use colour-coded chopping boards to avoid cross-contamination.
Cooking food	Cook thoroughly before consumption.
	During cooking, the temperature should reach 72 °C for two minutes. If keeping food hot, the temperature must be at or above 63 °C. A temperature (food) probe can be used to test the internal temperature of the food.

△ **Table 11.5** Safe hygiene practices

Controlled assessment link

It is important to consider health and safety when carrying our your making in the Controlled Assessment. Figure 14.9 on page 234 highlights important food safety checks.

11.5 Causes of food poisoning

Food poisoning is an illness caused by eating contaminated food or water. Thousands of cases of food poisoning occur each year and this number is increasing.

Food poisoning occurs if food is contaminated by:

○ harmful bacteria or other micro-organisms (pathogens)
○ toxic chemical contamination.

Some people, for example, pregnant women, elderly people, babies and those with a low resistance to infection, are more susceptible to food poisoning and extra care must be taken when preparing, and cooking food for these groups of people.

Symptoms of food poisoning include diarrhoea, vomiting, nausea, headache and fever. They may occur as quickly as one hour after eating or can

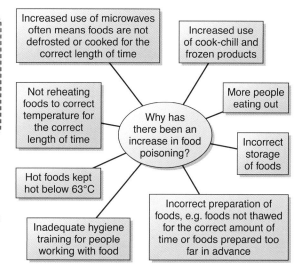

△ **Figure 11.18** Why has there been an increase in food poisoning?

take as long as 72 hours. The usual incubation period is 12–48 hours.

Bacteria

Many types of bacteria cause food poisoning, and the incubation periods, symptoms and methods of control vary accordingly. Most bacteria are killed by thorough heating, but some, such as Clostridium botulinum, produce spores which survive high cooking temperatures.

Food poisoning bacteria	Possible sources
Salmonella	Poultry, eggs, meat
Staphylococcus	Food handlers
Clostridium	Raw foods such as vegetables and meat
Bacillus	Cereals, especially rice
Campylobacter	Infected animals, birds and unpasteurised milk
Listeria	Raw, processed and cooked foods, for example, soft cheese
E. coli	Cattle, raw meat and raw milk

△ **Table 11.6** Bacteria which cause food poisoning

Key terms

Salmonella – a type of food-poisoning bacteria

Clostridium – a form of bacterial food-poisoning

Listeria – common food-poisoning bacteria

Bacteria multiply or reproduce by binary fusion. They require the following conditions to grow:

○ *Warmth* – bacteria thrive at temperatures between 37°C and 63°C – known as the danger zone. Temperatures above 72°C will destroy most bacteria, so food should be cooked until it is piping hot – hotter than 72°C for two minutes.
○ *Moisture (liquid)* – this is one reason why dried foods have such a long shelf life.
○ *Food* – bacteria prefer foods that are high in protein and are moist, that is, high-risk foods such as cooked meat and poultry, raw fish, cooked rice.
○ *Time* – in the right conditions bacteria can multiply quickly in a very short time.

The bacteria that cause food poisoning are called pathogenic bacteria. Most food poisoning is caused by bacterial contamination, which occurs for some of the following reasons:

○ poor personal hygiene standards of food handlers
○ poor hygiene during the production and serving of food
○ cross-contamination between raw foods and cooked foods, for example, raw meat to cooked ham
○ storage of high-risk foods at room temperature
○ poor preparation and cooking routines, such as:
  ○ not thawing foods properly
  ○ preparing food too far in advance
  ○ undercooking high-risk foods, for example, chicken
  ○ not allowing foods to cool before putting them in chill cabinets or freezers – 90 minutes to chill below 8°C
  ○ not reheating foods to the correct temperature (over 72°C) for a long enough time
  ○ keeping 'hot' foods below 63°C
  ○ leaving food on display at room temperature for longer than the maximum safe period of four hours
  ○ not checking temperatures accurately.

Use a temperature probe for food. Check thermometers in the refrigerator and freezer.

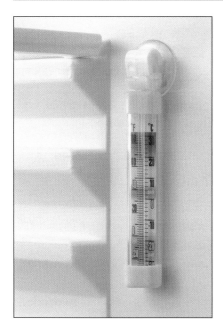

△ **Figure 11.19** Check the temperature of your refrigerator

Cross-contamination

During food processing, micro-organisms can transfer from raw to cooked foods, causing infection. This is known as cross-contamination.

To prevent cross-contamination you must avoid:

○ allowing raw and cooked foods to touch each other, for example, raw chicken and boiled ham

○ allowing the blood and juices of raw foods to drip onto cooked foods, for example, putting raw meat above cooked foods in the refrigerator

○ allowing bacteria to be transferred during handling or preparation, for example, from hands, work surfaces, equipment or clothing.

Rules for food hygiene

1. Wash hands thoroughly before handling food and between handling different types of food.

2. Keep raw and cooked foods separate and use different equipment to prepare them.

3. Pay particular attention to personal hygiene and wear clean protective clothing, cover cuts and never cough or sneeze over food.

△ **Figure 11.20** Hand washing

4. Keep all working surfaces and utensils clean. Use antibacterial spray for this.

5. Cover and cool all cooked food rapidly and refrigerate as quickly as possible. Store below 5 °C.

6. Do not put hot foods in the refrigerator as it will raise the temperature of all the foods in the refrigerator.

7. Keep pets away from food preparation areas.

8. Take care over waste disposal. Keep bins covered and empty and wash them regularly.

△ **Figure 11.21** Would these bins be acceptable in your kitchen?

9. Keep flies out of the kitchen

10. Reheat all food thoroughly, above the danger point of 63 °C, taking great care to avoid 'cold spots' in food heated in microwaves by turning and moving the food.

Exam practice questions

1. Knives must be used and stored correctly to avoid accidents and cross-contamination. Using a chart like Table 11.17, place the following statements under the correct heading.

Keep knives sharp
Cut on a chopping board
Use different knives for raw and cooked food
Store correctly in a knife box
Pass a knife by the handle

To avoid accidents	To avoid cross-contamination

△ **Table 11.17** Avoiding trouble

[5 marks]

2. State **four** safety rules you should follow when using electrical equipment. **[4 marks]**

3. State **two** hygiene and safety checks that a food manufacturer could carry out when choosing and buying ingredients. **[4 marks]**

4. State **three** hygiene and safety checks that a food manufacturer could carry out when preparing food. **[6 marks]**

5. Name the piece of equipment that could be used to test the internal temperature of food. **[1 mark]**

6. Define the term 'high-risk foods'. **[3 marks]**

7. State **two** symptoms of food poisoning. **[2 marks]**

8. Match the food poisoning bacteria with its correct possible source:

salmonella	rice
bacillus	eggs
listeria	raw vegetables
clostridium	food handlers
e.colio	infected animals
campylobacter	raw meat
staphylococcus	soft cheese **[7 marks]**

9. Explain what you understand by the term 'cross-contamination'. **[3 marks]**

10. Draw and label **three** items of protective clothing a food handler could wear. **[6 marks]**

Activities

1. Look at the rules for food hygiene. Select at least four.
Using the information, design a poster that could be displayed to inform people of the rules that should be followed when working with food.

2. Buffet food is usually high-risk food. Design and make a new food product suitable for a buffet party that is not going to be high-risk.

11.6 Safe food handling in the food industry

What is risk assessment?

Risk assessment means making an assessment of any risk to a food product during its production, and the required action to ensure the safety of the food.

The risk assessment system used within the food industry is known as the Hazard Analysis and Critical Control Point (HACCP). HACCP identifies specific hazards and risks associated with food production and describes how these hazards and risks can be controlled.

Many food companies now use the HACCP system to help with safe food production. All stages of the food process are assessed, from the raw materials, through the making process to the distribution and sale of the food product.

What is a hazard?

In food production, a **hazard** is anything that can cause harm to a consumer. For example, it could be:

○ biological, such as salmonella in chicken
○ chemical, such as cleaning chemicals in food
○ physical, such as glass or metal in food.

What is a risk?

In food production, the risk is the likelihood that a hazard might occur.

What is a critical control point?

A control point is the step in the making process where the hazards must be controlled. This step has to be carried out correctly to make sure that the hazard is removed or reduced to a safe level. Some hazards, such as micro-biological hazards, are high risk. The control points for these hazards are called **critical control points** (CCPs), as it is critical (essential) that the hazard is removed or reduced because it could result in food poisoning.

Benefits of HACCP to the food industry

○ Predicts hazards.
○ Prevents problems rather than responding to problems as they occur.
○ Saves money by planning ahead.
○ Critical control points mean that people are focusing on the important problems.
○ Response can be rapid.
○ Supports due diligence, that is, by showing and proving that all reasonable precautions have been taken to prevent the offence arising.
○ All staff are involved with product safety.
○ Helps make safe food products.
○ Meets legal requirements for safety.

Look at the HACCP for making a chilli con carne in Table 11.8, which shows how hazards have been identified.

Hazard analysis helps us to think about what could go wrong and how to reduce risks. The process of identifying hazards and working out how to reduce or eliminate them is called a risk assessment.

Process	Hazards	Control measures	CCP	Tests for control
Cook raw kidney beans for 40 minutes and drain	Dangerous chemicals in raw beans	Must boil rapidly for 10 minutes	Yes	Cook the beans at the correct temperature and for the right amount of time
Collect beef and other ingredients	Beef could contain bacteria	Make sure beef is stored separately at 5 °C or below	Yes	Check that the refrigerator is at or below 5 °C
Fry beef and chopped onions	Undercooked beef can be dangerous. Could contain salmonella	Make sure meat is cooked until it turns brown	Yes	Visual check for browning of meat
Add tomato purée, chilli seasoning and beans. Cook for 20 minutes	Tomato purée may be old and mouldy. Food may be undercooked	Check food is within shelf life Cook for sufficient time to reach 70 °C or above	Yes	Visual check of the date marks Cook at the correct temperature and time
If to be reheated, cover and cool quickly	Food may get contaminated from other foods	Make sure food cools to below 8°C within 90 minutes	Yes	Cool food to the correct temperature in the correct amount of time
Reheat to piping hot	Bacteria may be present	Test to see if 72 °C at edge and centre.	Yes	Reheat to correct temperature

△ **Table 11.8** Hazard analysis of making and reheating chilli con carne

Exam practice questions

1. What do the letters HACCP stand for? **[5 marks]**

2. What do you understand by the following terms:
   ○ risk assessment?
   ○ hazard?
   ○ risk?
   ○ critical control point? **[4 marks]**

3. Give **two** ways in which HACCP is used in the food industry. **[2 marks]**

Activities

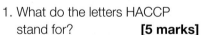

Draw a simple HACCP system for making a hard-boiled egg sandwich. Use the following processes to help you design the HACCP:

○ Store sandwich ingredients.
○ Boil the egg until hard, then cool in cold water.
○ Mash the egg with bottled mayonnaise for the filling.
○ Make the sandwiches.
○ Store the sandwiches for eating.

11.7 **Food safety and the law**

Several laws cover the regulations for the preparation, storage and sale of food. You will find it useful if you can identify and understand the main pieces of legislation.

The food industry has to be responsible for making sure its customers are protected from harm by using high standards of food safety.

Food Safety Act 1990

This Act ensures that all food produced in the food industry is safe to eat. All stages of food production are covered. The Local Authority and the Environmental Health Authority have the authority to enter premises and inspect food production methods.

Food Safety (General Food Hygiene) Regulations 1995

The regulations aim to ensure that there are common food hygiene rules across the EU. They affect anyone who runs a food business and ensure high standards of hygiene in the preparation and selling of food products.

Key points covered by the Food Safety (General Food Hygiene) Regulations 1995

- Food premises should be clean and in good repair.
- All preparation surfaces must be smooth, and easy to clean and disinfect.
- Design and layout of the premises should allow adequate cleaning and disinfection.
- Food areas must have adequate lighting and ventilation.
- Floors and walls must be non-absorbent and stay clean. Ceilings must be designed to minimise condensation and prevent the growth of moulds.
- Opening windows should be designed to prevent insects getting in, or be covered with a screen.

△ **Figure 11.22** A university canteen

- A pest control policy must be in place.
- Quality control checks must be carried out on ingredients.
- Food must be stored in hygienic conditions and protected from contamination.
- There should be adequate toilets and wash-hand basins.
- A supply of drinking water must be available when preparing and cooking foods.
- Core temperatures of food to be recorded during cooking.
- Equipment to be colour-coded.
- Equipment and packaging must be clean and made of a material that is easily disinfected.
- Food waste must be regularly removed from areas.
- Bins must be kept in good condition, fitted with lids and kept away from food stores and equipment. Bins should be easy to clean and disinfect.
- All food handlers must maintain a good standard of personal hygiene.
- Food handlers must wear appropriate, clean, protective clothing.
- Food handlers suffering from illness must not work in food areas. If feeling ill while at work they must report to their supervisor, who will send them home.
- Food handlers to change protective clothing and rewash/sanitise their hands when moving from low-risk to high-risk areas.

- All food handlers must be properly trained in food hygiene.
- Vehicles used to transport food must be clean, in good condition and designed to allow for cleaning and disinfection.
- Temperature-controlled vehicles must be designed so that the temperature can easily be monitored and controlled. Food should be stored at a temperature that will prevent the growth of micro-organisms. This means below 8 °C in a refrigerated van or below −18 °C in a freezer van.
- A distribution system should be established to record the orders and delivery dates.

The main offences

Selling or keeping for sale food which:

- is unfit for human consumption
- has been made harmful to health
- is contaminated
- is not of the nature, substance or quality expected
- is falsely or misleadingly presented.

The law is enforced by the local environmental health officer and the Trading Standards officer.

△ **Figure 11.23** The environmental health officer

Registration

Any premises where food is being prepared for sale, including vans selling ice cream or hot dogs, must be registered.

△ **Figure 11.24** Ice-cream vans must be registered

The Food Safety (Temperature Control) Regulations 1995

Some foods must be kept at controlled temperatures during preparation, transporting and storage, in order to help to control the spread of harmful micro-organisms such as listeria and salmonella, as these can cause very serious food poisoning. These micro-organisms grow rapidly at room temperature and foods must, therefore, be kept either very hot or very cold.

From 1 April 1991 a list of foods was given which must be kept either below 8 °C or above 63 °C if already cooked and waiting to be eaten.

The regulations clarify the three systems of temperature control as follows:

Chill-holding requirements

Any food which is likely to support growth of pathogenic micro-organisms or the formation of toxins must be kept at a temperature below 8 °C.

Hot-holding requirements

Food that has been cooked and needs to be kept hot must be at a temperature above 63 °C in order to control the growth of micro-organisms.

△ **Figure 11.25** Keeping hot food at the correct temperature – above 63 °C

Date marking

Virtually all foods, including frozen and canned foods, now have to carry date marks, in the form of either 'use by' or 'best before' dates.

Knowledge link
See page 143 on food labelling for further explanation.

If these Acts are followed, food businesses will have satisfied customers, a good reputation and, consequently, increased business. There will be less wastage of food, because food will have an increased shelf life, resulting in higher profits.

If the Acts are not followed this could result in food poisoning outbreaks, which might be fatal, resulting in complaints from customers that are difficult to defend. This could lead to civil action from the food-poisoning sufferers, which may in turn lead to fines and legal action costs.

Exam practice questions

1. The Food Safety (Temperature Control) Regulations 1995 outline three systems of temperature control. Give the temperature that this piece of legislation states for:
   ○ chill-holding
   ○ hot-holding
   ○ reheating. **[3 marks]**

2. Explain the benefits to a food manufacturer of following food hygiene and safety legislation. **[6 marks]**

Activity

Using the information in Table 11.9, create a mind map/bubble diagram to help you understand the implications of health and safety legislation for both the manufacturer and the consumer.

Relevant point	Explanation	Example/evidence
Ensures high standards of personal hygiene	Prevents contamination Prevents food poisoning	Protective clothing worn by workers No jewellery/nail varnish, and so on
Ensures high standards of safety	Control of high-risk foods, foreign bodies Health and safety of workers	Named high-risk food Any physical accident

△ **Table 11.9**

Cont.

Relevant point	Explanation	Example/evidence
Prevents cross-contamination	From raw to cooked foods	Raw meat to cooked meat Colour-coded equipment Safety of machinery
Staff training	Staff must all undergo training before being employed in the food chain	Foundation certificate in food hygiene
HACCP procedures	Assess and monitor risks	Any named control
Ensures appropriate control of high-risk foods	Temperature control in freezing/transportation/refrigerator/cooking/reheating	Any named temperature example Refrigerator 8 °C or below Freezer below −18 °C Cooking above 72 °C
Safety of equipment, machinery, storage equipment, transport	Equipment must be checked and cleaned regularly using sanitiser or disinfectant	Meat slicer, and so on Any suitable equipment
Microbial analysis must be carried out	Samples are taken regularly and checked in a laboratory	Any suitable named food product Food poisoning
Premises are inspected	Environmental health officers can visit at any time	Premises can be closed down if they are not up to the correct standard
Manufacturers must provide evidence of safe practices	Products are tracked through the factory	Cook-chilled products Batch numbers
Food labelling	Specific information must be included on labels	Contact details of manufacturer Storage instructions Reheating instructions Use by/sell by dates
Consumers have the legal right to complain	Legal action can be taken if there is a fault in a product	Any suitable example Fly in a loaf of bread
Good standards Poor standards	High reputation Closed down Fined	Increased sales Lose/poor sales Bankruptcy Product recall

△ **Table 11.9** *continued*

Stretch yourself

Describe the role of the environmental health officer in ensuring that food is safe to eat.

Key points

o Safety and hygiene rules should be followed when using tools and equipment.
o Cases of food poisoning are increasing.
o Food poisoning can result if food is not prepared, cooked and stored properly.
o Potential hazards are identified using a system known as HACCP.
o Hazards can be biological, chemical and physical.
o Many laws protect consumers and help to provide safe food.
o Rules and regulations support the preparation, cooking and storage of food so that it is safe to eat.

> ## Learning objectives
>
> By the end of this section you should have developed a knowledge and understanding of:
>
> - commercial food production methods: job/craft; batch production; mass production; continuous flow
> - how CAD and CAM can be used within food manufacturing
> - how quality control checks are used to produce consistent food products
> - how control checks can prevent problems in food production.

Introduction

Many manufacturers now use **computer-aided design (CAD)** and **computer-aided manufacture (CAM)** during the designing and manufacture of both the food product and the packaging. Quality assurance and quality control procedures are used in the food industry to set standards which meet consumer demands and expectations.

> ## Key terms
>
> **Computer-aided design (CAD)** – using computers for designing during food production, for example, packaging
>
> **Computer aided manufacture (CAM)** – using computers to control machinery during food production, for example, temperatures during baking

12.1 **Commercial production methods**

Several production methods are used in the food industry. The method used depends on the food product being produced. When selecting the best method of production, a food manufacturer would consider the following points:

- the number of food products to be made
- how often, for example, every day, weekly

- type of equipment available
- cost of the final product
- number of workers available
- level of skill of the workers
- money available for investment in new equipment/machinery.

One-off job/craft production

This is used when a single product is made, for instance, a wedding cake or novelty birthday cake.

> ## Key term
>
>
>
> **Job/craft production** – the production of a single product

Benefits of one-off production

- An individual or unique finished product.
- A high-quality product.

Limitations of one-off production

- Skilled staff required.
- Can take a long time to manufacture, as more processes are carried out by hand rather than machines.
- Can be expensive.

Batch production

This production system is used when small numbers of identical or similar products are

△ **Figure 12.1** Wedding cake

made. For example, each day a small bakery may make batches of Chelsea buns, bread rolls and teacakes.

Key term

Batch production – production of a specific number of a group of similar products at the same time

△ **Figure 12.2** Preparing bread using batch production

Benefits of batch production

o Small orders can be made.
o The same equipment can be used to make a variety of products.
o Slight adaptations can be made, without incurring too much cost, to meet consumer demand or to create consumer interest.
o Different fillings can be added to fruit pies.
o Different flavourings can be added to biscuits – chocolate, lemon, ginger.
o Different decorations can be used for icing cakes.
o Raw materials and components may be purchased in bulk, therefore reducing the cost.
o Only a small number of people are involved.
o Production costs are reduced as more products can be made in the same time it takes to make a one-off product.

Limitations

Waste can be high if the process fails.

Mass production

This production system is used when large numbers of one product are manufactured on an assembly line, for example, white sliced loaves, digestive biscuits, potato crisps, sandwiches.

o The manufacturing process is split into tasks and sequenced into an assembly line. Conveyor belts move the food product from one stage to the next as it is assembled.
o At each stage, specialised equipment or line operators carry out the tasks.

Key term

Mass production – producing products in a large quantity

Benefits of mass production

o Orders can be met quickly and efficiently.
o Raw materials and components are purchased in bulk, thereby reducing the cost.

△ **Figure 12.3** A mass-produced product

○ There is a low ratio of workers to the number of products produced, and workers do not have to be highly skilled.
○ Parts or all of the production line can be automated.
○ Large numbers of a product can be manufactured at a low cost.
○ After a large run is finished the production line may be adjusted to make another product.

> Key term
> **Assembled** – the component parts of a product put together

Limitations

○ Maintenance routines and checks must be very thorough and regular to avoid a breakdown, which would be very expensive to the company in terms of lost production.
○ Initial set-up is expensive, as large-scale, specialist equipment is required.
○ Many of the tasks carried out by workers can be repetitive and boring.

Continuous-flow production

This production system is computer-controlled and extends mass production by producing one specific product continuously, 24 hours a day, seven days a week, every year, in large quantities, for example, soft drinks, milk.

△ **Figure 12.4** A continuous-flow production line

> Key term
> **Continuous-flow production** – computer-controlled, producing products 24 hours a day, 7 days a week, 52 weeks a year

Benefits of continuous-flow production

○ Inexpensive to run once set up.
○ High-quality product is produced.
○ Small workforce is needed.
○ A consistent product is produced.
○ Orders can be met quickly and efficiently.
○ Raw materials and components are purchased in bulk, thereby reducing the cost.

Limitations

○ Maintenance routines and checks must be very thorough and regular to avoid a breakdown, which would be very expensive to the company in terms of lost production.
○ Initial set-up is expensive, as large-scale, specialist equipment is required.
○ Many of the tasks carried out by workers can be repetitive and boring.

12.2 Computer-aided design

Computers can play an important role in collecting and analysing information about the market sector. For example, they may be used in:

o desk research – looking at statistics over time to see if the market is growing in size; what products are already available; the value of the market; popular eating trends

o carrying out and analysing data from sensory evaluation tests for appearance, taste, texture, colour, saltiness or spiciness – helps to set the criteria for a successful product

o modelling costs/nutritional analysis/ratio and proportions of ingredients

o designing packaging and labels, advertising.

Advantages/benefits of using CAD

o Gives greater accuracy, for example, when working out the nutritional analysis of a product.

o Gives a professional finish, for example, graphics/artwork on food packaging.

o Allows certain tasks to be completed quickly, for example, speeds up the drawing process when producing annotated drawings of food products; graphs when presenting results from a questionnaire; graphical work for packaging.

o Colours and graphic effects can be modelled and tried out and the best ones chosen. The design can be varied easily if any of the details change or if special promotional offers are added.

o Modelling of a recipe can be carried out quickly and without wasting money actually trialling the product, for example, experimenting with different ingredients.

o Designs can be quickly sent by email, from the design stage to the manufacturing stage.

12.3 Computer aided manufacture

Production process systems are becoming increasingly automated and controlled by computers. The whole production line may be fully automated or large sections of the line may be involved.

How can CAD be used in food technology?

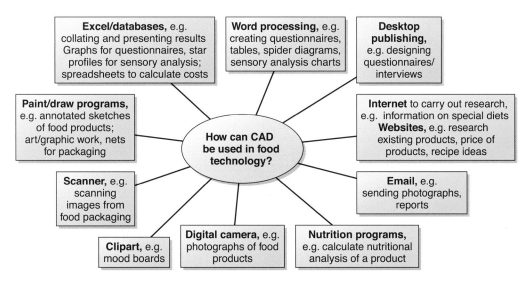

△ **Figure 12.5** Using CAD in the food industry

Automated manufacture is often referred to as computer-aided manufacture.

12.4 How computers can help to produce consistent food products

Computers are used to monitor the commercial production of food products.

Computer sensors monitor pH levels (levels of acids and alkalis). Acids and alkalis have an effect on the flavour, texture, appearance and nutritional value of food. For example:

○ foods with a high acidic level (like fruits) can cause mixtures to curdle, for example, if lemon juice is added before a sauce is made the milk would curdle; tomatoes can affect the consistency of a sauce, making it thin
○ foods with a low acidic level (like milk) may need to have their acidic level raised to ensure a smooth texture, for example, with yoghurt.

△ **Figure 12.6** Preparing dough for bread using computer-controlled equipment

Key term

Critical control point (CCP) – a point in production at which a food safety hazard can be reduced to a safe level

Advantages/benefits of using CAM	Examples
Saves time	Repetitive tasks can be carried out quickly, for example, cutting out several pastry tops rather than doing them one by one
Standardises production	Process can be repeated with accuracy and precision so a consistent finish is maintained, for example, consistent thickness of biscuits
Increases productivity	More products can be made at speed, resulting in lower costs, for example, white sliced bread
Increases reliability of finished products	All stages of production are controlled, and if products are below standard they are automatically rejected, for example, insufficient maillarding of bread products
Monitors the production system	Monitored through sensors which detect and record **critical control points**, for example, weight, temperature, colour, pH, tolerances, thickness and moisture changes in a product
Reduces need for storage	A 'just-in-time' system can be used, that is, nothing is made in advance and stored; made in response to consumer demand and delivered to maintain stock in the shops

△ **Table 12.1** Advantages of using CAM

Cont.

Advantages/benefits of using CAM	Examples
Increases safety	Workers will not be required to carry out hazardous tasks, for example, cutting processes
High standard of packaging can be produced and maintained	Cutting of packaging nets Printing labelling information on the packaging
Data handling can deal with the large amount of information	Monitoring of complex production schedules, for example, HACCP schedule, stock control

△ **Table 12.1** Advantages of using CAM *continued*

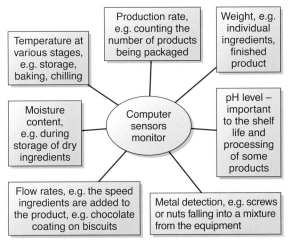

△ **Figure 12.7** How computers control and monitor the commercial production of food products

Ways computers are used in food production

Some manufacturers are now using computerised systems to assist in the control and monitoring of:

○ the sorting and grading of raw materials, for example, fruit and vegetables
○ the weight of the product before packaging
○ seals on packaging
○ colour and shade of finished products, for example, degree of brownness of bread products

○ decorations and shapes through visual images stored on the computer, for example, positioning of toppings on cakes
○ the bacterial content of products
○ stock control of raw ingredients and components.

However, visual checks are still carried out by the workers. Spot checks are carried out at any stage of the production line to check for quality and consistency.

 Controlled assessment link
As part of your development work in the Controlled Assessment, you need to plan for the manufacture of your product. Figure 14.9 on page 234 identifies considerations for mass-producing a product.

The effects on the workforce of introducing CAM into food production

If a food manufacturer decided to buy as much computerised equipment for the factory as possible there would be a number of effects on the workforce:

○ Staff will need training in how to operate the computerised equipment.

o The number of people employed will probably be reduced – the machines will do the job(s) of people, particularly lower-paid jobs.
o Individual staff costs may be higher because they have more responsible and skilled jobs.
o Highly trained computer operatives will be required.
o Engineers will be required.
o There will be problems if the computer system breaks down – staff may not be able to work.
o Jobs available could become monotonous and boring as people are less involved.

△ **Figure 12.8** Baking doughnuts using a computerised temperature-control system

12.5 **Quality assurance**

The word 'assurance' means 'a level of guarantee'.

Food manufacturers set criteria or specifications for every stage during the designing and manufacturing of food products so that the products are manufactured to agreed standards. The manufacturer then knows that the consumer will be supplied with food products that are safe to eat and of a reliable standard.

We know that when we buy these products we will get safe, good-quality products.

Quality assurance

Quality assurance checks might include:

o specification checks
o hygiene procedures
o monitoring waste
o sensory analysis.

Key terms

Quality assurance – a system that lays down procedures for making a safe, quality product

Quality control – a way of checking the quality of a product during or at the end of the production system

Quality control

In the food industry **quality control** is part of the quality assurance system. It involves checking the standards of a food product at three stages: as it is being designed, during manufacture and at the end of manufacture. It will also include the critical control points established as part of the HACCP procedure. Quality control checks ensure that the product meets the product specification.

Here is a list of quality control checks made on a batch of biscuits:

o Weighing biscuit ingredients – to obtain the correct consistency
o Mixing dough to the correct consistency – to have an even texture
o Rolling out the thickness of the dough – to obtain equal depth in the biscuits
o Cutting dough into accurate portions/portion control on extruder – to obtain equal/exact size/same shape of biscuits
o Temperature control of the product/use of food probe – to ensure bacteria is controlled/ even cooking for colour and crispness
o Time control during cooking – to ensure even cooking for colour and crispness.
o Colour sensor for cooked biscuits – to guarantee even colour

- Cooling time – to ensure standard degree of crispness (non-soggy)
- Counting into packages – to get correct numbers
- Sealing packages – to exclude air to keep biscuits crisp
- Metal detector – to make sure there are no foreign bodies
- Weighing finished biscuits – for equal products

- Moisture sensor – to ensure correct degree of crispness
- Monitoring the rate of production – the quantity/consistency of biscuits produced
- Alerting to any problems in the system – the quality of the biscuits
- Checking the number of biscuits made – to reorder the ingredients/stock

Exam practice questions

1. State what is meant by the letters CAD and CAM. **[2 marks]**
2. Give **two** examples of how CAD is used in the development of a new product. **[2 marks]**
3. Give **two** examples of how CAM is used in the development of a new product. **[2 marks]**
4. State **two** benefits of using CAD and **two** benefits of using CAM. **[4 marks]**
5. Copy and complete Table 12.2 to show how computer sensors can be used to monitor the commercial production of food products. **[7 marks]**

Computer sensors	Example
Metal detection	
pH level	
Flow rate	
Moisture content	
Temperature	
Weight	
Production rate	

△ **Table 12.2** How sensors are used in the food industry

6. You are asked to produce a batch of 50 cheese and onion pasties. State **three** ways you could ensure that all the pasties were identical. **[3 marks]**
7. Explain what is meant by (a) quality assurance and (b) quality control. **[4 marks]**

Activities

1. Create a visual representation of the different commercial production methods. This could be done by producing a table (see Table 12.3), bubble diagram or mind map. The information you produce should include:

   o the names of the different commercial production methods
   o their benefits and limitations
   o at least one example of a product that can be made by each method.

Production method	Benefits	Limitations	Example(s) of food products
Job/Craft			

△ **Table 12.3** Different commercial production methods

2. Copy and complete Table 12.4 to show the control measures you would use to ensure that each batch of cheese scones is of an identical standard.

Process for cheese scones	Control measure
Weighing and measuring ingredients	
Rubbing fat into the flour	
Grating cheese	
Rolling out the dough	
Cutting out the scones	
Baking the scones	

△ **Table 12.4** Control measures

3. Look at the following control system for making cake bars. For each stage of making, a control has been given, so the cake bars can be made to a consistently high standard. In pairs or small groups, discuss the following jumbled-up statements which explain why each control needs to be in place. Decide which statement fits each stage of making and record your answers in Table 12.5.

   Reasons:

   (a) Correct amount of air is added.
   (b) Ensure high standards of personal hygiene.
   (c) Same thickness of cake.
   (d) Ensure the same appearance each time.
   (e) Ensure same degree of browning and that cake is thoroughly cooked.
   (f) Prevent cake sticking to the tin.
   (g) Remove lumps and increase air.
   (h) Prevent curdling and a heavy-textured cake.
   (i) Achieve identical results each time the cake is made.   *Cont.*

Activities *continued*

(j) Accurate temperature.

(k) Prevent air from being knocked out.

(l) Same size bars each time.

Stage of making	Control	Reason
Preparing self	Wear apron, wash hands, and so on	
Weigh ingredients	Use electronic scales	
Preparation of cooker	Heat oven to 180 °C/gas mark 4	
Preparing Swiss roll tin	Grease the tin	
Creaming margarine and sugar	Electric mixer, full speed for 3½ minutes	
Adding beaten egg	Drop by drop, beating well after each addition	
Adding flour	Sieve	
Mixing in flour	Fold in with tablespoon	
Placing in tin	28 cm × 18 cm	
Baking cake	15–20 minutes	
Cutting the bars	14 bars 9 cm × 4 cm	
Decorating cake bars	Spread on butter cream to edges of bars	

△ **Table 12.5** Control system   *Cont.*

Activities *continued*

Melting moments

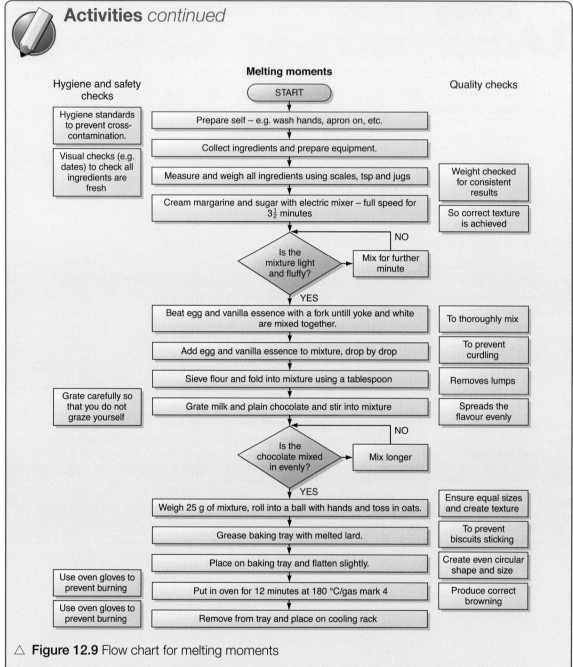

Hygiene and safety checks		Quality checks

START

Prepare self – e.g. wash hands, apron on, etc.

Hygiene standards to prevent cross-contamination.

Collect ingredients and prepare equipment.

Visual checks (e.g. dates) to check all ingredients are fresh

Measure and weigh all ingredients using scales, tsp and jugs

Weight checked for consistent results

Cream margarine and sugar with electric mixer – full speed for $3\frac{1}{2}$ minutes

So correct texture is achieved

Is the mixture light and fluffy? — NO → Mix for further minute

YES

Beat egg and vanilla essence with a fork untill yoke and white are mixed together.

To thoroughly mix

Add egg and vanilla essence to mixture, drop by drop

To prevent curdling

Sieve flour and fold into mixture using a tablespoon

Removes lumps

Grate carefully so that you do not graze yourself

Grate milk and plain chocolate and stir into mixture

Spreads the flavour evenly

Is the chocolate mixed in evenly? — NO → Mix longer

YES

Weigh 25 g of mixture, roll into a ball with hands and toss in oats.

Ensure equal sizes and create texture

Grease baking tray with melted lard.

To prevent biscuits sticking

Place on baking tray and flatten slightly.

Create even circular shape and size

Use oven gloves to prevent burning

Put in oven for 12 minutes at 180 °C/gas mark 4

Produce correct browning

Use oven gloves to prevent burning

Remove from tray and place on cooling rack

△ **Figure 12.9** Flow chart for melting moments

4. Figure 12.9 shows an example of a flow chart for melting moments that includes hygiene, safety and quality checks. Using a product you will be making, design a flow chart that includes hygiene, safety and quality checks.

Stretch yourself

Food products can be manufactured by different production methods. Discuss the points a food manufacturer should consider when selecting the best method of production.

Key points

○ Computers are used in a variety of ways in the food industry.

○ Computers are used for designing and manufacturing food products.

○ Necessary controls need to be put in place by food manufacturers.

○ Job/craft production is used when products are made specifically for one occasion.

○ Batch production is used when a specific quantity of a certain product is required.

○ Mass production is used when products are made in large quantities.

○ Continuous-flow production is used when the same product is made non-stop, for 24 hours a day.

○ Quality assurance means 'a level of guarantee' or 'positive declaration'.

○ Quality control is part of the quality assurance system which involves checking the standards of a food product during designing, manufacture and at the end of manufacture. Control checks ensure that the product meets the product specification and is of a quality standard.

○ 'Just in time' is a system which means that nothing is made in advance and stored.

 Learning objectives

By the end of this chapter you should have developed a knowledge and understanding of:

- the advantages and disadvantages of genetically modified foods to producers and consumers
- the role of modified starches in foods
- the importance of functional foods to producers and consumers
- how new technologies are used to produce new foods and ingredients.

13.1 **Genetically modified foods**

The use of new technology in the food industry is controversial, especially products made by modifying or engineering the genetic make-up of food. This might actually improve the quality of the food, for instance, blackcurrants can be modified to make them higher in vitamin C, tomatoes can be modified to improve their flavour or keeping qualities. It is now possible to 'switch off' the gene that is responsible for making a tomato go soft when it is ripe, thus making the tomato last longer. The most commonly grown genetically modified crops are potatoes, oilseed rape, sugar beet, maize and tomatoes. In animals it may mean that farmers can produce less fatty meat and animals can grow faster or be more fertile.

Advantages of genetically modified (GM) foods are:

- improvements to quantity and quality of food.
- can grow in adverse conditions, for example, drought
- herbicide and insect resistance
- high nutritional quality
- cheaper to produce.

However, there are concerns about GM foods:

- long-term safety is unknown
- environmental concerns, as the pollen does not stop in one place
- ethics – we need adequate labelling; from

January 2000 if a product has over 1 per cent of GM food it must be stated on the label (under 1 per cent does not need to be stated)
- there is a lack of communication between provider and consumer.

△ **Figure 13.1** Genetically modified crops

 Activity

Carry out research to find out what common foods contain GM ingredients.

13.2 Modified starches

In section 2.1 (page 60) we looked at the function of starches in food. Manufacturers often use modified starches in food products to improve the quality of foods. The most common types of foods that include modified starches are:

- frozen foods
- ready-made meals
- microwave meals
- sauces
- dressings
- soups
- desserts
- snacks.

Modified starches are available in many forms as maize, wheat, potato, oat and tapioca starches. They undergo a range of processes to alter them structurally in order to give specific properties. Examples of when modified starches are used are:

- in ready meals – to prevent sauces separating, so that the desired sauce thickness is maintained
- in instant soups/Pot Noodles – to produce a thick sauce as soon as hot liquid is added – no further heating is required
- in cold, gelling desserts – a cold liquid is added and the mixture thickens
- to stabilise emulsions so that they do not separate, for example, low-fat spreads, salad dressings.

△ **Figure 13.2** Examples of foods containing modified starches

13.3 Functional foods

Functional foods are foods that have health-promoting benefits over and above their basic nutritional value. Many foods are promoted in the supermarket as 'functional foods' because they contribute to good health.

Below are some examples of functional foods.

Probiotic foods

These include food ranges such as Yakult, Actimel and Müller Petit Filous yoghurts and drinks. These foods contain large numbers of naturally occurring live bacteria. These bacteria are often known as 'good' or 'friendly' bacteria. It is thought that they help to:

- maintain a healthy digestive system
- strengthen the immune system.

Prebiotic foods

These contain a carbohydrate which the digestive system cannot break down. They occur naturally in some foods, for example, leeks, onions and asparagus. Prebiotics help feed the good bacteria in the digestive system. They can improve the health of the digestive system.

Plant sterols and stanols

These help to reduce the absorption of cholesterol from the gut, therefore lowering cholesterol levels. Plant sterols are found in small amounts in fruits, vegetables, vegetable oils, grains, nuts and seeds. Foods containing sterols and stanols include Benecol®, Danone and Flora pro.activ products.

There are many other foods that are considered functional foods because of the health benefits they have. The number is likely to increase as scientists carry out more investigations into the benefits of eating certain foods.

△ **Figure 13.3** Examples of functional foods

13.4 **Nanotechnology**

Food experts are always seeking new sources of and novel uses for existing raw materials and ingredients, especially those containing healthy components and ones that will improve the quality of our food. One of the latest trends is nanotechnology, which is affecting all aspects of technology in a variety of materials. It is working with materials at a microscopic level.

In food science and technology, food is manipulated to one-billionth of a metre in scale. Its uses include:

○ nano-emulsions, which are being used to create double emulsions, which improve the texture of sauces
○ nano-food synthesisers, which can create or alter food molecules
○ nano-capsule protection, which can deliver a fortifying nutrient to our body, which can be released slowly, or can release a controlled flavour into a drink
○ nano-sensors, which record the changes in pH, temperature or the presence of pathogens
○ nano-bots, which are minute, microbe-destroying robots that can make food safe.

13.5 **Food trends**

The number of new food products and the range of foods available have increased as influences on consumers' lifestyles affect their food choices. You will know about new products in the supermarket that you have noticed recently, and perhaps you can think of some that have disappeared!

Health benefit	Functional food
Healthy digestive and immune system	Probiotic yogurts
Reduces the risk of heart disease	Omega-3 fatty acids found in oily fish such as mackerel
Reducing the risk of heart disease and blood cholesterol levels	Oats Soya products Products such as Benecol® and Flora pro.activ®
Urinary tract infections	Cranberries
Linked to reducing the risk of some cancers, for example, prostate cancer	Green tea Tomato and tomato products

△ **Table 13.1** How functional foods can benefit health

Recent trends

These are some of the food trends of the past few years:

○ An increase in the development of authentic ethnic foods – as we travel more around the world and learn about food from other cultures we want to try these dishes for ourselves.

○ More and more sandwiches are being eaten.

○ Traditional food products, such as bread and butter pudding and steamed puddings, have become more popular.

○ Healthy eating claims, especially low-fat or no-fat claims, are increasing.

○ The variety of vegetable dishes is increasing.

○ There are more new products targeted at children, for example, breakfast bars.

○ Organic foods and products suitable for vegetarians are increasing.

○ Party food is proving popular.

○ Healthier, low-fat versions of products are available.

○ There has been an increase in meals that can be taken at convenient times and are often eaten 'on the move'.

Trends for the future?

Here are some predictions for the future:

○ greater variety of choice and convenience, more products that can be cooked by microwave

○ demand for healthier foods and organic ingredients

○ greater demand for single portions

○ nostalgia products – food products from the past that will look and taste more 'home-made'

○ eco-friendly packaging

○ increased consumption of locally produced, sustainable foods

○ healthy ready meals targeted at children

○ innovative low-calorie products for weight-watchers

○ with heart disease and other diseases still a major issue, foods that can fight diseases are going to be popular

○ more indulgent foods, such as luxury desserts and chocolate products

○ less meat and a rise in the consumption of fruits, vegetables and whole grains

○ useful bacteria are going to gain entry into many other food items that are part of our daily diet

○ more snacking for busy people who just cannot stop for food

○ increase in the consumption of raw food in the form of salads and other enticing dishes (the benefits of raw food will be explored across the globe).

△ **Figure 13.4** Traditional steamed puddings with a new twist

 Stretch yourself

Investigate why natural foods have a better nutritional profile than processed foods.

Activities

1. Make a dish that illustrates the use of functional foods.

2. Using examples, write your own past and future food lists. Write your own ideas for the future.

3. Carry out a survey of people to find out what their favourite nostalgia food is. Ask older people what foods they can remember from the past. Write an article on nostalgia foods suitable to go in a food magazine.

4. Cook a traditional British pudding, but try to adapt it to meet the eatwell plate.

5. Plan a day's meals for an adult who is trying to reduce his or her cholesterol levels. Cook one of the dishes you have suggested.

Exam practice questions

1. Explain what is meant by a functional food. **[2 marks]**

2. List **three** functional foods that may help a person to reduce his or her blood cholesterol. **[3 marks]**

3. Explain what is meant by technology in relation to food products. **[4 marks]**

Introduction

The controlled assessment follows a journey of designing and making that has a strong focus on the practical. It begins with a task that is set in a context, and ends in a new product that is suited to the target group identified. There are 12 tasks to choose from, but your teacher will control the choice of task, and whichever task is selected will be known as the set task.

This chapter is about helping you to focus on what you need to do and why.

Here is an overview of the way marks are allocated for the controlled assessment. They are awarded for the completed project and not in a linear way. Guidance is clear:

	Maximum marks
Investigating the design opportunity	8
Development of design proposals	32
Making the design	32
Testing and evaluation	12
Communication	6
Total	**90**

△ **Table 14.1** How marks are allocated for controlled assessment

Remember that some of the marks relate to designing and some are for making and associated skills such as product analysis. The project should be evidence of 45 hours of work in total, with at least 20–25 hours spent on making activities. The project or record of your work should be completed within 20 pages, so it is important to be concise about what you record and how you record it.

In the following pages a clear guide will help you work through the controlled assessment task. Read each part carefully.

The project page indicator will help to structure the project. Read the following before you start.

14.1 **Preparation of the project pages**

On each project page include a title, giving the theme for the page. Alongside this, indicate an aim for that page as it helps the examiner to see what you are trying to show. Also briefly explain how you will achieve that aim, in other words, what your actions will be. It is useful to have your name and candidate number on each page too.

Showing photographic records of your progress is always desirable and it is *essential* that you photograph the final product.

So, each project page may include:

1. Title
2. Aim
3. Name
4. Actions explained
5. Evidence of your work, such as photographs, websites used, data notes.

In this chapter a route through the controlled assessment project is explained. You will find help at each stage in the following pattern:

○ Page indicators are given.
○ The title or theme is suggested so that it applies to any of the set tasks.
○ The aim is made clear and some information about the content of the page is given.
○ Where an example is provided, an accompanying commentary is given, to pick out the key points.

○ In some cases a 'strategy' or thinking tool is given to support you as you work.

○ A review of the page is given at the end so that you can check your work.

It is important to remember that these are only suggestions and that there are other ways to communicate your design-and-make journey, for example, using e-Portfolio systems.

14.2 **Working through the controlled assessment task**

Page 1

Title

The title of the page is 'Starting the controlled assessment in food technology'.

Aim

The aim here is to record carefully the design brief given by your teacher. This is the controlled assessment set task. Write out the context and the task. Your first steps should be to explain it in your own words and define keywords in the task. In this way you will come to understand the task and be able to see how you can make progress. The first page is also where you show a list of what research you need to do and why it will help you move through the task.

Commentary

In Figure 14.1 you can see how the student has set out her page clearly. The brief is shown and you can see the mind map which identifies aspects she has considered, such as health, cost, possible main ingredients and target group. Her understanding of the brief is clear and explained in her own words. She has shown some reasons for the research she intends to carry out. She has also made an attempt to start sorting out the criteria that will control what she chooses to do, as she has displayed some essential criteria for a school dinner product. This is a clear and well-ordered first page. An examiner would note that the student has identified her target group and look for links to the target group throughout the project.

Example

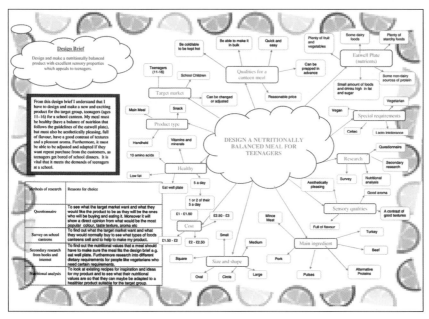

△ **Figure 14.1** Design brief and mind map

Content

○ Show the controlled assessment set task (the brief).
○ Define key terms.
○ Show evidence of thinking about the task.
○ Plan out research areas: some may be carried out immediately, some might be carried out later in the project.
○ Evidence any previous knowledge or key knowledge.

What does previous knowledge or key knowledge mean?

If you have a set task that asks you to create new cakes for a farmers' market using local ingredients, you may want to include evidence that you have had previous experience in cake making from your work in Year 9. You may well be aware of four differing methods of making cakes, such as the rubbing-in method, the creaming method, the melting method and the all-in-one method. If you tell the examiner this it is likely that you would not need to research cake making methods because you already have this *previous knowledge*. It would be more appropriate to use your research time for something else, such as studying the range of pre-packed cakes on sale locally and finding out their prices. Key knowledge might come from a starting point of the product analysis of existing farmers' market cakes.

Strategies to use when you are starting your project

1. Mind-map the task if this is easier for you
2. Use Socratic questions. This sounds complicated, but it just means use those questions beginning with W: 'What', 'Why', 'When' and even 'Where' or 'Who'.

Use the 'W' words in a chart to help you list your actions, with dates (see Table 14.2).

Review of page 1

Here are the actions you need to have completed on page 1:

○ Discuss the controlled assessment task (design brief). Think about it.
○ Using the computer if possible, write out your set task, as you may need a copy of it later in your project.
○ Record your previous knowledge from Year 9 or Year 10 food technology classes.
○ Make your plan for research using two different types as a minimum.

Pages 2 and 3

Title

Overview and evaluation of research

Aim

The aim on these pages is to demonstrate the way you link research to your set task.

Content

The page must evidence the following:

○ research for the controlled assessment that is applicable and accurate
○ evaluated research at the stage of the process when it is needed
○ identification of target group needs
○ at least two different types of research

What I need to research	Why this will help me	When I should do it by
Prices and types on sale	○ My products need to be priced competitively ○ I need to make 'unusual' or different products	By next lesson

△ **Table 14.2** Plan for research

○ use a maximum of two A3 pages for research evaluations

How do you go about researching?

All the controlled assessment tasks require you to make a new food product. The product must be suitable for a consumer. You must find out the needs of the consumer target group in some way. The way you do it is up to you. Suggested methods are using a short questionnaire or an interview, using questions as shown below.

Target group research

○ What type of food products do they need? A main meal, a snack, a showcase product or an everyday product?

○ What type of food storage method would suit their needs? A chilled item, a frozen or fresh item?

○ What sort of retail range would they desire for the product? Economy, low-budget, special treat, weekday meal, affordable luxury, splash-out expensive?

You can ask these questions to people who are in your target group. You do *not* need to create an elaborate questionnaire, as you do not need to include it in your project. Only include the evaluation from your questions, as these will guide your work.

Example

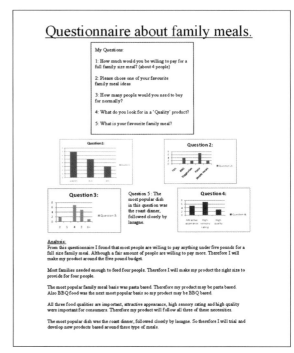

△ **Figure 14.2** Example of evaluation of questionnaire

Commentary

In Figure 14.2 you can see that the student has shown evaluation of the questionnaire she set. She has also explained the data and indicated how they help her focus the design of her new product.

Product research evaluation

Your research may include results from a supermarket survey, sometimes called existing product survey (see, for example, Figure 14.3). This is useful work. You may find out names of products, descriptions, packaging styles, weights and portions. These data can be included and presented in your research.

Example

NAME OF PRODUCT + DESCRIPTION	MAIN INGREDIENTS (percentage if given)	WEIGHT OF PACK	NUMBER IN PACK	COST PER PACK	COST PER 100 GRAM	KCAL CONTENT PER 100 GRAM	FAT CONTENT PER 100 GRAM	DESCRIPTION OF PACKAGING
Cheese and tomato pasta snack	Cooked Pasta (53%) (Water, Sieved Tomatoes (18%), Tomato and Basil Dressing (14%),	300g	n/a	£1.20	£0.40	173	6.8	Green labels covering a clear plastic container where the product was clearly displayed
Chicken fajita wrap-tortilla wrap containing chicken breast with mixed leaf and peppers.	Plain Tortilla (40%), Chicken Breast (20%), Fajita Vegetable Mix (13%),	185g	1	£2.00		142	2.2	Clear plastic packaging with a cardboard collar at the bottom of the product
British Fish and chips A white fish portion coated in crisp batter with a serving of chips.	Chips (58%), Alaska Pollack (22%), Wheat Flour, Vegetable Oil,	326g	1	£1.50	£0.37	205	8.6	Steaming product cut in half to see the cross section on a dark back ground
John West Tuna, sweet corn, pasta, crunchy water chestnuts and peppers with lime and cracked black pepper dressing.	Tuna (31%), Sweet corn (17%), Pasta Twists (14%),	240g	1	£2.15	£0.89	99	1.8	White background with product offset
Feasters chicken burger-Chargrilled, marinated whole chicken breast in a sesame seed bun with a sachet of mayonnaise.	Marinated chicken breast (46%) sesame seed bun (46%) mayonnaise (8%)	140g	1	£1.00	£0.71	206	5.1	Picture of the burger on a dark background with a green banner and drop of mayonnaise.
Spanish potato omelette- Spanish potato omelette with onion.	Potato (61%), Fresh Pasteurised Egg (24%), Onion (10%), Olive Oil, Salt	500g	1	£2.59	£0.51	121	6.8	Cardboard box with green and blue spots.

A chart to compare some existing products which could be suitable for selling in a school canteen (Supermarket survey)

△ **Figure 14.3** Analysis of existing products

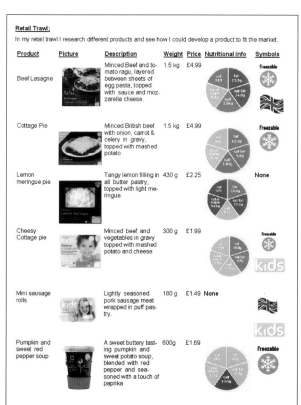

Example

◁ **Figure 14.4** A comparative shop

Commentary

Figure 14.3 is a thorough analysis of existing products that meet the needs of the target group. The evaluation is in depth – not only does it deal with the weight and the cost of the product, it also explores the cost, energy value and fat of a 100 g portion. Additionally, the packaging aspects have been considered.

Commentary

Figure 14.4 is another comparative shop. These are sometimes called a product trawl. It clearly shows use of ICT to capture images and also to gather data about the symbols and nutritional features that might appear on child-friendly products.

Nutritional research evaluation

For high marks it would be appropriate to include some nutritional research. This could be linked to your target group's needs or to existing food products, for example, the energy requirements of your target group or the healthy eating guidelines they might adhere to, such as reduction of saturated fat or excess salt. Alternatively, you may look at the amount of starchy carbohydrate in a range of pudding products in order to produce a dessert with similar nutritional values.

Recipe research evaluation

You must consider a range of 10–12 recipes that you might want to cook. Recipe research at this stage might be shown as a list of books used, websites visited or scanned pages. You need to come to a decision about dishes you may want to cook. At this stage recipes must be quickly checked and reviewed in the following way:

- o the number of servings or portions
- o the cost or expense involved
- o the availability of the ingredients
- o the cooking processes involved
- o the utensils or equipment required
- o the time it takes to cook – will it fit into the lesson time?

Later you will evaluate your recipes using the general design criteria.

Knowledge-based research evaluation

The topic comes from the context of the controlled assessment set task and will therefore vary. There are seven differing contexts and 12 set tasks with a clear focus. In Table 14.3 the knowledge-based research focus is provided.

Review of pages 2 and 3: Overview and evaluation of research

Aim to achieve up to four pieces of applied and accurate research.

Strategies to use when you are researching

Check you are showing evidence of at least two different methods of research as shown

- o Questionnaires: simple straightforward questions to find out the needs of the main target group of consumers
- o Data logging from existing products similar to the food product you plan to make
- o Interviews with your target group to gain insight into lifestyles and food choices
- o Internet-based research from websites of respected retail outlets or organisations
- o Using books for fact-finding research
- o Product analysis of existing products
- o Visits to discover and record findings such as farmers' markets, farm shops, retail outlets or school canteens.
- o The analysis and subsequent *evaluation* of your research is included.

Theme/context	Knowledge research focus
School products (two task options)	What makes a healthy school meal? What are the guidelines for meals for schoolchildren? Explore themed eating places and what type of food is served.
Farmers' markets (two task options)	When and where are they held and what sort of produce is sold? Are there any regulations about what is sold or how it is prepared? What are 'speciality foods'?
Ready-made products (three task options)	What health guidelines apply to food products? Which fruits and vegetables are popular in the UK? Where do they come from and when are they in season?
Children's food products (one task)	What is obesity and why should it be avoided? What is the energy value of food products? Which ingredients are low in calories and high in fibre?
Multicultural society (two task options)	What are the traditional foods of differing cultures? What does it mean to have fusion food and recipes? What is the availability of culturally themed eating in your town?
Faitrade (one task)	What does Fairtrade mean? What is the logo for Fairtrade? What sort of ingredients and products are Fairtrade? Why is Fairtrade important for our society?
Airline meals (one task)	What are the components of an airline meal? What sensory properties must be adapted in airline meals? What might be the dietary needs of consumers, for example, vegetarians? How can small servings be made attractive?

△ **Table 14.3** Contexts and knowledge-based research focus

Example

△ **Figure 14.5** Research evaluation and analysis of four areas

Commentary

Four pieces of research have been analysed here: a comparative shop (Figure 14.4), nutritional research (Figure 14.3), a questionnaire of the target group (Figure 14.2) and a disassembly of products (Figure 14.5). It is a good example, demonstrating a range of different methods of research that the student selected – questioning, investigating, data examination and product analysis. It is clear, with each written evaluation brought to a close with a summary of key points.

Page 4

Title

General design criteria

Aim

The aim is to take forward the analysis and evaluation of your research and make it contribute to your general design criteria. These criteria fit a range of products.

Content

A general design criteria list – use the computer for this if you can, as you will need to copy this for use later in the project.

Use points from your research evaluation, your target group needs evaluation and your set task focus to make up a list of general design criteria.

You must show these in your project. You will use these criteria to judge your 10–12 recipe ideas.

Review of page 4: general design criteria

The general design criteria list is very important. The criteria must come from criteria:

o   the controlled assessment set task (the brief)
o   the research findings
o   the need to make safe, high-quality food products
o   be used to evaluate recipe ideas.

Pages 5 and 6

Title

Working with general design criteria to evaluate recipe ideas.

Aim

To show a 'range' of recipe design ideas, up to a maximum of 12.

To annotate the ideas using guidance from the general design criteria.

Content

Show designs for food products that could meet the requirements of the set task and evaluate them.

How do you show design ideas?

Design in food means showing you have carried out a recipe search. Having found a range of appropriate recipes you need to refine your choices, rejecting recipes that do not meet the general design criteria. Sometimes you will have to adapt a recipe. It can be very helpful to annotate this, with notes on how to make it with different ingredients or alternative cooking methods. Ideas can be sketches, drawings or other graphical images. You do *not* need to copy out the recipes or include whole recipes, but you *do* need to add information to your images, sketches or recipe pictures. Annotation is essential to show the examiner your decisions and thoughts. You should provide a short description of the chosen recipe, pick out the main ingredients and state clearly how it meets some of the general design criteria. At this stage making is not needed.

Strategies to use during design ideas

- Sketching, describing and labelling;
- use of the scanner;
- use of recommended websites to review and collect recipes;
- annotating scanned recipes or hand-drawn images.

Commentary

In Figure 14.5a the student has used a recipe and scanned it. He has annotated the key features that show the recipe meets the general design criteria and is suitable for making in his practical lesson.

Example

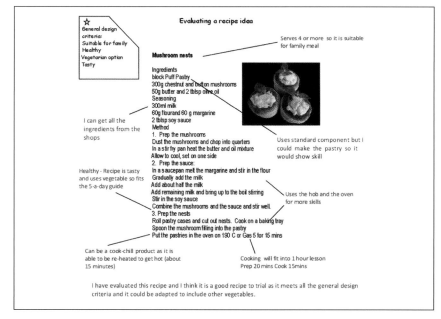

△ **Figure 14.5a** Evaluating a recipe idea

Review of pages 5 and 6

Working with general design criteria you must show:

o a selection of 10–12 recipe ideas you could make, named and described briefly

o recipes that use a wide range of ingredients and cooking processes

o annotations to evidence that the recipe ideas have been checked against the general design criteria

o identification of the best recipe ideas to trial (usually around six recipe ideas)

o use of recipe images, pictures or sketches to communicate ideas.

Page 7

Title

Moving from general design criteria to product design specification

Aim

o To evaluate your design ideas by checking they meet the general design criteria.

o To identify six recipe ideas that you will trial.

o To draw up a product design specification.

Content

Show evidence of evaluation of the range of recipe ideas. A chart is the most likely way of presenting this information.

Commentary

Figure 14.6 shows a full review of recipe ideas charted against product design specifications. You can see a table layout, with the product design specification points down the side and the ideas across the top. This enables a thorough evaluation of each of the recipe ideas.

Example

Evaluation of my design ideas

Design Specification	Idea one	Idea two	Idea three	Idea four	Idea five	Idea six	Idea seven	Idea eight	Idea nine	Idea ten
Must be suitable for teenagers, and have good sensory properties	7/10- won't smell great, but crispy and nice to look at	9/10-looks good, should smell good, and will taste good	4/10- not very nice looking and won't smell of anything. Should taste good!	6/10-will look good but won't smell of much but should taste for teenagers.	8/10-will look good and taste good, and is very suitable for teenagers.	7/10- the bread will smell nice, but the textures might not go well together.	7/10- will look and taste good but wont smell of much.	8/10-looks good, smells good but texture won't be brilliant.	9/10- will look good and smell good, suitable for teenagers and taste good	3/10- not very suitable for teenagers but ok sensory properties.
It must be prepared and cooked in one hour	5/10- should be easy enough, but preparation takes forever	8/10- should be done in an hour if rushed	8/10- easy to make and prepare so won't take long.	4/10- I find fish hard to make and prepare.	10/10- very easy to make and prepare.	3/10- lots of preparation involved, will take a long time.	8/10- should be easily made in one hour.	10/10- very easy to prepare and make.	5/10- should be easy enough to make in an hour	5/10- sauce would take a while to make.
It must contain at least one five a day and be nutritionally balanced	5/10- contains one five-a-day, but has too much protein.	8/10- contains two five-a-days and has all the right nutrients in it.	4/10-fatty cause it contains pastry, but contains two five-a-days.	7/10- sauce quite fatty but good with vegetables and fish is healthy.	8/10- sauce is fatty, but everything else is good.	8/10- Healthy and low fat, but could contain more protein.	7/10- contains pastry which is fatty, but otherwise good.	8/10- pasta could be wholegrain, but otherwise good.	10/10-low fat and contains a two-five-a-days.	4/10- contains a lot of sugar and would not have as much vegetables in it.
It should contain pasta (carbohydrate) and chicken (protein)	5/10- contains chicken but not pasta.	10/10-lots of chicken and pasta.	4/10- contains a lot of chicken but no pasta.	0/10- chicken and no pasta.	9/10- chicken and pasta, though there could be more chicken.	5/10- chicken but no pasta.	5/10- chicken but no pasta.	10/10- pasta and chicken will be present.	10/10- pasta and chicken contained.	4/10- no pasta and not much chicken.
It should contain a sauce (cheese preferred)	0/10- no sauce	10/10- cheese sauce is contained	5/10- contains tomato sauce	5/10- contains a white sauce.	10/10- cheese sauce is contained	5/10- tomato sauce but is white.	5/10- sauce but it is white.	5/10- sauce but it is white.	5/10- sauce but it is white.	5/10- sauce but it is sweet and sour.
It should be suitable for more than one person but also to be shared.	5/10- can be shared but is not made for more than one person.	9/10- can be shared with more than one person.	2/10- can be shared with difficulty, can be made for more than one person.	3/10- can be shared with difficulty, but not really shared.	9/10- very easy to make for several people and share.	2/10-can't be shared easily, but can be made for several people.	3/10-can be made for more than one person but can't be shared.	9/10- can easily be made for several people and can be shared.	9/10- can easily be made for several people and can be shared.	7/10-can be shared with difficulty and can be made for several people.
It should be a handheld product.	9/10-very handheld	7/10- could be handheld if put in a dish	5/10- again a good handheld product	5/10- can be made to be handheld, but could be difficult	7/10-can be handheld if put in a dish.	9/10-very handheld	6/10- can be handheld if put in a dish	8/10- can be handheld if put in a dish.	7/10- would be handheld if put in a dish	5/10- difficult to make this product handheld.
It should be layered	7/10- it's layered with bread.	10/10- layered with pasta.	2/10- can you call this layered with pastry?	8/10- layered with potato	0/0- not layered at all	4/10- sort of layered with bread.	8/10- layered with potato	0/10-not layered at all	10/10- layered with pasta	3/10- layered as there is chicken on top
It should be based on a British cuisine.	5/10- quite British but could be Italian	9/10- its more Italian than British	6/10- it's a little bit like a samosa	8/10- quite British	4/10- more Italian	6/10- original and British	10/10- original and British	4/10-more like Italian	4/10- more Italian	5/10- more Chinese
It should contain carrots and sweetcorn.	0/10- neither carrots or sweetcorn	10/10- sweetcorn and carrots	10/10- carrots and carrots	10/10- sweetcorn and carrots	10/10- sweetcorn and carrots	10/10- sweetcorn and carrots	10/10- carrots and carrots	5/20- sweetcorn with peas	10/10- sweetcorn and carrots	10/10- carrots but with carrots
It shouldn't cost more than £2.00 (per person)	5/10- shouldn't cost more, but it might do if I use good ingredients	9/10- for one person, it should be cheap	9/10- for one person, it should be cheap	4/10- fish is expensive, but should be cheap	9/10- pasta is cheap, to make	8/10- quite cheap but chicken can be expensive	8/10- should be cheap for one person	9/10- pasta is cheap and easy to make	8/10- should be cheap	8/10- rice is cheap and easy to make
It must be high in fibre.	5/10- wholemeal bread has fibre	9/10-lots of fibre in bread	4/10- not much fibre in pastry	5/10- fibre in the vegetables	8/10- fibre in pasta	6/10- fibre in carrots and vegetables	6/10- fibre in carrots and sweetcorn	6/10- fibre in peas and carrots	9/10- sweetcorn and vegetables contain fibre	4/10- vegetables but nothing else

△ **Figure 14.6** Evaluating design ideas

Strategy

Evaluation is an essential process to show in the project. Evaluating the recipe design ideas enables you to prepare a plan of action for making a selection of the recipes. It also helps in developing a product design specification.

Evaluation at this stage must also check that the recipes you want to make:

o show a number of different skills, processes or techniques

o use a range of ingredients

o meet the needs of the target group.

How to develop your product design specification

Use your general design criteria and expand them to contain some measurable criteria. If you want a healthy product for teenagers, for example, and you have criteria relating to limiting the fat, or simply stating 'be low in fat', you could make the criteria measurable. Give a range for the amount of fat you want to include in your product, for example, not more than 4 g fat. Similarly, with the energy content you might wish to specify between 650 and 800 kcal for the product.

Example A

> ## Design specification
>
> **Essential criteria**
>
> * My product should be snack–size and hand–held (questionnaire results)
> * Cost should be a maximum of £1.50 (questionnaire results)
> * For 11–16 year olds who are in full-time education (design brief)
> * My product needs to be fully encased (questionnaire results).
> * Include a sauce (questionnaire results)
> * Include a type of meat (questionnaire results)
> * Serve one person (questionnaire results)
>
> **Desired criteria**
>
> * Pack with transparent window (evaluating existing products)
> * Be labelled with appropriate information (evaluating existing products)
> * Instructions on storage (evaluating existing products)
> * Warning if the product contains allergen foods (evaluating existing products)
> * Serving suggestion (evaluating existing products)
> * Not less that 150 g per portion (other products provided a benchmark)
> * Provide 11 to 16 year-old dietary requirements (nutritional research)

△ **Figure 14.7** Product design criteria

Commentary

Figure 14.7 shows a product design specification that shows essential and desirable criteria. It is helpful to see where the criteria have originated from, as shown by the comments in brackets.

Review of page 7

This page of the project should show:

○ evaluation of the design ideas
○ six recipes identified to take forward to making trials

○ if the recipes are simple, details of a few more dishes you could make in order to demonstrate a range of skills
○ your product design specification
○ your plan for a series of practical sessions.

What to include in a product design specification

○ Size of product, such as individual portion product, family size
○ Type of product, such as main meal, luxury product, celebration dish
○ Main components, for example, pastry with chicken sauce and three vegetables
○ Nutritional references, for example, low salt, 300–350 kcal, high fibre
○ Storage details, for example, frozen ready meal, cook-chill, takeaway
○ Cost, for example, low cost, high cost, budget or luxury, between £3 and £5
○ Reference to sensory properties, for example, golden-brown, moist, spicy
○ Reheating instructions as appropriate
○ Shape and style of presentation meeting the needs of the target consumer
○ Weight of end product.

What is the difference between the general design criteria and the product design specification?

A product design specification is related directly to the final product and shows a list of criteria linked to that product. Look at the examples in Table 14.5 and note the differences. In the general design criteria specification the points are general. In the product design specification the criteria are tighter and tolerances are reduced. It is essential that a final product has a product specification and recipe in order that it can be manufactured repeatedly.

General design criteria	Product design specification criteria
Suitable for 4 servings	Must weigh 800 g–850 g
Offer healthy options	Must provide over 10mg vitamin C per portion
Contain some vegetables Meet 5-a-day rule	Must contain three portions vegetables

△ **Table 14.4** Differences between general design criteria and product design specification

Pages 8, 9 and 10

Title

Trials of best recipe design ideas

Aim

o To make six of the best ideas in order to test how the product meets the criteria.

Example

o To evidence your practical testing and evaluating skills

Commentary

In Figure 14.9 the pages are full, with no wasted space. The practical session has been recorded in detail, including quality checks and safety checks. Additionally, there are photographs that help the examiner to see what has been made. The product has been tested against the key points of the product design specification and ideas for further development have been explored.

Content

Record of practical sessions.

Strategy

Your making of the recipe design ideas must be recorded to show a range of testing procedures, including:

o an annotated photo of the product after you have made it
o checks that the outcome meets the key points of the product design specification

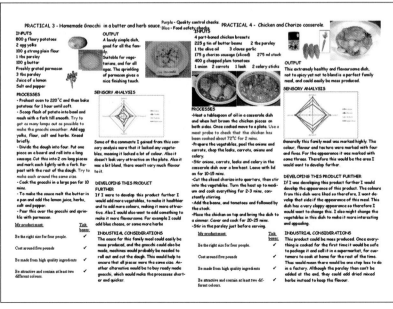

△ **Figure 14.9** Recording practical work

- sensory testing charts with evaluation comments – show you can use at least two different methods of sensory testing
- evaluation by the test chef (that is you!), a target group member and an expert (your teacher)
- a brief nutritional review to identify major nutrients to include or avoid in the product
- suggestions for development of the product to improve it for the target group
- data such as the product weight, size and shape
- the methods used and functions of some of the major ingredients in your product
- an estimate of the cost, if appropriate, of the whole product and per portion.

Use several methods to aid evaluation, such as sensory profile webs, charts, post-it notes, annotated photographs and nutritional software printouts. You can use a log or diary to make notes during practical sessions to help with accurate recording.

Example

Food Technology GCSE   Practical diary note page
Name ....Teacher ....

DATE	PRODUCT (or experiment or analysis)	Key points to note	How did it meet the specification?
Nov 18	Malaysian chicken curry	Chicken thighs used	Affordable Cultural Ready meal
	Equipment used: Food processor Stir-fry pan Chiller	Suggested testing method: Sensory via target group Chef's responses Nutritional data Against the design spec Expert	Digital camera used Yes

Making notes:	Design issues/Sensory testing
How many processes did you use? .... Could you change or adapt them?	Identify main flavours and textures What is the cost of your dish? Comment on the amount/portion/looks
Nutritional aspects: What are the main nutrients in the dish? Could you change or adapt them? Do they meet your target group needs?	Safety/Quality controls List the main safety aspects you used List some quality controls used
Has this practical been written up in your portfolio?	Grade/comments for assessed practical:

△ **Figure 14.10** A practical log

Review of pages 8, 9 and 10

Recording your work in practical sessions is about showing your ability to:

- cook creative, high-quality products skilfully and safely
- test and evaluate your own work
- be organised, thorough and accurate
- use your pages as evidence of the practical work you have undertaken.

Commentary

The practical log shown in Figure 14.10 demonstrates a variety of methods of testing as the practical work is being undertaken. The use of evaluation methods is clear; on completion the evidence would support the practical work carried out by a student.

Page 11

Title

Reflection and future planning

Aim

To review and develop your project.

Content

You should show evidence of some reflection on the initial six ideas that have been trialled. Development follows the making of the best six recipe design ideas. It is appropriate at this stage to list some points that show you have *reviewed* the practical work against the product design specification and the brief. You also need to show that you are thinking about what comes next. Which product will go forward to development?

Example

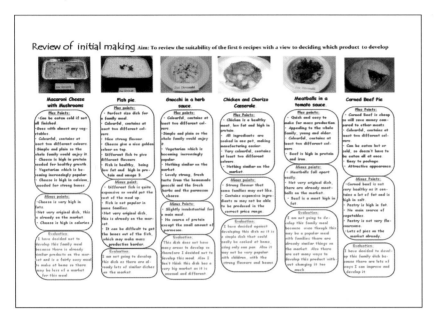

Review of initial making Aim: To review the suitability of the first 6 recipes with a view to deciding which product to develop

Macaroni Cheese with Mushrooms

Plus Points:
- Can be eaten cold if not all finished
- Goes with almost any vegetables
- Colourful, contains at least two different colours
- Simple and plain so the whole family would enjoy it
- Cheese is high in protein needed for healthy growth
- Vegetarian which is becoming increasingly popular
- Cheese is high in calcium, needed for strong bones

Minus points:
- Cheese is very high in fats
- Not very original dish, this is already on the market
- Cheese is high in calories

Evaluation:
I have decided not to develop this family meal because there is already similar products on the market and is a fairly easy meal to make at home so there may be less of a market for this meal

Fish pie.

Plus points:
- Perfect size dish for a family meal
- Colourful, contains at least two different colours
- Nice strong flavour
- Cheese give a nice golden colour on top
- Different fish to give different flavours
- Fish is healthy, being low fat and high in protein and omega 3

Minus point:
- Different fish is quite expensive so would put the cost of the meal up.
- Fish is not popular in some families
- Not very original dish, this is already on the market
- It can be difficult to get the bones out of the fish, which may make mass production harder.

Evaluation:
I am not going to develop this dish as there are already lots of similar dishes on the market

Gnocchi in a herb sauce.

Plus Points:
- Colourful, contains at least two different colours
- Simple and plain so the whole family would enjoy it
- Vegetarian which is becoming increasingly popular
- Nothing similar on the market
- Lovely strong, fresh taste from the homemade gnocchi and the fresh herbs and the parmesan cheese

Minus Points:
- Slightly insubstantial for a main meal
- No source of protein except the small amount of parmesan

Evaluation:
This dish does not have many areas to develop so therefore I decided not to develop this meal. Also I don't think this dish has a very big market as it is unusual and different

Chicken and Chorizo Casserole.

Plus Points:
- Chicken is a healthy meat, low fat and high in protein
- All ingredients are cooked in one pot, making manufacturing easier
- Very colourful, contains at least two different colours
- Nothing similar on the market

Minus points:
- Strong flavour that some families may not like
- Contains expensive ingredients so may not be able to be produced in the correct price range

Evaluation:
I have decided against developing this dish as it is a simple dish that could easily be cooked at home using only one pan. Also it may not be very popular with children, with the strong flavours and beans

Meatballs in a tomato sauce.

Plus points:
- Quick and easy to make for mass production
- Appealing to the whole family, young and older.
- Colourful, contains at least two different colours
- Beef is high in protein and iron

Minus points:
- Meatballs fall apart easily.
- Not very original dish, there are already meatballs on the market.
- Beef is a meat high in fat

Evaluation:
I am not going to develop this family meal because even though this may be a popular meal with families there are already similar things on the market. Also there are not many ways to develop this product without changing it too much

Corned Beef Pie

Plus Points:
- Corned Beef is cheap so will save money compared to other meats
- Colourful, contains at least two different colours
- Can be eaten hot or cold, so doesn't have to be eaten all at once
- Easy to package
- Attractive appearance

Minus Points:
- Corned beef is not very healthy as it contains a lot of fat and is high in salt
- Pastry is high in fat.
- No main source of vegetables
- Pastry is not very flavoursome
- Lots of pies on the market already.

Evaluation:
I have decided to develop this family dish because there are lots of ways I can improve and develop it

△ **Figure 14.11** Reflection and future planning

Commentary

Figure 14.11 shows evidence of reviewing. A photograph of the product is evaluated by a systematic method, bringing out the plus and minus points of each recipe tested. It is clear what decision has been made and which recipe is to be developed.

The outcome of the review helps explain which recipe product will be taken forward to the next stage of development. Planning development might involve considering some of the social, moral, environmental and sustainability issues related to ingredients you have used in the recipes.

Strategy

Use the strategy in Table 14.5 on page 237 to show 'Development planning'. This deals with issues other than appearance, sensory factors, cost and nutritional issues, which have already been shown in your practical records.

Remember that you should integrate the following issues throughout the project and not just deal with them in isolation.

Review of page 11

Reflection and future planning is essential for the quality of the second half of the project. It is necessary to show:

○ a review of initial practical cookery outcomes
○ how you have selected a product/recipe to move forward to the 'Development stage'.

Page 12 and 13

Title

Confirming the Product design specification and planning product development trials.

Aim

○ To confirm the product design specification for your new product.
○ To show ideas for development work.

Social values	Will your product meet the needs of different cultural groups within your target group? Can your product be used by other target groups? Is your product affordable? Could your product be sold in all regions of the UK?
Moral issues	Are all your ingredients safe? Would your recipes be acceptable for all groups in society? Does your product induce any health-related conditions?
Environmental factors	Are your ingredients from environmentally responsible factories? Can your packaging be reduced, reused or recycled? Might your product be criticised for environmental pollution (air miles, pesticides, fertilisers)?
Sustainability planning	Are you using locally sourced ingredients? Are any of your ingredients organic? Have you considered biodiversity (substitute ingredients that could be used if the source of the ingredient runs out)?

△ Table 14.5

Content

A product design specification must be provided in the project. A product design specification is a clear set of criteria that your final product must meet. You will use this list to evaluate your product. It is likely to take half a page. Use the remaining half of the page to show planning for development work.

Commentary

The student in Figure 14.12 has listed her points for the product design specification and has explored ideas for development work. She may not do all the developments, but she has shown the examiner that she has lots of experimental ideas. Finally, she has planned a logical number of practical sessions, with a clear focus for each one.

Example

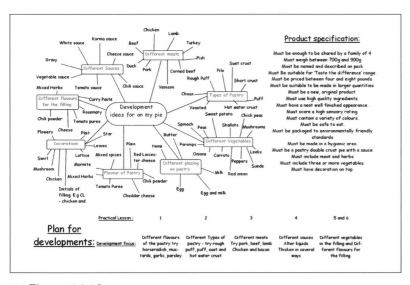

△ Figure 14.12

Planning product development trials

To plan a range of practical cooking in order to develop your chosen recipe and make it a new product that satisfies the criteria of the set task.

Development is sometimes called recipe engineering. It involves exploring new possibilities for a recipe, such as coming up with ideas to change, substitute, add or remove ingredients. Some of the ideas will be a success and some may fail. Either way shows good development performance. A record of thorough testing of your recipe is the key. The practical work becomes 'experimental' and the outcome produces samples to evaluate. It would be unusual to cook a whole recipe during this stage.

What is development?

Identification and development of components of a product

For example:

The layers in a cheesecake:	**1.** biscuit crumb layer	**2.** cheese-based mousse layer	**3.** fruity topping	**4.** cream swirls
The layers in a lasagne	**1.** type of pasta	**2.** meaty sauce	**3.** white sauce	**4.** toppings

△ **Table 14.6**

Identification and development of individual ingredients in a recipe

For example:

Vegetable soup	**1.** the stock	**2.** vegetables	**3.** herbs, spices and flavourings	**4.** accompaniments

△ **Table 14.7**

Identification and development of ingredients in part of a product

For example:

Pastry	**1.** type of flour or flour mixture	**2.** type of fat or fat mixture	**3.** glazing products

△ **Table 14.8**

Identification and development of methods of making a product

For example:

Cake products	1. creaming method	2. rubbing-in method	3. all-in-one method	4. melting method

△ Table 14.9

Development through time-reduction efficiency experiments

For example:

1. use a microwave for parts	2. Hand versus electrical equipment	3. pre-make parts	4. use standard components	5. change process stage

△ Table 14.10

Development via nutritional profile experiments

For example:

1. use low-fat version of ingredient	2. add or change ingredients	3. use different cooking method

△ Table 14.11

Development via costing experiments

For example:

1. substitute expensive with cheaper ingredients	**2.** remove ingredients	**3.** use technological advances for example, smart materials

△ **Table 14.12**

Example

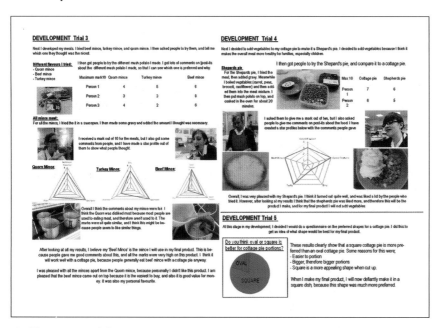

△ **Figure 14.13** Development trials

Commentary

The development practical work in Figure 14.13 has been written up to tell a story of trialling a part of a product and then getting feedback from users in the target group. A variety of methods of gathering evidence are shown and discussed, from using post-its to filling in score charts. Photographs help to show which part of the product has been tested.

Strategies

At this stage it might be appropriate to show evidence of product analysis. Select a product in the style of the new product you are developing, examine it thoroughly and record your findings. Present your analysis in the project to show a comparison between this product and the one you are making. It will confirm that you are intending to create a new product that fits in the retail market.

Review of pages 12 and 13

The planning product development trials page must show:

○ a review of initial practical work
○ a clear product design specification list
○ a plan for development practical work sessions.

Pages 14–18

Title

Records of development trials

Aim

To show development towards a final product

To justify the final product specification

Content

Show evidence of investigating and carrying out a series of experiments to achieve the best possible end product. For each developmental cookery session evidence clear thinking by:

o stating your aims
o listing changes and substitution ingredients
o recording your work via photographs of samples
o recording product appraisal, including sensory testing and nutritional details
o identifying successes and failures and explaining them in relation to the task

o providing conclusions that meet your target market needs, such as cost, size and storage.

Commentary

The development record in Figure 14.14 shows a specific aim and details the skills and methods to be used. Data have been collected and a photograph provides evidence of the practical work. A conclusion has been made to assist the final product specification.

Review of pages 14–18

When recording your development practical work:

o show plenty of practical work
o use photographic evidence if possible
o record the outcome processes related to quality and safety
o confirm the final product specification
o consider adaptations for manufacturing the product – you do *not* need to create a manufacturing specification.

Example

Development number 3

Development to find out which type of sponge is best out of low fat sponge, dark chocolate sponge (control) and fondant sponge

Method: cream together butter and the sugar then add egg (for the low fat use margarine and only one egg) then add flour. For the low fat sponge add cocoa powder and for the control use melted chocolate. Then bake for 10-20 mins. For the fondant follow the fondant recipe but spread the mixture out on a cake tin and cook for slightly longer.

Skills used: creaming, melting chocolate, baking, sieving, whisking

Question	Low fat	Dark chocolate	
Best taste	0	10	5
Best appearance	1	7	7
Best texture	3	9	3
Works with the rest	1	11	3
total	5	37	18

Nutritional info	Low fat	Dark choc	fondant
energy	450	550	600
protein	3	5	5
carbs	16	16	23
fat	15	25	20

Conclusion: I will use the original dark chocolate sponge for the sponge layer in my chocolate trifle because it works the best with all of the other ingredients and it gives the best flavour, texture and appearance.

Evaluation: the results tell us that the low fat option was fairly bad as it is unreliable and often does not rise and give the full flavour of its full fat counterpart. The fondant was fairly good but it was too thick and heavy to work with the rest of the dessert. Dark chocolate was the best in the results as it had the best flavour and was soft and light.

△ **Figure 14.14** Record of development trials

Pages 19–20

Title

Final product with production plan

Aim

To show the making of the final product with a detailed production plan, and to evaluate the performance of the final product.

Content

Presentation of the final product must include:

○ a photo of the final product
○ a full list of ingredients/standard components for all component parts of the product, including quantities and safety controls
○ a nutritional label for your product that uses computer-aided design
○ a list of functions of the ingredients you have used.

It should also show:

○ your making plan, with control checks and hygiene checks
○ finishing techniques used
○ a full list of equipment used, with safety checks
○ reheating and user instructions specifically for your target group
○ a comprehensive evaluation of the product against your product specification
○ evidence that the final product meets the needs of the user.

Example

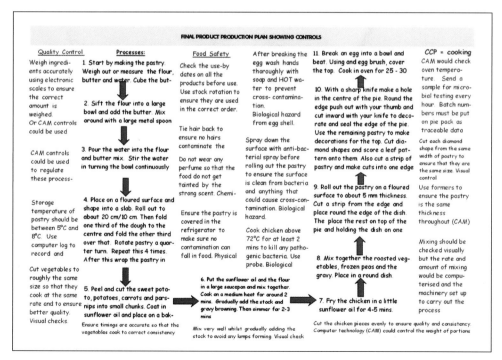

△ **Figure 14.15** Final production plan

Commentary

Figure 14.15 is a final production plan. It shows all the details of how the student has made the product. The student has included a step-by-step guide to the making and explained the function of the ingredients used.

This production chart shows the controls that are needed to make a safe and high quality food product. They relate to the final product, which is a roast dinner pie.

Review

The final product pages must contain:

o a photograph of the final product
o a detailed production plan
o evidence of reviewing the final product for suitability
o planning notes for the manufacture of the product, for example, suitability for production, future potential of the product.

14.3 On completion of the project

Once you have completed your project, you should:

o check your punctuation, spelling and grammar throughout your pages
o make sure you have indicated which controlled task you have been working on
o check that the pages are in the correct order
o check your use of technical vocabulary – Is it accurate? Have you used names for processes? Have you explained functions of ingredients?
o check that your project tells a story of the making and development of a new product
o check that your folder shows your name and candidate number clearly.

Index

Key terms shown in **bold**

244